D1320878

ALL OF THE MARVELS

ALSO BY DOUGLAS WOLK

James Brown's Live at the Apollo

*Reading Comics: How Graphic Novels Work
and What They Mean*

ALL
OF THE
MARVELS

An Amazing Voyage into Marvel's Universe and 27,000 Superhero Comics

DOUGLAS WOLK

P

PROFILE BOOKS

First published in Great Britain in 2021 by
Profile Books Ltd
29 Cloth Fair
London
EC1A 7JQ
www.profilebooks.com

First published in the United States of America by Penguin
Press, an imprint of Penguin Random House LLC

Copyright © Douglas Wolk, 2021

Designed by Meighan Cavanaugh

This book is not sponsored or endorsed by Marvel Worldwide Inc. or
any of its affiliates, divisions, subsidiaries or parent companies.

1 3 5 7 9 10 8 6 4 2

Printed and bound in Great Britain by
Clays Ltd, Elcograf S.p.A.

The moral right of the author has been asserted.

All rights reserved. Without limiting the rights under copyright reserved above, no part of this
publication may be reproduced, stored or introduced into a retrieval system, or transmitted,
in any form or by any means (electronic, mechanical, photocopying, recording or otherwise),
without the prior written permission of both the copyright owner and the publisher of this book.

A CIP catalogue record for this book is available from the British Library.

ISBN 978 1 78816 928 8
eISBN 978 1 78283 912 5

FSC
www.fsc.org
MIX
Paper from
responsible sources
FSC® C018072

For Sterling, who read with me

Ink runs from the corners of my mouth.
There is no happiness like mine.

—Mark Strand, "Eating Poetry"

The story of Doom can *end*, you say?... Then I'm a
better story than *you*.

—Doctor Doom, to Loki, in *Loki: Agent of Asgard* #6

CONTENTS

ALL OF THE MARVELS

1

THE MOUNTAIN OF MARVELS

The twenty-seven thousand or so superhero comic books that Marvel Comics has published since 1961 are the longest continuous, self-contained work of fiction ever created: over half a million pages to date, and growing. Thousands of writers and artists have contributed to it. Every week, about twenty slim pamphlets of twenty or thirty pages apiece are added to the body of its single enormous story. By design, any of its episodes can build on the events of any that came before it, and they're all (more or less) consistent with one another.

Every schoolchild recognizes the Marvel story's protagonists: Spider-Man, the Incredible Hulk, the X-Men. Eighteen of the hundred highest-grossing movies of all time, from *Avengers: Endgame* and *Black Panther* down to *Captain America: The Winter Soldier* and *Guardians of the Galaxy*, are based on parts of the story, and it has profoundly influenced a lot of the rest: *Star Wars* and *Avatar* and *The Matrix* would be unimaginable without it.

Its characters and the images associated with them appear on T-shirts, travel pillows, dog leashes, pizza cutters, shampoo bottles, fishing gear, jigsaw puzzles, and bags of salad greens. (Some of the people who love the story also love to be reminded of it, or to associate themselves with particular characters from it.) Its catchphrases have seeped into standard usage: "Spidey-sense," "you wouldn't like me when I'm angry," "I say thee nay," "healing factor," "no—*you* move," "bitten by a radioactive spider," "puny humans," "threat or menace?," "true believers," "'nuff said." Parts of it have been adapted into serial TV dramas, animated cartoons, prose novels, picture books, video games, theme-park attractions, and a Broadway musical. For someone who lives in our society, having some familiarity with the Marvel story is useful in much the same way as, say, being familiar with the Bible is useful for someone who lives in a Judeo-Christian society: its iconography and influence are pervasive.

The Marvel story is a mountain, smack in the middle of contemporary culture. The mountain wasn't always there. At first, there was a little subterranean wonder in that spot, a cave that was rumored to have monsters inside it; colorful adventurers had once tested their skills there, and lovers met at its mouth. Then, in the 1960s, it started bulging up above the surface of the earth, and it never stopped growing.

It's not the kind of mountain whose face you can climb. It doesn't seem hazardous (and it isn't), but those who try to follow what appear to be direct trails to its summit find that it's grown higher every time they look up. The way to experience what the mountain has to offer is to go *inside* it and explore its innumerable bioluminescent caverns and twisty passageways; some of them lead to stunning vantage points onto the landscape that surrounds it.

There is no clear pathway into the mountain from the outside. Parts of it are abandoned and choked with cobwebs. Other parts are tedious, gruesome, ludicrous, infuriating. And yet people emerge from it all the time, gasping and cheering, telling one another about the marvels they've seen, then rushing back in for more.

/////

Marvel Comics, as an artistic and commercial project, began in the early 1960s, initially as the work of a handful of experienced comics professionals—artists Jack Kirby and Steve Ditko, editor/writer Stan Lee,* and a few others. The superhero stories that had dominated American comic books in the late '30s and early '40s had mostly fallen out of style at that point, but instead of returning to that faltering genre as it had been, Kirby, Ditko, and Lee combined it with aspects of the genres that had supplanted it: the uncanny horror of the monster and sci-fi stories Ditko and Kirby had been drawing more recently; the focus on the emotion of the romance anthologies Kirby had helped to invent in 1947; the gently jabbing wit of the humor titles Lee had been writing for many years. That hybrid formula—absorbing monster comics and romance comics and humor comics *into* superhero comics—turned out to be irresistible and durable. Marvel's early stories responded to the atmosphere of their historical moment, sometimes explicitly in their content and always implicitly in their themes.

Then Kirby, Lee, Ditko, and their collaborators figured out how to make the individual narrative melodies of all of their comics harmonize with one another, turning each episode into a component of a gigantic epic. That led to a vastly broader artistic collaboration: ever since then, its writers and artists have been elaborating on one another's visions, sometimes set in the same place and time but often separated by generations and continents.

The big Marvel story is a funhouse-mirror history of the past sixty years of American life, from the atomic night-terrors of the Cold War to the technocracy and pluralism of the present day—a boisterous, tragicomic, magnificently filigreed story about power and ethics, set in a world transformed by wonders. In some of its deeper caverns, it's the most for-

---

*For the prehistory of Marvel, see chapter 5; for more on these three, see chapter 7.

bidding, baffling, overwhelming work of art in existence. At its fringes, it's so easy to understand and enjoy that you can read a five-year-old an issue of *The Unbeatable Squirrel Girl* and she'll get it right away. And not even the people telling the story have read the whole thing.

That's fine. Nobody is *supposed* to read the whole thing. That's not how it's meant to be experienced.

So, of course, that's what I did. I read all 540,000-plus pages of the story published to date, from *Alpha Flight* to *Omega the Unknown*. Do I recommend anyone else do the same? God, no. Am I glad I did it? Absolutely.

I've spent some of my happiest days exploring the mountain of Marvels, and I wanted to get a better sense of what was in there so I could help curious travelers figure out how they might get inside it and how they might find the parts they'd like best. (I went all out so you don't have to; if you liked an *Avengers* movie and are interested in dipping a toe into its characters' comics, or read *X-Men* as a teenager and wonder what it's looked like since then, I'm here to help you have fun with that.) I also wanted to see what the Marvel narrative said as *a single body of work*: an epic among epics, Marcel Proust times Doris Lessing times Robert Altman to the power of the *Mahābhārata*.*

As a cluster of overlapping serials, with dozens running in parallel at any given time, it has a different relationship with time and sequence than most kinds of narrative art have. It doesn't really have a beginning—well, it does, but since mid-1961, where the story began is not where any member of the audience has ever been meant to join it. Instead, the Marvel story gives the reader tools to figure out the context from any entry point, reading backward and sideways as well as forward. Each individual piece of it, on its own, is *fun*—engaging, exciting, pleasing to the

---

*The *Mahābhārata*, in its critical edition, runs about 13,000 pages, which is roughly as many as all of the issues of *The Incredible Hulk* to date.

eye—or, at least, meant to be fun. But there's another, different kind of fun that comes from piecing together the big story.

Marvel's narrative also has a peculiar relationship with authorship. Legally, its "maker" is a corporation, one that's gotten bigger over time as its body of intellectual property has changed hands. In practice, it was made by a specific group of people whose names we (mostly) know, and whose particular hands are (usually) unmistakable on any given page. But it's also almost always been created collaboratively: if you think any one person is the sole creator of a particular image or plot point, you're probably wrong, which is why it's a mistake to think of any one person who's worked on a Marvel comic book as its "author."* On top of that, the nature of "continuity"—an important word in this context—is that every episode has to dovetail with (or at least not contradict) everything by other writers and artists that came before it or appears alongside it.

From a reader's perspective, though, that was one of Marvel's great innovations. You can follow any series on its own, without having to pay any mind to others; if you just want to see what Moon Knight's up to this

---

*Even the question of who created Marvel's best-known characters is also often more complicated than it looks. It's easy enough to assess who came up with Marvel's first superheroes of the 1960s, the Fantastic Four: Jack Kirby and Stan Lee. (Except that the Human Torch's name and basic design had been created by Carl Burgos back in 1939.) Captain America? Kirby and Joe Simon in 1941. How about Doctor Strange? That was Steve Ditko, according to Lee's own words (he wrote "'Twas Steve's idea" in a 1963 letter to fan Jerry Bails). Iron Man? That's a little trickier. Lee plotted his first story, but Larry Lieber wrote its dialogue, Kirby drew the first cover and designed the character's initial costume (which barely resembles the familiar red-and-gold one, designed by Ditko a bit later); Don Heck drew the initial story and invented what its protagonists Tony Stark and Pepper Potts look like.

Daredevil? Well, now you're running into trouble. Lee wrote the first story, and Bill Everett drew it, but the cover was drawn by Kirby, who might have designed Daredevil's original costume, too, although the much more familiar red costume was first drawn by Wally Wood starting in the seventh issue. When you talk about the now-familiar look and feel and mythology of "Daredevil," though—the tormented Catholic romantic who leaps around the shadows of Hell's Kitchen and fights ninjas and Wilson Fisk—you're mostly talking about what Frank Miller added to the character in the '80s, along with his artistic collaborators Klaus Janson and David Mazzucchelli. (Except that Wilson Fisk had been created by Lee and John Romita Sr. fifteen years earlier.) And so on.

month, you're good. But characters and plotlines bounce freely from one series to another, and events in any individual issue can have ramifications in any other, the same week or years later. Every little story is part of the big one, and potentially a crucial part.

That sense of shared experience, of seeing dozens of historical threads and dozens of creators' separate contributions being woven together, is a particular joy of following the Marvel Universe (with a capital *U*), as both the company and comics readers call it.* The Marvel story is not the first or only one that works like that—DC Comics, Marvel's largest competitor, and other comics publishers have adopted the "universe" template too— but it's the largest of its kind.†

It wasn't even meant to work *that* way, at first; it wasn't conceived organically in any way. The story has been driven, at every turn, by the dictates of the peculiar marketplace that sustains comics, and in recent decades by the much more profitable business of media and merchandise derived from stories that originated in comics. It grew accidentally, and it's accrued meaning accidentally, through its creators' memory lapses and misreadings and frantic attempts to meet deadlines. Even so, it's accrued a *lot* of meaning.

The Marvel story is about exploration—about seeing secret worlds within the world we know, and understanding possibilities of what we haven't yet experienced—and its parallel serials and wildly divergent creative perspectives even within a single serial make that broader understanding possible. It's high adventure, slapstick comedy, soap opera, blood-spattered horror, tender character study, and political allegory, usually all in the same week. It encompasses magnificent craft and dumb hackwork, and enduring the latter is sometimes helpful preparation for

---

*The "universe" part is because the story's scope isn't limited to Earth; parts of it take place deep in outer space, or in more metaphysical territory.

†That's part of why this book is about Marvel, rather than DC or some other shared universe. For all the superhero comics that DC has published since 1938, it was very slow to integrate them into anything like a coherent fictional world—and that world was rebooted in 1986 and again in 2011, discarding most of its established history.

appreciating the former. It grew with its audience, and then grew beyond successive generations of its tellers. In form and substance, it's a tribute to the astonishing powers of human imagination and to the way that human imaginations in concert with one another can do far more than they could individually. It's a tale that never ends for any of its characters, even in death.

Those characters—and there are thousands of them—include some extraordinary ones, in whose fantastic excesses you, as a reader, might potentially see parts of yourself, or see what you might hope to become or fear becoming. On any page, you're likely to encounter someone like a computer science student who can talk to squirrels and is friends with an immortal, planet-devouring god;* or an android who saved the world thirty-seven times, then moved to the suburbs of Washington, D.C., and built himself a family in a catastrophically failed attempt to be more human;† or a vindictive, physically immense crimelord who has become the mayor of New York, and whose archenemy is the alter ego of the blind lawyer who serves as his deputy mayor;‡ or a woman who discovered as a teenager that she could walk through walls, was briefly possessed by a version of herself from a dystopian future, trained as a ninja, later spent months trapped inside a gigantic bullet flying through the cosmos, and is now a pirate captain;§ or a tree creature from another planet who makes remarkably expressive use of his three-word vocabulary.¶

Marvel's shared-universe schema offers an exceptionally fun way of thinking about ethical behavior that's more complicated than "good guys and bad guys." The story's alliterative heroes, from Peter Parker to Miles Morales to Jessica Jones to Kamala Khan, rarely come into their power

*Squirrel Girl and Galactus, respectively; see chapter 20.
†The Vision.
‡The Kingpin, aka Wilson Fisk, and Daredevil; see * on p. 5.
§Kate Pryde; see chapter 10.
¶That's Groot, who's best known for having appeared in the *Guardians of the Galaxy* movies, and in the comics series of the same name beginning in 2008. An early, slightly more eloquent version of him first turned up on the cover of 1960's *Tales to Astonish* #13, bellowing "*Behold!* I am *Groot*, the invincible! Who *dares* to defy me?"

willingly; their abilities are less often something they've achieved than an unanticipated burden. Its villains are rarely beyond redemption, and are as likely as not to become its heroes or even its saviors. Even the worst of them have their reasons.

Over the course of six decades, the story has developed its own bizarre, sort-of-coherent cosmology. Marvel's Earth is the center of its universe, the most important place in all of creation. It's also "Earth-616," only one of many possible versions of the world that appear within the story. A former surgeon, who lives in a Greenwich Village town house with the ghost of his dog, perpetually defends the planet against occult attack and has seen it destroyed and rebuilt, good as new, more than once. The nexus of all of its realities is deep within a swamp in the Florida Everglades, guarded by a monster who can't abide fear. An ancient being who lived in an oxygenated zone of the moon witnessed all of the alternate possibilities for how its important events might have turned out, until he was murdered and his eyes stolen. The throne of the Marvel Universe's Hell is empty; its Norse pantheon's home once crash-landed in Oklahoma.

Some of the questions the Marvel story asks and (the short versions of) the answers it offers:

- What do gods do? (They create; they judge; they destroy.)
- What do monarchs do? (They protect their nations, even when that makes them monstrous.)
- Is there anything beyond the world we know? (There is more than we could ever possibly imagine.)
- What happens when we grow up? (We may try to put away childish things, but we can't, or shouldn't. The best thing that can happen is that we turn those things into something bigger and more beautiful.)

More than anything else, though, the Marvel world is a place of scientific miracles and of technological progress that transforms the lives of everyone within it. Its most prominent and most fallible champions are the ones with doctorates. The telling of the Marvel story begins with a rocket flight gone wrong; the main engine of its American century is a race for technology to create the perfect soldier; its chief exponents of terror are a cult of scientists hoping to strike blows against corporate control. Some of its best-loved characters are "children of the atom," the next step in evolution, sparked by the nuclear age. Earth-616 is recognizably our world, made stranger and richer by wonders of science—a world in which deep knowledge has always been a shield against incomprehensible horrors.

I wanted to gain deep knowledge of the story itself—to learn all there is to know about it—and I dedicated a couple of years of my life to that effort.* But Marvel has also published a lot of stuff that *isn't* part of that story, by some definition, and I had to draw the line somewhere. I came up with three questions to narrow down what I would obligate myself to read:

1. *Was it a comic book published by Marvel during the period bounded by 1961's* Fantastic Four *#1 and 2017's* Marvel Legacy *#1?*

   The first issue of *Fantastic Four* is where the "Marvel Age" conventionally begins—although I ended up reading *everything* Marvel published between 1960 and 1962 anyway, and finding a slightly earlier starting point for what I think of as the story. (The endpoint was just so that I'd have an endpoint; I didn't actually stop reading there.)†

---

*That wasn't *all* I was doing during those years. Even so, more than one friend, on hearing about the project, immediately compared me to the cartoonist Bob Burden's absurdist mid-1980s character Flaming Carrot, who "read over 5000 comic books in a single sitting to win a bet. He won, but his mind could not take the strain."

†The covers of those two issues suggest how much the way the story is told had changed in fifty-six years. Jack Kirby's *The Fantastic Four* cover is crammed with language and action, insistently explaining who everyone is and what's going on; Joe Quesada's *Marvel Legacy* cover focuses tightly on a few characters looking at something we can't see, and spares room only for the text of its title. (There are also elements the two images share: the interrupted arc of a circle, and a monster opening its mouth to scream.)

2. *Did it involve characters owned by Marvel?*

    This actually ruled out a lot of stuff. The "ownership" rule set *Conan the Barbarian* and its related series, for instance, outside the scope of

The covers of the two comic books that were the bookends for this project: *Fantastic Four* #1, 1961 (drawn by Jack Kirby), and *Marvel Legacy* #1, 2017 (drawn by Joe Quesada and Kevin Nowlan).

this project*—at least until after 2017—so I washed my hands of them. Ditto for *Star Wars* and *G.I. Joe*, whose licensed series never crossed over with the Marvel Universe, as well as the many creator-owned comics published by the Epic and Icon imprints. Likewise with movie adaptations, and nonfiction biographies of Pope John Paul II and Mother Teresa, and adaptations of L. Frank Baum's Oz books, and *Care Bears*, and *Marvel Classics Comics*, despite a very clever attempt I once saw to demonstrate that Fandral the Dashing from *Thor* appears in disguise in Sir Walter Scott's *Ivanhoe* and consequently in its *Marvel Classics* adaptation.

---

*If you're thinking about bringing up the Serpent Crown, I'll give you a nickel not to.

On the other hand, Marvel has published a few series that involve characters licensed from elsewhere interacting with Marvel's characters—*Master of Kung Fu, ROM: Spaceknight, Micronauts*, and *Godzilla* are prominent examples. All of those were within the scope of the project, and I read all of them.

3. *Could the version of Spider-Man who stars in* The Amazing Spider-Man* *reasonably turn up in it without the benefit of time travel, whether or not he actually does?*

This was the Great Excluder—or, as I came to think of it, the Great Time-Saver. There are a handful of series that have been wholly owned by Marvel but whose characters have never interacted with those in the big fictional universe—*Strikeforce: Morituri* comes to mind. There are also a lot of series about alternate versions of the Marvel characters: the Marvel Age imprint of stories for younger readers; most of the MAX imprint of adults-only takes on familiar characters; the MC2 line of stories about second-generation superheroes in a possible future; *Spidey Super Stories*; adaptations of various animated series; and so on. I let myself pass over those. But then there was Ultimate Marvel, a separate and distinct continuity that ran from 2000 to 2015 in comics whose titles all included the word "Ultimate." The Ultimate titles and the main Marvel line eventually became closely connected, so I read all 600-plus Ultimate comics.

The time-travel clause was a work-around to get me off the hook from reading a giant pile of Western and war comics. It didn't stop me from reading all of Marvel's post-1958 horror and romance anthologies, though.

---

*You know the game "Six Degrees of Kevin Bacon"? The protagonist of *Amazing Spider-Man* is basically that: the character who's met everybody. The only significant Marvel character who's been on Earth at the same time as Spider-Man without yet encountering him face-to-face is Millie Collins (whose sitcom series *Millie the Model* ran 207 issues, ending in 1973)—and Spider-Man's ex, Mary Jane Watson, has worked with Millie.

And I did end up reading the entirety of the alarmingly clueless *Red Wolf*, a short-lived Western series about a Native American superhero, rather than limiting myself to the issues set in what several 1973 covers called "the holocaust of TODAY!"*

The remaining twenty-seven thousand or so issues, though,† were all on my reading list, and if you're wondering how I tracked them all down, that wasn't the hard part.‡ The hard part was finding enough hours in the day to read them all.

I didn't read them in order, of course; that would have been unbearable. Instead, I grazed. I'd read *Spider-Woman* for a while, then an *Iron Man* miniseries, then some comics drawn by Leonardo Manco, then various appearances by the monstrously huge dragon Fin Fang Foom, then a bunch of early-1970s romance comics, then whatever new issues I'd bought that week.

How did I read them? Any way I could. I read them on couches, in cafés, on treadmills. I read them as yellowing issues I'd bought when they were first published, or scored at garage sales as a kid, or snagged from a dollar bin at a convention as an adult. I read them in glossy, bashed-cornered paperbacks borrowed from the library. I read them as bagged-and-boarded gems borrowed from friends. I read them as expensively "remastered" hardcover reprints, and as .cbz files of sketchy provenance, and as brittle stacks of pulp that had been lovingly reread until they'd nearly disintegrated. I read a few from a stack of back issues somebody abandoned on the table next to mine as I was working at a Starbucks one day; it just happened to include an issue of *Power Man and Iron Fist* I'd

---

*By which they meant, among other things, that it involves a Mohawk policewoman named Jill Tomahawk who says things like "And I'm a good cop, too—even if I *am* a woman! So don't try to zap me with any male chauvinistic pig-ism!!!"

†My spreadsheet claims there were exactly 27,206 of them, but I don't entirely trust it. There were some edge cases, too: an *ALF* Annual that parodies the "Evolutionary War" crossover from the same year; a *Ren & Stimpy* issue in which Dan Slott wrote Spider-Man for the first time; that sort of thing. I went ahead and read all of those, because why not?

‡The Marvel Unlimited digital service, which includes upward of twenty thousand issues, helped a lot—it has some major and minor gaps, but it was invaluable for my purposes.

been looking for. I read a hell of a lot of them on a digital tablet. I read them in the economical black-and-white "Essential" collections Marvel pumped out between 1996 and 2013, and in ragged British pulp weeklies from the '70s. I read them from the peculiar CD-ROM collections Graphic Imaging Technology published in the mid-2000s, with hundreds of indifferently scanned issues of *Amazing Spider-Man* or *Ghost Rider*.*

And I had an absolutely great time. The best of them, old and new, were astonishing, as thrilling and imaginative as popular entertainment gets. There was also plenty of sophomoric, retrograde stuff, rushed out to serve an audience of credulous kids or bloodthirsty nostalgics. I was often aware that I was gorging myself on something made for cherry-picking and nibbling, indulging the worst part of the collector's impulse: the part that strives for completeness rather than for enjoyment. Fortunately, by the time I'd waded too far into the piles of *Nightstalkers* and *Skull the Slayer* and *Marvel Double Feature: Thunderstrike/Code Blue* to turn around, a small but useful transformation had come over me.

I realized that I'd become able to find *something* to enjoy in just about any issue, new or old. Sometimes, it was a detail that connected to another one on the story's perpetually expanding canvas. (It's a truism about superhero comics that nobody ever stays dead, but it's more broadly true that *nothing* in them goes away forever. Any character or gizmo or situation that's ever appeared in the Marvel narrative is fair game for any of the story's subsequent tellers; someone a decade or three later will inevitably come up with a plot in which Crystar the Crystal Warrior or Arcanna Jones or the Leader's Brain-Wave Booster can serve some purpose, and it will be richer for a reader who recognizes that element from the first time around.)

---

*I didn't *intend* to read any at the Burning Man art festival in the Nevada desert in the summer of 2019; the only comics I had brought with me were a few copies, to give away, of 1998's *X-Force* #75, in which the team attends the same event, transparently disguised as the "Exploding Colossal Man" festival. But somebody had set up a little memorial shrine for Stan Lee, and at its base there was a box labeled READ ME, containing some battered but intact fifty-year-old issues of *Amazing Spider-Man* and *Thor* and *Tales of Suspense*, and what was I going to do, *not* read them?

Other times, it was some display of a creator's idiolect. Longtime comics readers know that one of the delights of following particular characters for years is seeing the moments at which they act *in character*, doing something unexpected that's still absolutely consistent with what we know of them. There's a very similar joy in observing comics creators being who they are—when there's a line of dialogue or a line of ink that could have come from nobody else's hand.

Most often, though, what made otherwise iffy older comics come alive for me was the ways they reflected the moments at which they were made. Before "collectibility" infected them, periodical comic books were sold alongside newspapers and designed to be thrown out with them, and they're kind of a much more colorful, metaphorical version of the same thing. Comics dramatize the cultural conflicts and fears of their time, and that subtext is often clearer in dull or hacky comics than in aesthetically satisfying ones.* Even the apparatus around the stories themselves illuminates their historical context. (You can learn a lot about the race and gender politics of the 1970s and '80s by reading the letters to the editor that were printed in *Hero for Hire* or *The Punisher* or *Ms. Marvel*, or looking at the ads that interrupted those stories every few pages.)

My background is in pop music criticism, and one of the things I've learned from it is that if a piece of art of any kind becomes popular, that means there's something about it that commands an audience's attention and gives them pleasure in a way that other things, even similar things, don't.† There are lots of commercial failures that are artistic triumphs, of

---

*The "Living Mummy" feature that ran in *Supernatural Thrillers* from 1973 to 1975, for instance, is . . . a real mess, actually, but a fascinating mess, an evocation of the early '70s' conflation of archaeology and mysticism, as well as the craze around the "Treasures of Tutankhamun" tour. It includes what might be Marvel's first same-sex couple, as well as some wild psychedelic artwork by Tom Sutton in its final episode.

†I occasionally hear the argument that popular success in culture has to do only with what big corporations decide to shove down the throat of the public. The backing of a capitalist machine can absolutely help resonant art reach its audience, but all the money in the world can't make a hit out of something nobody wants. To quote W. H. Auden, "Some books are undeservedly forgotten; none are undeservedly remembered."

course, and I'll wave the flag for plenty of those in the chapters that fol-low. But every hit comic book, like every hit record, has something excep-tional about it,* and part of the job of critics who are interested in this particular subfield is to figure out what those exceptional things are. It can be hard to do, and sometimes I can't manage it; that's my failing. Sometimes I can see what's exceptional but am not moved by it myself; that has more to do with my tastes and preferences.

Again, though, the fact that Marvel's comics have always been so en-tirely a commercial enterprise means that the ones that have thrived in the market at any given moment, regardless of who has been writing or drawing them, responded to some kind of craving in their audience of that moment.† The early parts of the Marvel story were unabashedly power fantasies for children. As superhero comics' narrative style has grown up along with their audience, those fantasies' messier subtexts have bubbled up and been addressed head-on. Looking at close to sixty years of *Spider-Man* or *Captain America*, you can clearly make out the rise and fall of particular cultural aspirations and of the storytelling modes that con-veyed them.

As you explore the Marvel story, it becomes another world you can call your own, one that's constantly expanding and full of unfinished won-ders. You can no more exhaust its possibilities than the real world's. (I have tried.) And spending time in that world can make you better equipped to live in the real one: more curious about how its systems fit together; more willing to explore what you don't yet understand, and accept that you can't know everything; more open to hope in the face of catastrophe; more aware that no matter how overwhelming your own life may seem, it's only part of a much bigger picture.

---

*Thanks to Robert Christgau, whose formulation I'm stealing here.
†Sometimes they find mass appeal by taking artistic risks; they're cheap enough to pro-duce that failed experiments aren't ruinous.

2

WHERE TO START, OR HOW TO ENJOY BEING CONFUSED

n the time I've been working on this book, I've run into one question more than any other—in person, on message boards, or passed along from friends of friends: *I want to read this stuff too. But where do I start?*

That is a very easy question to answer glibly ("Anywhere you want!") and a tricky one to answer more specifically. Marvel's body of comics looks from a distance like an impenetrable web of series and stories. Up close, it's even denser and messier than that: it's a great gnarl of interconnected webs, a constantly expanding fractal form of histories and characters and contradictory evidence and impossible reversals. There is always a "previously" and always a "to be continued." There are relaunches and resurrections, parallel universes and alternate timelines. No matter where you come in, it's later than it might be.

Everything in a serial superhero comic book is balanced, wholly or partly, on knowledge of some earlier story. Everything *spoils* some earlier story. There is always a thrill, a shock, a bit of storytelling sleight of hand that you deny yourself by coming in too late. But you have to.

The only hope, prospective readers think too often, is to start at the beginning. I beg of you: *Don't do that.* Even if you "like doing things in order" and "want to get a sense of history," don't do it. Please. I promise you, that's not what you want to do.* You will not make it far, and you will not enjoy it, and enjoying it is the whole point.

But (I hear you asking) why *not* start at the beginning, with *Fantastic Four* #1 (or the first appearance of your favorite character), and let the story unfold as it did for people lucky enough to be paying attention back then? For one thing, Marvel's comics, even at the outset, were not designed to be read in a specific, unified order: the edict of the comics business was that "every issue is somebody's first," and when a particular issue was off the newsstands, it was *gone.*† Even when new issues built on events from older ones, their creators had to work from the assumption that readers probably wouldn't have access to those antecedents.

More significantly, a lot of those early 1960s comics are unrewarding and off-putting, especially if you're coming to them cold in the twenty-first century. They were often wildly original for their time; they were also often breathlessly dumb, hacked out at sloppy speed for an audience of children who were expected to stick them in the trash when they were done. If you're used to the rhythms and tone of contemporary entertainment and decide to look at, say, the comics that led up to the *Daredevil*

---

*"But I'm a completist," people sometimes say when I implore them not to try to read everything in order—or, if they play a lot of video games, "I'm a completionist." Then, I tell them, you can get an extra side benefit from superhero comics: they can be a tool to help relieve you of that burden.

†If you were very interested in a particular back issue, maybe you could trade with a friend who was done reading it or get really lucky and find a copy at a garage sale. Otherwise, you'd have to extrapolate from footnotes and recaps. Marvel didn't start reprinting relatively recent storylines in book form until 1987—Frank Miller and David Mazzucchelli's *Daredevil* sequence "Born Again" seems to have been the first—and reprinted their '60s comics only in single issues and scattershot anthologies until the Marvel Masterworks books debuted that year.

TV show, you might not make it all the way through *Daredevil* #1. You can only remind yourself that early Ant-Man or Human Torch stories are "historically important" for so long before your eyes glaze over.

This is not to say that there are not circumstances under which you would want to read comics created in what are now archaic modes. Some of them have a lot to offer, and a few are extraordinary. They're just not the ones you want to read *first*, for the most part.

So: if "at the beginning, of course," is not the right answer to the question of where to begin, what is? Another approach is to go for the consensus favorites—the best and most important issues and sequences. That's a better idea, but it's still deceptively tricky, because "best" and "most important" are often totally different things. "Important," in particular, is a slippery term: Importance to subsequent parts of the story? To the aesthetics of comics in general? To what longtime readers remember fondly?

There's a sort of circular assumption that comes up surprisingly often without being articulated: that the most significant metric of quality for a particular comic book is how often later comic books allude to it.* That tends to mean "importance" is granted to an episode of a long serial that shakes its foundations, or to the introduction or death of a major character. Those moments of change, though, can't mean much to a reader who's not already familiar with what's *being* changed. Nobody who's read and enjoyed a dozen comics about Wolverine thinks the one most coveted by speculators—his first appearance, in *The Incredible Hulk* #181†—was the best one; that's just the moment when an object of cathexis arrived.

Canons of "classics" also tend to reinforce themselves: they're considered the most important because everyone knows they're the most impor-

---

*In the ghastly parts of comics culture that focus on back issues as concrete financial investments, there is a single-minded fascination with first appearances of recurring characters. *The Uncanny X-Men* #201, for instance, commands inflated prices because it includes the first appearance of the character Cable. Except you would never guess that from reading it, and indeed nobody involved in creating it had any idea that the newborn infant who appears on five pages of that issue would grow up to star in multiple series as a grizzled, one-eyed old man with a penchant for enormous guns.
†Fine. His first appearance was in #180, technically. But that one either.

tant. That means that, as in any other medium, they skew more and more toward old stuff over time. In 2014, Marvel let fans vote on its seventy-five greatest stories ever. The results were a mishmash of individual issues, long serials, and storylines that spanned dozens of series. Of the top twenty, though, sixteen had been published at least two decades earlier, and seventeen either introduced characters who later appeared extensively, killed off characters who had been around for a while, or both.

Good comics, though, are often very much of their moment. They're serials; the only ones that survive are those whose readers are willing to wait to find out what happens next. From my current perspective, the comics of the early 2020s have a lot to offer, but I hope twenty years from now I'll feel the same way about the comics of the early 2040s, and I bet some of the recent ones I adore right now will seem, at best, a little odd and fusty. As much as the past weighs on the present within the Marvel story, being familiar with old comics is rarely a prerequisite for enjoying new comics, and when it is, that's a failure on the storytellers' part.

A third and still better option for where to begin is to start with something one of your friends likes. Superhero comics are a *social* medium. A stack of battered copies of *Ms. Marvel*, or an *X-Statix* volume with cracks in its spine, is a memento of a shared experience—a set of images to rhapsodize over or argue about, a collection of reference points its readers have in common. For all its flaws, the culture around comics is exceptionally good at communicating enthusiasm. We love to talk about the stories that have delighted us, and to help other people discover stories they'll love too.

That's also the point of this book, really. I'm not going to rattle off a list of volumes that anyone will enjoy (there's no such thing) or proclaim a canon of "The 300 Issues You Must Read." What I *can* do, as someone who's traveled the entirety of this territory, is act as a tour guide.

Our tour will take a strange, looping route. It won't show you all the geysers and redwood forests and subterranean crystal palaces that are hidden within the mountain of Marvels; there's much more to see than a book could do justice to. Instead, it will lead you past a whole lot of trailheads—the beginnings of paths through the story you might find rewarding or diverting. (The appendix at the end of the book is a sort of map of the whole thing.)

We're not quite ready to start yet, though. Before the tour itself begins, I'm going to explain the weird customs of mainstream American comics and Marvel's comics in particular, and of the ways their readers talk about them (that's in chapter 3). And before *that*, I need to clarify a few things that this book might be but is not; give you two warnings, one very short and one very long; and tell you about the three different meanings of time and chronology as they apply to the Marvel story.

WHAT THIS BOOK IS NOT

- This is not a book about the comics form in general, or even about its American incarnations in particular. It does not imply that the commercial end of the American superhero genre is the same thing as the comics medium, or the "most important" or "best" part of it.
- It is not an argument that all of the comics I looked at are good, or that most of them are good.*
- It is not a defense of Marvel's business practices, currently or historically, or of the business practices of any of their corporate parents, nor is it a defense of any of these comics' creators as people.
- It's also not a defense of these comics' retrograde, myopic history of representation, in terms of both the characters who appeared on their pages and the people who created them.
- It not only does not defend, but actively disavows, the elements of mainstream comics readership that try to keep it the province

---

*Some of them are really good, though.

of straight white men, with boxes full of back issues, who want everything to stay exactly like it was when they were kids. (The only kind of "gatekeepers" who have any business being around comics are the ones who make sure the gate stays wide open to anyone who wants to come join the fun.)

- It is absolutely not an argument that reading all of Marvel's comics is an ideal or even advisable way to approach them. Enjoying things is not a competition, and there is no such thing as a "real fan" or "fake fan." You like what you like the way you like it. This book is about a story that I experienced in an excessive, exhausting, delightful way; I hope it can help you find a way of your own.

That leads us to our warnings:

THE SHORT WARNING: ON FOLLOWING THE PATH

This warning is precisely the opposite of the one that applies to most tours of mysterious terrain: you *must* stray from the path. Don't treat this book as a syllabus or reading list to be followed in sequence. Skip around! Trust your taste! If a story calls out to you, go follow it as far as you like!

THE LONG WARNING: ON CONFUSION

You are going to be baffled at first; there's no way around that. It is absolutely okay—unavoidable, in fact—not to get everything that's going on in a modern superhero comic. To not want to *fail to understand* any part of a story is a reasonable desire on the part of readers, but one of the great pleasures of reading Marvel's comics is the pleasure of being confused and then finding a way out of confusion.

Sometimes, that confusion is just the effect of a narrative that doesn't spell everything out at first—withholding information and then revealing it later,* or revealing it in sidelong ways, is one of the most effective tools in a storyteller's arsenal.† More often, a new reader's confusion comes from recent comics' constant allusions to older ones, the history piled upon history that pushes readers who are too wary of *not-knowing* all the way back to the beginning, or all the way out of the story. The only comics that *assume* the reader knows the relevant background already, though, are poorly constructed comics, because that assumption is an actual barrier to understanding.

Modern superhero comics don't often explain up front who everybody is or what their relationships are, but that doesn't mean they don't explain it at all; a story whose antecedents will have been seen by some but not all of its audience has to get across essential information subtly and in passing, rather than through clumps of potentially redundant exposition. And *no* creator expects that their readers are familiar with the whole Marvel story to date. (That can seem odd if you're used to relatively self-contained sorts of stories.) There is history behind what's happening in the story, and its dramatic effect is often greater if you know more of that history, but most of the dramatic effect remains intact if you don't. What

---

*You may, at some points in this book, encounter spoilers—plot information whose revelation was meant to be a surprise at the time it was originally published. That's okay: the way the story is told is always more important, and includes more pleasant surprises, than the bare facts of the story. Well-planned plot twists quickly turn into well-remembered moments that are worth discussing openly.

†The excellent 2012 *Hawkeye* series, written by Matt Fraction and drawn by David Aja, Annie Wu, and others, is a fine example of that; frustrated communication is its central motif. The story's internal timeline is scrambled from its very first page—the process of reading it demands some work to figure out how its pieces fit together. One issue is presented from the point of view of Hawkeye's dog, Lucky: its only legible words of dialogue are the few Lucky understands, its color palette is limited (to the yellows and blues that dogs can see!), and his "narration" takes the form of associative maps of little icon-like images (a trick lifted from Chris Ware's comics). Another issue takes place after Hawkeye has lost his hearing: this time, the legible dialogue is what little he can lip-read, and a few crucial passages appear as American Sign Language diagrams. As Aja has pointed out, if you, as a reader, aren't sure you fully understand what's being said in that issue, that's not a failure of the comic, or a hurdle meant to exclude you from enjoying it—it's specifically the point of the way this story is being told, a suggestion of the experience of disability.

the story wants from you is not your knowledge but your curiosity. You are not "unprepared"; you are already the ideal reader.*

Even when Marvel's comics involve intricate networks of reference, paying attention to where those connections might be in any particular story is almost always enough to catch what's going on and figure out where to learn more. To grab an example that's close at hand (and one that's both solidly enjoyable and referentially dense), here's how you might approach the baffling aspects of *Captain Britain and the Mighty Defenders* #2, by writer Al Ewing and artists Alan Davis and Mark Farmer, published in the summer of 2015.

On its surface, it's a fairly straightforward story about a conflict between two neighboring cities, resolved by people in colorful costumes smashing things, and it's satisfying enough on that level. On an allegorical level, it's also a very thinly veiled attack on the reactionary stances of the British political party UKIP.

But that issue is also a mind-bendingly (and typically) complicated mass of allusions, inversions, and commentary. For starters, *Captain Britain and the Mighty Defenders* was one of forty-odd miniseries published in conjunction with another miniseries, the "event comic" *Secret Wars.*† It's not set on the Earth on which most Marvel comics take place, but on Battleworld, a mass of "fragments of worlds that no longer exist" that have

---

*"But what about you, person who wrote this book?" I'm not the ideal reader—I'm over-qualified.

†That's the 2015 *Secret Wars*, not to be confused with the 1984 miniseries *Marvel Super Heroes Secret Wars*, to which it's a thematic sequel, or the 2004 miniseries *Secret War*, with which it has little in common. Patience: we'll get there (see chapter 18). What's an "event comic"? A story that's signaled in advance as affecting a wide swath of the fictional landscape. Event comics most often operate on a sort of hub-and-spoke model: there's a central miniseries in which big things happen, and the consequences of those things play out in tie-in issues of ongoing series, as well as in spin-off one-shots and miniseries about other characters and the general infrastructure of the Marvel world. The idea is that if, say, you want to see the effects of the *World War Hulk* event miniseries on Iron Man or Ghost Rider, you can follow their plot strands into their own titles, and if you want to see how the news media of Marvel's world tackle what happens in *World War Hulk*, you can also read *World War Hulk: Front Line*, but if you skip them, you still won't miss anything in *World War Hulk* proper.

been assembled into walled-off fiefdoms. Its title is a variation on *Captain America and the Mighty Avengers*, a series written by Ewing that had ended several months earlier (in Marvel's comics, the Avengers are a long-running, government-licensed superhero team with a malleable lineup; the Defenders are a much looser, more intermittent superhero team that famously lacks a raison d'être), and Davis and Farmer are closely associated with a version of the Captain Britain character.

That particular Captain Britain isn't in this story, though. The cover shows a woman with a sword confronting a giant robot; she's Dr. Faiza Hussain, who was introduced as a supporting character in the *Captain Britain and MI-13* series in 2008, and became (another iteration of) Captain Britain in 2013's *Avengers Assemble* #15AU.* The sword is Excalibur, the one from Arthurian legend, which is both the title of an earlier Marvel series (drawn by Davis and Farmer in the early 1990s) and a handy piece of shorthand for "we're going to make a point about British culture here."

That is *a lot,* and we haven't even opened the issue yet. On the first page of the story, we are introduced to Big Boss Hill, "Baron and Thor of Mondo City," who's wearing a costume that combines visual elements of the costumes most often worn by Thor and the Punisher.† We can gather from context that Mondo City is run by a sort of military junta, and that she's in charge of it. But there are other details an experienced superhero comics reader might notice. Hill's name and appearance are borrowed from the character Maria Hill, who has intermittently run the Marvel Universe's paramilitary agency S.H.I.E.L.D.; in the stories set on Battleworld, "Thors" are police. (The lettering in Big Boss Hill's word balloons is in the "chiseled" typeface normally used for Thor and other gods.) The "Boss" formulation alludes to Boss Cage, a character (from yet

---

*The odd form of that issue number indicates that it takes place in the alternate timeline called Age of Ultron.

†Both of those long-running characters have starred in movies of their own. They occupy entirely different spheres: Thor is literally a Norse god—more of him in chapter 12—and the Punisher is a non-superpowered military vet who has devoted his life to shooting "criminals."

another series, *Dark Avengers*) distinctly inspired by the British comics character Judge Dredd— who is *not* a Marvel character, but whose stories Ewing has also written. In fact, the way a shadow falls across Hill's outfit on the first page on which we see her suggests the badges worn by police in *Judge Dredd* comics. The implication, then, is that Big Boss Hill is a ruthless law-and-order type who commands the respect of her allies.

It goes on in that vein. For the sort of reader who likes to have everything spelled out, this can be intimidating: there's obviously so much context and subtext, and it's all zooming by. A helpful way to approach it as a novice, then, is

The first page of *Captain Britain and the Mighty Defenders* #2, 2015, written by Al Ewing and drawn by Alan Davis and Mark Farmer.

to start making note of proper names and curious details. Why is "Yinsen City" called that? Might it be significant that there's a cop named Magniconte, or a psychic named Frost? Does the strange design of a "sentient torture chair" mean something? Is the kid called Spider Hero meant to be anything more than a weird knockoff of Spider-Man? (Yes all around, of course, and even after reading tens of thousands of issues, I had to look up Magniconte.)

Do you *need* to know the answers to any of those questions to understand and enjoy what's happening in the comic? Absolutely not. If you want it to just be a story about a conflict between two cities, with a lot of on-the-fly worldbuilding, then that's what it is. But if you start investigating the answers to your questions, you might discover, for instance, that Ho Yinsen was the engineer who helped to create Iron Man and sacrificed his life so that Tony Stark could survive in 1963's *Tales of Suspense* #39, and that in the alternate reality seen in 2013's *Iron Man: Fatal Frontier* (another Ewing-written story), Yinsen survived instead of Stark and became a superhero named Rescue, and that Rescue is also the superhero name adopted in 2009 by longtime *Iron Man* supporting character Pepper Potts, and that Ho Yinsen's name is echoed by that of Maya Hansen, the inventor who appeared in Warren Ellis and Adi Granov's 2005 *Iron Man* storyline "Extremis," and you are *off to the races.*

Enjoying that process of not-knowing and finding out requires a certain humility as a reader. You need to be willing to say, "I don't know who that is," or "I don't get what she's doing," or "I have no idea what Hercules is talking about," or "Why does that planet have a face, and what's up with its goatee?" You also need to be willing to *continue* to not know some things: finding the answers to your questions will give you some possible paths for what to read next, but there's no way to take all of those paths, and sometimes things are just confusing by design or by accident. Again, the incompleteness is part of the fun of this endless, imperfect, collaboratively created story. An open question that a particular episode of it poses might be resolved by the creators who asked it, or by other creators later on, or by nobody at all. (Or by you: all of the story's current tellers were once part of its audience.)

Once you get your bearings—and that will happen very quickly—other interesting things might happen. You might discover characters who turn up only occasionally, but delight you whenever they do. (Ms. America Chavez. Batroc the Leaper. Diamondback. Amadeus Cho. The Shocker!) You might spend hours digging through grubby bargain bins in search of a fifty-cent copy of an issue of *Marvel Tales* with one of Fred Hembeck's "Petey" stories—"the adventures of Peter Parker long before he became Spider-Man." (Worth it.) You might become real-life friends with someone you first encountered by discussing minutiae of Black Widow's chronology on a message board. (So, wait, the *Gambit* special has to happen between pages 10 and 11 of *Champions* #7?) You might chat with your favorite creators online or at a convention, and discover them to be smart and charming. (Well . . . not *all* of them are.) You might also eventually find yourself reading stacks of some comic book you know perfectly well is terrible, just to see *what happens* in it, or to see fledgling artists working toward their mature powers, or to fill in the context for some other story you've enjoyed. That's not so bad; you'll still get some pleasure from it, just a different kind.

I'm making it sound like immersion in this stuff is *all* fun, which it's not. Caring about superhero comics will empty your pockets, break your heart, and fill you with red-eyed indignation. They linger over stupidity and violence, and prey on their audience's emotional identification and sense of incomplete understanding; there is cruelty and unfairness to creative geniuses stamped into every page. The whole structure is balanced on a disintegrating pile of flimsy, trivial amusements created for children of the baby boom.

What makes it worthwhile—for me and for at least some other people who follow serial superhero comics—is that there is a particular, deep kind of joy that comes from that practice. Read half a dozen of Marvel's better comics, and you might get the buzz of a good adventure story, see some striking artwork, and be introduced to a few memorable characters. Read a hundred, and you start to get a sense of what their devotees find special: that they add up to a collaborative story, built for delight, whose various tellers' specific visions are its most important aspect. Read a thousand, and every little detail of them becomes charged with meaning, as another world (which is also a stranger, more vivid version of our own world) is slowly revealed to you—a world of constant spectacle and drama, so broad and complicated that its mysteries perpetually unfold over hundreds of pages every week.

THE THREE CHRONOLOGIES

There are three different chronologies that it's important to keep separate in your head as you read this book, and as a reader of the big Marvel story: the chronology of publication, the chronology of events within the story, and the chronology in which you read the story. The first is governed by time, the second is governed by creators, and the third is governed by you and your personal interests and decisions.

/////

The first chronology—the order in which individual comic books were created and published—is the most obvious one. We know, in most cases, exactly when particular issues appeared on newsstands or in comics stores, and that's useful for thinking about the history of how they were made and how they were understood by their initial audience.

Again, Marvel's comics are always products and reflections of the moments in which they were made; reading them, you can see how those moments' politics and aesthetics and hopes for the future turned into little paper artifacts that carry episodes of a gigantic, continuous story. They also reflect the work of particular creators (and their collaborations) over time, and the evolution of the business and technology of comics. It's fun to look at how a favorite artist's work changes as they discover their voice, or to observe how and why issues of *Thor* from 1967 and 1992 and 2017 seem so different from one another.

/////

The second chronology—the order and timeline in which the events within the Marvel story occur—is much stranger. Close up, it looks a lot like the first chronology. A is followed by B; what happens in this month's issue of *Moon Girl and Devil Dinosaur* can usually be presumed to take place after what happened in last month's. Sometimes it can take a little bit of sorting out, as when there are two serials about the same character being published at the same time. (One has to happen before the other, and it's usually clear which is which later on.)

More broadly, Marvel's internal chronology happens on a massive parallel scale. The fifty or sixty series they publish at any one time are all on the same timeline, and affected by events in one another. Sometimes they're coordinated very tightly, and when that works, it's glorious—like hearing dozens of distinct melody lines snap into contrapuntal harmony.*

These stories can involve flashbacks and flash-forwards, which isn't that special in itself—every kind of narrative art has access to those. An odd and special thing about this kind of long-term serial storytelling, though, is that comics creators can alter the internal chronology of their own work or others', *long* after the fact, by way of the ingenious device known as a "retcon," short for "retroactive continuity." (The Norse mischief god Loki, in his role as a Marvel character, calls it "a story so big and mad and brilliant that it goes back in time and changes other stories.")

Pull back a bit, to the point where you can perceive more of the second chronology, and it starts getting really weird. For one thing, it doesn't actually map onto the first chronology at all. *Fantastic Four* #1 appeared sixty years ago, and

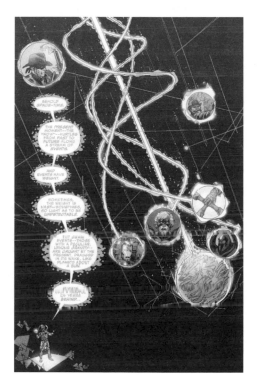

Galactus explains the "sliding timeline" in *The Ultimates* #5, written by Al Ewing and drawn by Kenneth Rocafort.

---

*It doesn't always work, but train wrecks can also be fun to watch if you're not on the train.

roughly fourteen years have passed between then and now within the story, but new comics are set in the present day, not in 1975.

The generally accepted solution to that problem is the "sliding timeline," a wonderfully convenient bit of undiluted sophistry. The clock of the story starts running with *Fantastic Four* #1, and the events of that issue take place about fourteen years before right now, *whenever "right now" is*.* Anachronistic elements of old comics, like Aunt May watching *The Beverly Hillbillies* on TV in *Amazing Spider-Man Annual* #1, are "topical references," inserted into the published versions of the story to backdate them.† And of course a month doesn't go by between the end of one issue and the beginning of the next—sometimes a long string of issues happen very quickly. Spider-Man, we can assume, doesn't have an adventure every month; he has something more like an adventure (or two or three) every day.

The sliding timeline doesn't solve every chronological problem, particularly when significant events within stories are pegged to historical phenomena. Nick Fury served as a sergeant in World War II and was still running S.H.I.E.L.D. in 2015? No problem: a 1976 issue of *Marvel Spotlight* establishes that a miraculous serum keeps him from aging normally. Tony Stark built the Iron Man armor while he was in captivity, around fourteen years ago, during the ... Vietnam War?‡ Well, it was during *some* war: 2010's *Iron Man: Requiem* sends him back to the cave where he built the armor, which now appears to be in Afghanistan, as his mind is failing.

---

*Galactus endorses a version of that perspective in 2016's *The Ultimates* #5: "Some events—those with a peculiar, unique gravity—are caught by the present. Dragged in its wake, like planets about a sun. Always just a handful of years behind."

†Another example: *The Amazing Spider-Man* #1.1, from 2014, appears to take place immediately after Spider-Man's first appearance, in 1962's *Amazing Fantasy* #15—but it involves laptop computers and mobile phones, which didn't exist then. That's fine, though: since that first story took place about fourteen years ago, any technology that was around by the mid-2000s is fair game, and the *absence* of laptops and cell phones from the earliest published Spider-Man stories was a "topical reference."

‡*History of the Marvel Universe* #2, from 2019, suggests that a lengthy conflict in Siancong (a fictional country, first mentioned as Sin-Cong back in 1965's *Avengers* #18) was *that big war in Asia a while ago*, and the "real" subject of "topical references" to Vietnam in older comics.

("Maybe it doesn't matter," he mutters to himself. "Whether it's here or in Vietnam or Cambodia or Rwanda or Bosnia or Iraq." It probably doesn't.)

And of course some irreconcilable errors and contradictions sneak in anyway—if you're looking for those, you'll find them. Characters seem to age at different rates, some appear to get older and then younger again depending on who's writing them (Kitty Pryde's age is infamously mutable), and there are more than a few loops and bumps of causality. But if you squint and think creatively and maybe cheat a little, almost any area of the timeline can be nudged into an order that makes some kind of sense.*

I find this second chronology endlessly fascinating. It's also nerd cliché #1, the stuff of countless well-actuallys. Thinking of these comics this way (the not-entirely-unfair accusation goes) overlooks their real wonders—artwork and language, imaginative invention, unforgettably vivid characters—in favor of treating them like a tricky jigsaw puzzle. I don't see a contradiction between those ways of thinking about them, though. The way shared-universe comics play with time is part of what makes them unlike any other kind of art: a collaboration among hundreds of storytellers, across decades, with some of the significant work done by their audience.

/////

Speaking of the audience: The third chronology of the Marvel story, and the most important by far, is the order in which *you* experience it. For the parts that are available to you, that order is determined only by you. To imagine that it's possible to do that "wrong" is to deny your own powers, both literally and figuratively.

---

*I've contributed a little bit of labor to the Marvel Chronology Project, a group of fans who have compiled an online concordance of every appearance by every recurring character—not in the order of publication, or even the order of events, but still another chronology: the order each individual character experienced them. (What's the difference between the order of events and the order of experiences? Time travel!) The MCP's discussion boards are full of voluminous, polite, Talmudically precise efforts to figure out how everything can fit together.

In relation to their story, Marvel's characters are, mostly, constrained by time's arrow, and by the (admittedly mutable) laws of physics of their environment. You, the reader, are not. For your purposes, as you navigate through these comics, you have a time machine, a teleporter, and a universe-jumping device. Why not use them? The pleasure of continuity isn't about making sure you're experiencing a multithreaded story in the "right" order: it's realizing how the pieces fit together and feeling the links of causality snap into place in your head.

You can read these comics in any order you like, following narrative threads or individual characters or specific creators' work, investigating a piece of history that's led to something interesting you've just seen, wandering in any direction as the mood strikes you. You can even do something no character within the story can do: revisit any part of it, any time you want, with everything you've read (and everything you've become) since the first time you saw it, allowing you to get greater joy and deeper understanding out of it.

3

CURSE OF THE WEIRD (FREQUENTLY ASKED QUESTIONS)

The culture around superhero comics can be forbidding and baffling, or bubble over with welcoming kindness. When people who have been part of that culture for a while take the latter route, we're doing it right: we want to invite everyone in to have fun with us. Sometimes we use technical jargon, not because we're trying to keep anyone out, but because it's convenient and we're used to it, and because we're maybe kind of socially inept. (Sorry.) American superhero comics—"cape comics," we sometimes call them, self-mockingly— also have a lot of peculiar storytelling conventions, most of which have to do with the ways the medium and the genre have evolved. So this chapter is an attempt to lower some of the barriers that Marvel-curious readers may run into, and to answer some questions I've seen come up repeatedly. None of this requires memorization or anything; some of it may seem obvious or arcane; all of it is meant to make this tour easier and more enjoyable for you.

What makes a superhero comic book good?

That is a deceptively tricky question, but rather than going off for the next forty pages about the construction of taste, I'll note that there are two basic principles that can make finding comics *you* enjoy much easier. One is that *creators are at least as important as characters.* You like Spider-Man? I like Spider-Man too! A lot! But that doesn't mean a randomly selected Spider-Man comic will do anything for either of us. If you particularly like the *Daredevil* comics by Ann Nocenti and John Romita Jr., other *Daredevil* comics may give you more of what you like about them, but different comics written by Nocenti or drawn by Romita are even more likely to be your kind of thing.*

The other is that artists are at least as important as writers. It's faster to write comics than to draw them,† so there are often issues or sequences that are written by one person and drawn by a few people. But look-and-feel is artists' territory, and so are character acting and (usually) staging and (occasionally) plotting.

What's the difference between comic books, graphic novels, and trades? How have those formats affected the stories within them?

Comic books are how most of Marvel's stories are serialized: twenty- to thirty-page issues, usually published as stapled pamphlets on a roughly monthly basis. They're subsequently collected as trades (short for "trade paperbacks," as opposed to the smaller "mass market" paperback format used for some prose books) or hardcover collections, each of which gener-

---

*Sometimes cape comics' alchemy requires both particular creators and particular characters. I'm fond of Nocenti's work, and Romita's, and inker Al Williamson's, and of *Daredevil* in general, but put them together and it's *exactly* my jam.
†The exception to this rule, as to many others: Jack Kirby, who could draw (and plot) faster than almost anyone could write.

ally contains five or more issues of a particular series; those ostensibly stay in print as long as there's enough demand for them. "Graphic novel" has come to be a term of art for any square-bound book of comics; it can refer to anything from collections of short, unrelated stories to long nonfiction narratives. But "original graphic novels," in the context of mainstream comics, are stories published in book form without having previously been serialized. (Marvel publishes a handful of those each year.)

Book publishing and digital publishing have massively transformed the Marvel story because they've transformed the way its audience has access to its earlier parts. It wasn't until sometime in the early 2000s that it became standard practice for most American publishers to reprint *every* serial comic as books, as it became clear that there was a subset of readers who were willing to "wait for the trade," and that bookstores and libraries were opening up shelf space for graphic novels. That also shaped the content of new comics, naturally: writers started pacing stories for five- or six-issue volumes.

Marvel Unlimited, a digital all-you-can-read service, was launched in late 2007. (By then, collectors had already scanned pretty much everything Marvel had ever published and made it available online to those who knew where to look, but Unlimited was officially authorized and easy to access on mobile devices.) It's a fairly recent development that the bulk of the big Marvel story has become easily accessible to a curious reader,* and a lot of recent comics reflect that change. Instead of on-page recaps and bottom-of-panel editorial notes citing past issue numbers, they can gracefully allude to older stories in passing, since there are readers

---

*The bulk of it, not all of it. Some series are officially out of print because of rights issues, like *ROM* and *Godzilla*; some have never been reprinted or officially made available digitally because not many people are clamoring for them. And a few stories seem to have been entirely lost, like most of the CyberComics produced by Marvel for America Online between 1996 and 2000, which could only be read via AOL. *Gambit* #12 from 2000, for instance, includes a footnote referring to a *Gambit* CyberComic called *The Hunt for the Tomorrow Stone*—but, apparently, Marvel doesn't have archival copies of *Tomorrow Stone*, and neither do its creators. It's just *gone*, vanished into the internet ether.

who will catch those allusions, then pass the word along to others who will look them up.

I really liked the latest Marvel movie. What comic is it based on? Are there more comics that continue its story?

None of Marvel Studios' movies are *entirely* drawn from particular comic books' plots, but a few of them incorporate elements from specific stories. *Captain America: Civil War*, for instance, has a central conceit of a conflict between Captain America and Iron Man, which was also part of the premise of the 2006 *Civil War* comics. *Avengers: Infinity War* has some characters and pieces of its plot borrowed from *Thanos Quest* (1990), *The Infinity Gauntlet* (1991), and *Infinity* (2013)—though not really from the 1992 *Infinity War* comics miniseries. The 2021 TV series *WandaVision* echoes *The Vision and the Scarlet Witch* (1985), *House of M* (2005), and *The Vision* (2016) in its tone and themes, and lifts some imagery from a 1989 sequence of *West Coast Avengers*. And virtually every named character in Marvel's post-2008 movies and TV shows has an equivalent in the comics, though some have a closer resemblance than others.

That said, some of the X-Men-related movies made by 20th Century Fox are loosely based on well-loved X-Men comics of the past. *The Wolverine* is derived from the 1982 *Wolverine* miniseries, and *X-Men: Days of Future Past, Apocalypse,* and *Dark Phoenix* draw on particular comics storylines. (*X-Men: First Class* has very little in common with the comics of the same name, though.)

As for the reciprocal relationship, there are a handful of comics that directly adapt Marvel Studios' movies, or are set in the movies' fictional universe. They're hamstrung by having to try to imitate what happens on a theater's screen, without the benefit of either film's particular tools (continuous motion, sound, physical immersion) or a lot of comics' particular tools (expressive visual style, freedom from direct representation, deep worldbuilding). They can't add much to the movies, either, since anything significant in terms of plot or characters is reserved for the screen anyway.

Rewind a second. The movie universe is different? It seems like there are so many universes, multiverses, timelines—how do I keep them all straight if I just want to read about the one real Iron Man?

They're *all* real, or rather none of them are real, but I know what you mean: you want to know which comics with Iron Man in them involve the same version of the character you will see if you pick up this month's issue of *Iron Man*. The answer is "most of them, and if not, they'll probably let you know."

That said, the multiverse is a long-standing device in the Marvel story. The idea is that there are a whole lot of alternate universes that are *kind of* like the one in which most of the story takes place, but different in specific ways; under certain circumstances, it's possible to travel between them. So even stories about versions of Marvel characters that are explicitly *not* set in the same environment as *The Avengers* and *The Amazing Spider-Man*, from the infelicitously titled *Ultimate Comics New Ultimates* to *Peter Porker, The Spectacular Spider-Ham*,* do also "happen," just in some parallel universe or other.

As I noted in chapter 1, Marvel's main universe is often referred to as "616," a useful concept whose name is something of an inside joke. In the 1960s, DC Comics explained the difference between the superhero stories they were then publishing and the ones they'd published between 1938 and the mid '50s by saying that the earlier ones had happened on a parallel world, "Earth-Two," and that the current ones took place on

---

*Peter Porker is exactly what you'd guess: a variation on Spider-Man, with all of the characters changed to funny-animal types with punning names. It managed to run seventeen issues between 1985 and 1987. (The jokes are occasionally pretty good, as when a dancing Mary Jane Water Buffalo declares "This 'Stop Making Nests' soundtrack by the Squawking Heads is awesome. David Bird's voice just reeks of contemporary avian angst!") Spider-Ham continues to show up here and there in comics, and made a memorable appearance in the *Spider-Man: Into the Spider-Verse* movie.

"Earth-One." Lots of subsequent DC stories involved parallel worlds, some of them numbered.

Marvel also occasionally played with parallel worlds in the '60s and '70s, but didn't bother to give them numbers until an early-'80s Captain Britain story mentioned in passing that the familiar Marvel universe, and by extension its Earth, were numbered 616. The implication was that there was nothing particularly special about it—that it was not the Platonic ideal from which all others were derived, but one of many possibilities— and that idea stuck.*

So what's a timeline? In Marvel's comics, time travel can, under certain circumstances, result in the past being changed, which effectively results in the creation of a new version of a universe that branches off from the old one at that point.† (Don't think too hard about it.)

What does "continuity" mean? What's canonical? How do I tell? What does it matter?

Continuity in comics means roughly the same thing it means in, for instance, film editing: the idea is that all the events we see in comics set within universe 616 are *pretty much* compatible with one another. When they're not, there may be an explanation forthcoming—or one may be invented at some point.‡

---

*The world in which the MCU movies take place is Earth-199999. The benighted, superhumanless world in which you and I live is Earth-1218. Our universe was destroyed at some point in the course of a 2012–2015 storyline in *New Avengers*—see chapter 18—but has apparently since been reconstructed, given that you're reading this.
†There's an in-story organization called the Time Variance Authority that makes sure all of that works the way it should, or tries to.
‡Sometimes, that requires a sort of emergency carpentry. My favorite example is the problem of 1976's *Marvel Team-Up Annual* #1 and *Marvel Team-Up* #53, which involve the X-Men, including Phoenix, and take place when Charles Xavier is experiencing precognitive nightmares. Between the time Phoenix first appears, collapses, and is rushed to a hospital in *X-Men* #101 and the time the "Xavier's nightmares" plot is resolved in *X-Men* #105, there doesn't seem to be any moment at which all the relevant characters are available to appear in the *Team-Up* stories. The solution some inspired nerd came up with is that between panels of a hospital scene in *X-Men* #101 a good deal of time surreptitiously goes by in which Phoenix recuperates and rejoins the X-Men, they go off and have an adventure in the southwestern U.S. in *Marvel Team-Up*, and then she goes *back* to the

A canon is a body of stories to which other stories can refer as history or background. They "happened," as far as subsequent stories are concerned. Every comic book that is both published by Marvel and set inside what looks like its main shared universe is canonical to every other one, unless it explicitly and irreconcilably contradicts them. That rule applies on a series-by-series basis, and it's usually pretty easy to figure out.* Does it matter? Only as much as you want it to.

---

hospital. When *Marvel Team-Up* #53 was reprinted in 1992's *Marvel Tales* #262, it was accompanied by a short, newly written and drawn story in which the X-Men are attacked on their way home from that *Marvel Team-Up* issue, and Phoenix is injured and has to be rushed to a hospital. It's not a *good* story, by any reasonable metric, but it does the work of whacking a board into place over the hole.

*Here's an example: 2015's *Spidey* #1, by writer Robbie Thompson and artist Nick Bradshaw, is the first issue of a series set at the beginning of Peter Parker's career as Spider-Man, when he was still in high school (as he was in the comics published from 1962 to 1965). The story's first pages recapitulate a lot of familiar images from the first Spider-Man story—the spider bite, the wrestling match, the dead uncle. But we also see him fighting the White Rabbit, a villain who didn't appear until 1983's *Marvel Team-Up* #131. Can we imagine that there was a *different* White Rabbit he fought much earlier? That's stretching things.

Then, still early in the first issue, there's a scene in which Gwen Stacy is seen as one of Peter Parker's classmates and acquaintances in high school, and that's where we pull the brake. The 616 Peter and Gwen didn't meet until college, and lots of stories would cease to make sense if they *did* know each other in high school—which means that *Spidey*'s creators are signaling, for those who care, that it doesn't take place in the main Marvel universe but is off in a universe of its own. If that's not a detail that would stick out to you as a reader, then it doesn't matter for your purposes; you can just enjoy *Spidey* as a comic book about a high school–aged Peter Parker, written and drawn in a modern style.

For the sake of comparison, look at 1995's *Untold Tales of Spider-Man* #1, by writer Kurt Busiek and artists Pat Olliffe and Al Vey. It's also a "Peter Parker in high school" story, and begins with the young Spider-Man fighting a never-before-seen character called the Scorcher. Peter is wearing the big round glasses he wore in his earliest stories (until they were broken in *Amazing Spider-Man* #8); he has flashbacks to encountering the Lizard, Doctor Doom, Doctor Octopus, and the Vulture, all of whom he had met by *Amazing Spider-Man* #6; and, as Spider-Man, he meets Gwen Stacy's father, Captain George Stacy of the New York City Police.

That's *not* a problem. George Stacy first appeared even later than Gwen, in *Amazing Spider-Man* #56, but nothing about his 1960s appearances is contradicted by his having spent a few minutes with Spider-Man sometime earlier. All of the details in the first issue of *Untold Tales* suggest that it *is* 616-canonical, and indicate exactly when it takes place. And again: for a reader to whom those details don't signify anything in particular, that doesn't matter! It's just another comic book about a high school–aged Peter Parker, in a style contemporary to the mid-'90s.

I tried reading something that looked like a first issue, and I'm disoriented—it seems like a bunch of stuff has happened already?

There are a few different reasons serial comics might do that. One is that they're starting a new story *in medias res*—diving into the action so they can get readers engaged with the story first and explain themselves later. Another is that they're deliberately concealing something to be revealed later, or suggesting that the parts they're not explaining aren't important. Also, one storytelling technique Marvel has used repeatedly in the past few years is abruptly yanking the timeline of a series forward and indicating that a lot of big developments have taken place while we weren't looking; it's left as an exercise for the reader to notice what's different and imagine how it might have happened.

The other reason a story that's signaled as a starting point might be confusing, of course, is that it's poorly written. That happens sometimes too.

If I like a character, do I have to read everything they're in to understand what's going on with them?

No more than you have to follow your friends around 24/7 to understand what's going on with them.

Why are there so many series with nearly identical titles?

Often, that happens when a section of the fictional universe is popular enough to support multiple series with different creative teams and, sometimes, different casts and tones. (*X-Men, Uncanny X-Men, New X-Men, All-New X-Men, Dark X-Men, Astonishing X-Men, Amazing X-Men,* and *Ultimate X-Men*, for instance, are all slightly different things; whether the distinctions between them are meaningful or not depends on how much you like the X-Men.) Sometimes it happens accidentally: *Astonishing Tales* and *Tales to Astonish* are discrete entities. There are only so many hyperbolic adjectives to go around.

Did I hear about some kind of reboot a few months ago? Can I just start there?

Sure, but it's not really a "reboot": in serial fiction, rebooting means throwing out most or all of the old stories and starting over. Marvel has never done that. They do have "relaunches" every year or two: a coordinated advertising campaign* for some or all of their series, often resetting their numbering back to #1. That's just to announce that it's a point designed for readers to join the big story in progress—a new season, in effect. If there's a new *Amazing Spider-Man* #1, the events of the previous 800-odd issues of *Amazing Spider-Man* still happened to the character, but it's specifically designed to be extra-friendly to people who haven't read any of the earlier ones, or haven't read Spider-Man comics in a long while.

Speaking of *Amazing Spider-Man* #1: Why are there five different comics called that?

Comics buyers are much more likely to care about issue #1 than issue #437, so a new #1 signals that there's a new creative team or new direction of some kind for the series. Since the late 1990s, renumbering has most often implied something along those lines. In 2017, almost all of Marvel's ongoing series' numbers jumped to what they *would* have been had they been numbered consecutively from the beginning (resulting in *Amazing Spider-Man*, for instance, leaping directly from #32 to #789). Subsequent relaunches of various series have listed that "legacy number" (indicated with LGY) below the regular issue number.†

---

*They usually have names that imply *it's really okay to start here, honest*: 2012's Marvel Now! was followed by All-New Marvel Now!, then All-New, All-Different Marvel, then Marvel Legacy, then Fresh Start.

†The convention Marvel uses is to put the year of the most recent renumbering of a series between the title and issue number, e.g., "*Amazing Spider-Man* (2015) #32." Making it easy to keep track of when specific issues came out relative to one another is important for my purposes here, so in the body of this book's text, I generally refer to the year of the cover date; that means I'd refer to the same issue as "2017's *Amazing Spider-Man* #32."

The covers of the five different comics called *Amazing Spider-Man #1*, clockwise from 1963 (drawn by Jack Kirby and Steve Ditko), 1999 (John Byrne), 2014 (Humberto Ramos), 2015 (Alex Ross), and 2018 (Ryan Ottley).

And speaking of "legacies," what are "legacy characters"?

Occasionally, a newly introduced character will be based, in name or appearance or other ways, on an older character. Marvel's first legacy character appeared in the first issue of *Fantastic Four*: the Human Torch, an updated version of a character from the 1930s.

A few more legacy characters turned up in the '70s and early '80s, mostly women who were connected to male superheroes: Spider-Woman, Ms. Marvel, She-Hulk. Series about teams begat auxiliary teams—the X-Men were joined by the New Mutants, the Avengers by the West Coast Avengers. Tony Stark gave up being Iron Man for a while and was replaced by James Rhodes; after Stark returned, Rhodes got his own suit of armor and his own series as War Machine. By the mid-'90s, nearly every long-running series had at least one spin-off about related characters.

Legacy characters can also illuminate the differences between a given character's role (in the sense of a name, costume, and power set) and the specific person who has taken on that role—and that device is very useful for introducing major new characters who don't belong to the homogeneous demographic that got to be superheroes in the 1960s and '70s. Hence Miles Morales, Riri Williams, Kate Bishop, Kamala Khan, Amadeus Cho, and Lunella Lafayette, who have all been starring in series with familiar titles over the past few years: *Spider-Man*, *The Invincible Iron Man*, *Hawkeye*, *Ms. Marvel*, *The Totally Awesome Hulk*, and *Moon Girl and Devil Dinosaur*.

That led to certain readers—generally older, whiter, and male-er than otherwise—getting into the habit of making bad-faith arguments about Marvel's comics in the mid-2010s. The complaint that turned up in venue after venue was that Marvel was publishing *Spider-Man* without Peter Parker, *Thor* without Odin's son, *Iron Man* without Tony Stark, *Captain America* without Steve Rogers, *Wolverine* without Logan, *X-Men* without

---

There are also a handful of issues with numbers that aren't positive integers—#0, #14AU, #-1, #258.3, and so on—which usually just means "This is a special story that has some kind of relationship to an issue with a number close to this one."

"the real" Wolverine or Cyclops or Professor X, *Hulk* without Bruce Banner, *Hawkeye* without Clint Barton, and no *Fantastic Four* at all.

That's a kind of complaint that almost always reads as code. Marvel was publishing a *Spider-Man* with a Black and Latino protagonist, a *Thor* with a woman protagonist, an *Iron Man* with a Black woman protagonist, a *Captain America* with a Black protagonist, a *Wolverine* with a woman protagonist, a *Hulk* with an Asian American protagonist followed by a *Hulk* with a woman protagonist, a *Hawkeye* with a woman protagonist, and a bunch of *X-Men* series that, admittedly, often felt rather adrift. Meanwhile, Peter Parker and the former Thor and Tony Stark and Steve Rogers and Clint Barton and Ben Grimm and Johnny Storm and Logan had all continued to appear in *just about as many new comics as ever*. It's not that the old characters went away (apart from Reed and Sue Richards, who took a two-and-a-half-year leave of absence before returning in mid-2018*); it's that the new characters who tried on their roles weren't white men.

Another familiar bad-faith question about legacy characters is "Why can't new comics be about totally new superhero characters, not derived in any way from extant ones? Don't legacy characters reveal an essential lack of creativity?" It's a bad-faith argument because, given modern market conditions, series about characters who fit that description are nearly impossible to sell. The last one Marvel published that caught on was *Runaways*, and that debuted in 2005. (The last one they've tried, as of this writing, was 2016's *Mosaic*, which lasted only eight issues.)

When did superhero comics suddenly get so political?

This is yet another question that is often asked in bad faith, most often by people who dislike the progressive political content that is often part of superhero comics but have no objection to reactionary political content. Let's put it this way: the first issue of *Captain America Comics*, whose cover depicted Captain America socking Hitler on the jaw, was published

---

*See chapters 4 and 18.

in late 1940, a year before Pearl Harbor—
which is to say that Joe Simon and Jack
Kirby created Captain America specifically *as* an argument for the U.S. to enter
the Second World War. Superhero comics have never *not* been political.

**I keep running into unpleasantly
sexualized art in mainstream comics,
and especially when I look at older
comics I see some really nasty racial
representations too. How do I get my
superhero fix in the face of that?**

Unfortunately, that stuff is there
sometimes. Remember that if you encounter something gross enough to ruin
your enjoyment of a comic book you
were predisposed to enjoy, the error
belongs to the people who made that

Captain America punches Hitler
on the cover of *Captain America
Comics* #1, cover-dated March
1941 and drawn by Joe Simon
and Jack Kirby.

comic; it's not your responsibility to deal with it or to push through it. But
the creators of comics are specific people. Keep your eyes on their names.
Making note of whose work you like and whose work makes you cringe
can be a pretty effective filter.

**Spider-Woman/Reed Richards/Jean Grey would never do/say
[the thing they're shown doing/saying]!**

They just did, canonically. Now you get to figure out what to do about
it. You can find a way to resign yourself to the fact that a character is not
always quite the way you imagined them to be (people do sometimes act
"out of character" or change over time). You can wait for some kind of explanation of why they're acting differently than usual (altered behavior or
speech patterns are sometimes a signal, in storytelling, that *things are*

not what they seem*). Or you can decide that a particular story's interpretation of a particular character is not your thing.

Wait, I thought Captain America/the Hulk/Moira MacTaggert was killed a while ago! What's up with them being alive again? How can all these characters keep coming back to life?

That's just narrative convention now. It used to be said that "the only two characters who don't come back are Uncle Ben and Bucky Barnes,"† but Marvel occasionally has killed off characters who'd starred in their own series, for keeps: Omega the Unknown died in 1977 and Captain Marvel in 1982, and both of them are still dead.‡ When the 1992 "Death of Superman" sequence sold millions of copies for DC Comics, though, publishers realized that briefly dispatching well-loved characters, then bringing them back, was a reliable way to turn nostalgia into money.§ A wave of significant deaths and returns followed.

In the early 2000s, when Joe Quesada became Marvel's editor in chief, he decreed that "dead is dead," and that miraculously resurrecting characters was no longer cricket. By the middle of the decade, though, death's revolving door was rotating freely once again, and when Captain America was "assassinated" in 2007, very few readers believed they'd seen the last

---

*Occasionally, comics creators will put a spin on each other's interpretations. In 1981's *Uncanny X-Men* #146, for instance, Arcade strikes a match on Doctor Doom's armor, to which Doom doesn't respond at all. Two years later, in *Fantastic Four* #258, one of Doom's look-alike robots explains that it got a scratch on its armor because Arcade struck a match on it, but didn't kill Arcade because "I judged it conceivable you might have need of him later"; Doom destroys the robot ("Need? Doom needs no one"). And in 2014's *Loki: Agent of Asgard* #6, Doom explains that he makes his robots look like himself so that nobody ever knows whether they're dealing with the real Doom: "I once let Arcade strike a match on me, just to maintain that confusion."
†Then Bucky Barnes came back.
‡There have been a few other Captains Marvel since then, including the one in the 2019 movie.
§It was enough of a cultural watershed that even a few Marvel comics reacted to it. Vampire detective Hannibal King knelt by Superman's grave in *Nightstalkers*, and Ghost Rider appeared on his own series' letters page, announcing: "Your super-strength couldn't save you, man from Krypton... and for your death... I must seek vengeance!"

of him. Neil Gaiman and Andy Kubert's 2003–2004 miniseries *Marvel 1602* put it neatly: its seventeenth-century version of Reed Richards says, "I posit we are in a universe which favours stories. A universe in which no story can ever truly end; in which there can be only continuances."

The intractable problem is that characters who matter enough that their deaths are dramatically meaningful also matter enough that the endless narrative needs them. They'll have to come back eventually, and everyone knows it. So clever writers have started playing with *that* expectation: 2019's *X-Men* relaunch establishes that any of its protagonists can be resurrected as necessary, and the premise of the 2018 *Immortal Hulk* series is that Bruce Banner, the Hulk, longs to stay dead but keeps coming back to life.

What's a comics fan? Do I count as one? Do I have to be one?

"Fan"—originally derived from "fanatic," subsequently given much tamer and happier connotations—is a really slippery term, but I think of it as meaning someone whose self-image includes "enjoying comics." If you consider yourself to be a fan, then you're a fan, by definition. You are not required to act on that part of your self-image the way anyone else does, or to the same extent, and you have every right to be suspicious of anyone who claims otherwise. You can also read anything you like *without* having to make "fandom" a part of your identity. This is entertainment, not citizenship.

/////

With that, the tour is ready to begin. Most of the rest of this book focuses on a set of specific bodies of work within the big Marvel story—the work of particular writers and artists on particular series or narrative moments. I picked them because they're especially rewarding on their own, and because they represent and point toward broader categories of interesting and enjoyable comics (again, these are trailheads), with an eye toward surveying the chronological, creative, and tonal range of what the story has been in the past sixty years.*

Everything in the Marvel story, though, is connected to everything else, and made richer by its context—so each of the long chapters follows some of those sequences' connections to other parts of the Marvel story, before and after and during the time of their initial publication. Between those chapters, there are interludes—quick glimpses of other kinds of cross sections of Marvel's comics and the history around them. And at the end, there's an appendix: my attempt to take an overhead view of the whole story, show where the sequences I've discussed fit within it, and summarize the plot and themes of Marvel's first half million pages in a few thousand words. (If you are the kind of reader who is more comfortable knowing what the big picture looks like before you can start focusing on details, you may want to look at that appendix before you go on; otherwise, I recommend holding off until you get there.)

I'll repeat my warning one more time: *You must stray from the path.* And now we're off to our first stop, the crossroads of infinity.

---

*And what did I regretfully leave off that short list, you ask? *So much*—but the comics I didn't write about here informed the way I approached the ones I did write about. Jim Starlin's 1974–1977 Adam Warlock sequence is very dear to me, but I've already written about it at length in my 2008 book, *Reading Comics: How Graphic Novels Work and What They Mean*, so I touch on it only briefly in this one. The same goes for Marv Wolfman, Gene Colan, and Tom Palmer's 1972–1979 *Tomb of Dracula*. Nick Spencer and Steve Lieber's *The Superior Foes of Spider-Man* (2013) and Tom King and Gabriel Hernandez Walta's *The Vision* (2016) are both wonderful in their own ways, but I was already hitting the 2010s pretty hard. There are four radically different periods of *Daredevil* that I like a whole lot, respectively created by Frank Miller with Klaus Janson and David Mazzucchelli (1981–1983 and 1986); Ann Nocenti, John Romita Jr., and Al Williamson (1988–1990); Brian Michael Bendis and Alex Maleev (2001–2006); and Mark Waid with Chris Samnee and others (2011–2015); but they also overlap in some way with a lot of other comics I discuss here. The "cosmic Marvel" titles that ran from 2004 to 2011—*Annihilation, War of Kings, Guardians of the Galaxy,* and so on—are a whole thing. James Robinson and ACO's *Nick Fury*! Charles Soule and Javier Pulido's *She-Hulk*! J. M. DeMatteis and Liam Sharp's *Man-Thing*! *The Incredible Hercules, You Are Deadpool, Doctor Strange: The Oath, Mockingbird, War of the Realms: Giant-Man*—I could go on. Wait, how is Kieron Gillen and Jamie McKelvie's *Young Avengers* not in here? It's so good! Anyway, I apologize for leaving out your favorite comic. It almost made the cut.

4

THE JUNCTION TO EVERYWHERE

ur tour of the Marvel story has to start *somewhere*, and there's one particular issue—one page, actually—that announces itself as a special kind of vantage point.

Fantastic Four #51 (June 1966)
STAN LEE, JACK KIRBY, JOE SINNOTT

Stan Lee and Jack Kirby's 1961–1970 run on *Fantastic Four* was the first superhero series Marvel published in that era, and effectively the flagship comic of the line:* the adventures of Ben Grimm (the Thing); his genius-scientist friend Reed Richards (Mr. Fantastic); Reed's girlfriend, Sue Storm

---

*It's worth noting that by 1966, the first year for which sales statements are available, *Amazing Spider-Man* was outselling it—and, at the time, *Archie, Superman, Batman,* and *Tarzan* all outsold anything Marvel published. Aside from a few heavily hyped issues, *Fantastic Four* has never been Marvel's bestselling title, but it's their landmark, the place where Kirby and Lee planted the standard of their aesthetic.

(the Invisible Girl); and Sue's brother, Johnny Storm (the Human Torch, a new take on a name and design that went back to 1939's *Marvel Comics* #1). A bold, yellow box on the cover of *Fantastic Four* #3 declared that it was THE GREATEST COMIC MAGAZINE IN THE WORLD!! With the next issue, that became the strapline, and "The World's Greatest Comic Magazine!" stayed above its title for the next forty years.

The Kirby and Lee *Fantastic Four* is an incredible feat of universe-building and genre-hybridizing, smooshing together most of the breeds of comics in which both creators had been working for twenty years: an adventure-serial comic that's *also* a superhero comic and *also* a monster comic and *also* a romance comic and *also* a teen-humor comic and *also* a sci-fi comic, all at once. (Interestingly, it's not a crime comic, although both Lee and Kirby had dabbled in that genre when it was popular a decade earlier. The Fantastic Four are referred to as "crime fighters" in early issues, but the law and its enforcement are effectively irrelevant to what they do.) With some variations, that basic combination—superheroes + monsters + romance—became the basis of most of Marvel's early successes, and some of their later ones too.

The first hundred issues of *Fantastic Four* are Marvel's bible and manual, the rocky orange blood cells in the weird green veins of its story. Kirby and Lee hurled extraordinary concepts out into the world they were making, issue by issue, page after page. Some grew roots and leaves, others became foundation stones.

If you're talking about the glories of Kirby-era *Fantastic Four*, you're especially talking about a couple of years in the middle of it, the 1965–1967 stretch when the series was at its most ambitious and thrilling, pushing into uncharted spaces every month. And in the middle of that era—and almost exactly halfway through Lee and Kirby's *Fantastic Four* (102 issues, 6 annuals, a barrel-scraping fragment or two later on)—there's #51: "This Man... This Monster!"

Fantastic Four #51 remains a sentimental favorite for a lot of long-time comics readers, especially for an issue in which no famous character debuts or dies. It touches on some of the biggest themes of the broader Marvel story: monsters, doubles and shadow selves, redemption. Created at frantic speed* and designed to keep impatient kids entertained, Lee and Kirby's collaborations were powerfully resonant, and "This Man . . . This Monster!" is pulled taut by opposites braced against each other: journeys inward and outward, spectacle and introspection, cosmology and style, art and commerce, imperfection and perfection.

Midway through the issue, there's a very famous page. It's an image of unreality, an impossible psychedelic landscape, mostly constructed as a photographic collage

Jack Kirby's photo collage from *Fantastic Four* #51, 1966, with dialogue by Stan Lee and inks (on the figure of Reed Richards) by Joe Sinnott.

of circular forms and inverted mountains, but with two conventional comics elements pasted onto it. Near its center, there's a small image of Reed Richards, drawn by Kirby with inker Joe Sinnott,† and a word balloon with Lee's text in letterer Artie Simek's handwriting. Kirby, in those days, wrote notes in the margins of each page he drew, explaining their action to Lee and suggesting what the characters might be saying. His

---

*Kirby drew *Fantastic Four* #51 at a moment when he was cutting down his workload from inhuman (the 120 pages a month he'd been drawing just a bit earlier) to backbreaking (a mere 78 or 79 pages a month); Lee, besides editing the entire line, scripted seven full comics that month and half of an eighth.

†Sinnott was the quiet member of the *Fantastic Four* creative team: after inking issue #5, he returned with #44 and continued to ink the series almost continuously for the next fifteen years.

comment on the original artwork for the collage page is "Reed drifts in dimensional space—it's both weird and beautiful." Lee's dialogue for Reed seizes on two of the key words from Kirby's note and wraps an exquisite, hyperbolic jumble of language around them: "I've *done* it!! I'm drifting into a world of limitless dimensions!! It's the *crossroads of infinity*—the junction to *everywhere*!"

That's exactly what Lee and Kirby's *Fantastic Four* is, as a whole. It's the capital city of Marvel's universe, the central wellspring of its extraordinary elements. It's a story about emotional intimacy that's also about geographical and metaphysical exploration; it's a story about family that's also about monsters. (Family means the people who are inalienably part of who you are. A monster is a concept you fear given a physical form, and it's what you need to protect your family from.) *Fantastic Four* is an ensemble story, but it includes two characters who are so extraordinary that they absolutely dominate its overall shape: the Thing and Doctor Doom, who have parallel if unequal roles in its dramatic structure.

Only the first of those two appears in "This Man... This Monster!" Ben Grimm, the Thing, is an outsider whose sense of exile mostly comes from his own perceptions of himself. He grew up in rough circumstances (on Yancy Street, a nonexistent place whose name is distinctly Old New York), alongside a gang that still delights in pranking him. He's smarter than he usually lets on, but he got out of poverty by making himself physically powerful, winning a football scholarship to the college where he met Reed.

And then that backfired on him: the origin story of the Fantastic Four is the story of how his body became that of a monster, an impossibly strong pile of orange rocks in a parody of a human form. He tries to soften his literal sharp edges by wisecracking, but his jokes have a bitter, self-deprecating aftertaste. "It's clobberin' time!" is his catchphrase, and it's a funny one—"clobber" is the kind of word a guy who grew up on Yancy Street would use, and nobody else in *Fantastic Four* would ever think to—but it's also rueful: the subtext is "brute force, the one thing I'm good at, is finally useful!"

There's no dialogue on the first page of *Fantastic Four* #51, just the title and credits and a bit of Lee's whipping-up-the-crowd patter, and mostly an image of the Thing standing on a city street in the rain at night. As usual, he's naked except for his "costume," a pair of blue trunks; the downpour is falling on the rocks he has instead of skin, pooling around his massive feet. He's not wet or cold—he can't really feel anything. We've seen him in action many times, but there is no action here. He's motionless and a little slumped, even more asymmetrical than usual.

What Kirby has drawn is very obviously a picture of depression, and on the next page, as Ben starts moving again, Lee confirms it. The first words Ben thinks are a mantra of despair: "I'll never be human again!"* He's convinced that he's blown it for good, that he's not even a person, that all he can do is try to act like one. He doesn't perceive himself as a hero: contrast him with ultra-genius Reed, who got his powers and immediately started calling himself "Mr. Fantastic." If the heroic center of the family is all about the mind, what does that make someone who's all body? Ben's understanding of himself is that he's a monster—something that his loved ones should be defended against.

After Ben mopes for a few panels, a scientist† beckons him in from the rain and pours him a cup of drugged coffee, then steals his powers, appearance, and identity. The scientist is bitterly jealous of Reed Richards's success. Now in the Thing's form and impersonating his speech patterns, he agrees to assist Reed with an experimental exploration of "sub-space" (the "world of limitless dimensions," later called the Negative Zone), while planning to betray him. When the experiment goes disastrously awry, he has a change of heart and sacrifices himself to save Reed. The real Ben,

---

*For its first few years, *Fantastic Four* perpetually teased the possibility of Ben's return to human form, and that's remained in its well of occasionally recycled plot elements—in the mid-1970s, Ben was briefly human and wore a Thing suit to approximate his powers, for instance. But a Thing who has agency over the form he takes is a lot less interesting than a Thing who's an unwilling monster.

†The scientist is never named in the course of the Lee and Kirby story, though he was given a name, Ricardo Jones, in an issue of *Web of Spider-Man* twenty-five years later.

now in human form, has gone to visit his girlfriend, the blind sculptor Alicia Masters, but as he reaches her door (at the moment the impostor dies), he turns back into the Thing and runs away.

That's the plot,* which doesn't make a lick of sense if you think about any aspect of it for half a second, although anyone who objects to it on those grounds really *is* made of stone. The story has the emotional force and clarity of a fable, and it touches on the biggest questions of Lee and Kirby's *Fantastic Four*: Is the quotidian world all there is? (Not by a long shot, but we need to be brave to find out what's beyond it.) What anchors us and gives our actions meaning? (The bonds of friendship and of family; our personal understandings of ourselves and the world, as flawed as they might be.)

It's also extraordinary as artistic expression. Kirby takes the space to show off his spectacular visions at every turn. A full, breathtaking page is devoted to an enormous machine—Reed calls it a "radical cube," but it looks more like an M. C. Escher drawing of a car engine. Kirby's approach to staging and lighting is so mightily stylized that it barely looks like his own work from five years earlier, much less anyone else's. And he has a whole visual dialect of his own: the spattered, variable-size dots that surround characters here as they enter sub-space are still referred to as "Kirby crackle" when other artists use them in any context.

Lee's script doesn't flaunt his gifts as much—he's mostly concerned with clarifying Kirby's images and keeping the story in motion—but nearly every line of dialogue tells us something about its speaker through voice alone. (The Thing, feeling the drug with which he's been dosed kick in: "I don't get it! I can hardly keep my peepers open! I'm *bushed*—!") There's a lot of exposition going on here, as was the custom of the time: the characters tend to narrate everything they're doing. Lee keeps that lively, too, though. "It's taken long months of patient planning to lure the Thing into

---

*Most of the plot anyway. The Human Torch, who had gone off to college in the previous issue, only appears in an interlude that introduces a never-mentioned-again subplot about football players.

this room, by using my short-range subliminal influencer!" explains the scientist to himself, opening the door to a closet filled with another piece of mind-bending Kirby machinery.

Fantastic Four Annual #3 (October 1965)
STAN LEE, JACK KIRBY, VINCE COLLETTA

At the opposite pole from the melancholy introversion of "This Man ... This Monster!" is the story of Reed and Sue Storm's wedding day, published eight months earlier. *Fantastic Four Annual* #3 is almost entirely devoted to a gigantic, playful action scene involving virtually every superpowered character from Marvel's first four years. (Lee and Kirby themselves turn up as would-be wedding crashers.)

The first character we see in *Annual* #3, though, is *Fantastic Four*'s other most durable creation, and the counterpart to the Thing: Doctor Doom, the perfect villain. Victor Von Doom is (usually) the despotic ruler of the small Eastern European nation of Latveria. Doom is convinced that his is the greatest mind of his time, and he has an accomplishment to back that up: he's built a working time machine.* His driving ambition, although he never says so out loud in the Kirby and Lee era, is to become God; he's certain that the gig is rightfully his anyway.

Doom is *genuinely* monstrous. He never removes the armor with which he has covered his flesh, or the metal mask he built so that nobody could ever see his scarred face.† He's prideful, supercilious, and illeistic, devoid of compassion, prone to bursts of contemptuous rage. He maintains his power through violence, and it's of paramount importance to him to appear

---

*In the grand Marvel narrative, when someone needs to travel through time, they most often resort to finding some kind of access to Doom's time platform.
†The condition of Doom's face was a matter of some debate for a while. He had injured it in an explosion in college, *Fantastic Four* indicated fairly early on. Kirby suggested that he had only sustained a tiny scar and adopted the mask out of vanity; in the 1980s, John Byrne's *Fantastic Four* proposed that Doom had done a great deal more damage to his face with the newly forged, red-hot mask itself, which seems fitting.

Doctor Doom glowers behind a newspaper in *Fantastic Four Annual #3*, 1965.

to be in absolute control at all times. (Compare him to Ben Grimm, who longs to be free of his impervious rock hide.) All we see of Doom in this issue's opening image is his eyes, surrounded on all sides by his armor and cape, rhapsodic blurbs, and a newspaper headline about the wedding that takes up the better part of the page. But that's all he usually lets anyone see of him anyway.

Doom wants to rule the world, it subsequently becomes clear, because he believes the world would be better that way. (He may, in fact, be correct about that, or at least partly correct.*) In the stories Kirby drew, we most often see Doom in the business of consolidating his power, or plotting his revenge on Reed Richards, as he does here, rather than something more broadly nefarious. We are to understand that he's a villain because he fights the Fantastic Four, and that the Fantastic Four are heroes because they fight him; his understanding is just the reverse.

The narrative center of *Fantastic Four*'s Lee and Kirby era is Reed, Sue, Johnny, and Ben growing closer together as a family, becoming the core of a circle of friends and lovers and allies. That circle expands much more quickly once Reed and Sue are married, as new characters and concepts start bursting out of *Fantastic Four* at every turn. The Inhumans, Galactus, the Silver Surfer, and the Black Panther all debut within the following year and become recurring members of the cast. Both the scope

---

*In the 1987 graphic novel *Emperor Doom*, he does indeed rule the world for a while, but finds that the paperwork involved with the job is too tedious for him to bear.

of the series and its visual style keep growing and changing; at the time, there wasn't yet a "classic" form to which it was expected to revert.

Fantastic Four Annual #6 (November 1968)
STAN LEE, JACK KIRBY, JOE SINNOTT

The final big change in the family during the Fantastic Four's first decade comes three years later: the birth of Sue and Reed's son, Franklin Richards, in an issue that also debuts the last of Lee and Kirby's notable *Fantastic Four* monster/antagonists, Annihilus. He's an alien conqueror who looks like a cross between a beetle, a bat, and a radiator, in the traditional villainous colors of green and purple, and he's somehow scary anyway. (Kirby could pull off pretty much any design.)

The plot is, once again, not very substantial, and its setting returns to the sub-space territory of "This Man... This Monster!" As Sue is about to give birth, the cosmic radiation in her bloodstream causes life-threatening medical complications, so her teammates go to the Negative Zone to retrieve a doohickey that can somehow fix things; mayhem involving Annihilus ensues.

But "plot," by this point in the series, is no more the selling point of *Fantastic Four* than "modesty." It's about style and spectacle: bizarre landscapes, bursts of Kirby crackle, surreal photo collages, impossible machinery, overwhelming action. Kirby often draws only three or four big panels on each page, and renders everything so dynamically that the reader may instinctively duck. Lee is left trying to make sense of the thrilling chaos ("Johnny... look out! It's an all-engulfing *sonic sponge!*"), and to keep the wisecracks and melodramatic utterances flowing.

The McGuffin is acquired, the day is saved, and Franklin is born,* and with that, the barreling momentum of *Fantastic Four* slows to a crawl.†

---

*He wasn't named on panel for over a year.
†That's also right about when the pretense that the Marvel story was progressing in something like real time ended. Franklin aged roughly nine years over the next forty-seven

Lee has often been quoted, without a specific citation, as claiming that what comics readers wanted was not change but "the illusion of change." Franklin's birth, seven years into *Fantastic Four*, was a genuine change—two of the group were now parents, the other two uncles—and the last one the series would see for a while.

Fantastic Four #116 (November 1971)
ARCHIE GOODWIN, JOHN BUSCEMA, JOE SINNOTT

The dimming of *Fantastic Four*'s kinetic energy may have come about because Kirby and Lee's working relationship was beginning to break down.* At some point, Kirby apparently decided that he wasn't going to develop any more new characters for Marvel, and his last dozen or so issues of *Fantastic Four* before he quit with 1970's issue #102 are palpably grudging.† With Kirby gone, *Fantastic Four* was stuck. This wasn't a case like *Spider-Man*, where a new artist could provide a fresh spin and a way forward:‡ the only way to do *Fantastic Four*, it seemed, was Kirby's way, and Lee departed not long after.

Fantastic Four #116 is the first issue to have been written and drawn without either of the series' creators. (Lee's name still appears first in its credits, as editor.) Archie Goodwin and John Buscema do well-practiced impressions of Lee's and Kirby's styles, and Joe Sinnott's inking is as rugged and dynamic as ever. Reading it is an incredibly uncomfortable experience, like eating dinner in the house where you grew up, with the

---

years' worth of comics. The *Fantastic Four* superfan known as "Tuk" has proposed that, within the story, Franklin is *why* that happened: he's subsequently established as an impossibly powerful mutant, and he knows it's going to be a big problem when he grows up, so he's bending time around himself and everybody in his parents' circle.
*See chapter 7.
†A few scraps of Kirby's *Fantastic Four* subsequently appeared here and there, but he returned to the Fantastic Four in earnest only once: in 1978, he wrote and drew *What If?* #11, "What If the Original Marvel Bullpen Had Become the Fantastic Four?" In his meandering story, Stan Lee becomes Mr. Fantastic, and Kirby himself becomes the Thing.
‡See chapter 6.

strangers who live there now pretending to be your family members. On the cover, Doctor Doom is leading the Fantastic Four into battle, with Reed Richards nowhere to be seen—a sideways acknowledgment that the people who are supposed to be in charge are gone.

It appeared at an awkward moment of transition for Marvel. The "Bullpen Bulletins" hype page that appeared in that month's comics told part of the story: "This is it! Ten years to the month since the first immortal issue of *Fantastic Four* ushered in the Marvel Age of Madcap Madness—and have we got an anniversary surprise for you! 'Cause this is the month when each and every one of our award-winning mags goes king-size to fifty-two pages (that's counting the four-color covers, natch) for a mere 25¢. . . ." The new format instantly failed; the next month, the line went back to thirty-six-page issues for twenty cents, rather than the fifteen cents they'd cost two months earlier.

All *Fantastic Four*'s next hundred issues' worth of writers and artists could do was act as if Lee and Kirby might come back next month and pick up where they left off. The series' exploratory spirit moved on to other comics. There were almost no durable new characters or settings introduced in *Fantastic Four* for the rest of the 1970s, or the '80s, or the '90s. A few plots recurred with tedious regularity: One member is incapacitated, or quits, and is briefly replaced, then returns. The Thing turns into powerless Ben Grimm, then turns back again. Doom returns, and is defeated. Galactus returns, and once again doesn't devour the Earth. The group splits up, then reunites.

Fantastic Four #271 (October 1984)
JOHN BYRNE, GLYNIS WEIN

Even so, the *Fantastic Four* of those decades has bright spots. John Byrne, who wrote and drew the series from 1981 to 1986, is as fervent a Kirby revivalist as anyone, and again recycled some of those staple plots. (The Thing is briefly replaced by She-Hulk, then returns. Galactus returns, and yet again doesn't devour the Earth. Sue Richards gets pregnant again, but her daughter is stillborn.) But he's also a graceful, engaging storyteller, and found opportunities to flesh out the series' familiar characters—especially Doctor Doom and Sue, whose costumed identity he gave a long-overdue revision from the Invisible Girl to the Invisible Woman.

This issue, Byrne's cleverest homage to Kirby, involves Reed Richards describing his earliest clear memory: an encounter, years earlier, with an alien monster called Gormuu. Both the flashback's premise and Byrne's artwork for it evoke not the Kirby of mid-'60s *Fantastic Four*, but the Kirby of Marvel's early-'60s monster comics*—the gigantic creatures with doubled letters in their names, the "triptych" panels showing progressive action, the distant perspectives on the sorts of scenes that Kirby would later render in hyperdynamic close-up. The Gormuu incident, Reed explains, gave him a sense of desperate urgency about hastening the rocket launch that opens *Fantastic Four* #1.

The visual presentation of Reed's story underscores the direct connection between those monster comics and the early *Fantastic Four*. Reed is telling that story, though, because he's feeling parts of his past slipping from his memory's grasp (while the readership of his comics had turned over to the point where many of them wouldn't have been able to make that stylistic connection). And the reason he's trying to recapture them cuts directly to the series' familial, emotional core: "I can't remember my mother's eyes," he says.

Power Pack #16 (November 1985)
LOUISE SIMONSON, JUNE BRIGMAN, BOB WIACEK, GLYNIS OLIVER

One of the oddest successful Marvel series of the 1980s, *Power Pack* was, like *Fantastic Four*, about a family: four preteen children, Katie, Jack, Julie, and Alex Power, whose parents don't know they're superheroes. It

---

*See chapter 5.

was the first superhero comic to be written and drawn by women (writer Louise Simonson and artist June Brigman) for more than a few issues. Despite its young cast, *Power Pack* was sometimes a grim, scary comic—the kids live in Marvel's hazardous New York City, and are often overwhelmed by their own abilities—but their origin (they're given superpowers and a talking spaceship by a sort of magical alien pony) is the sort of thing a four-year-old might make up.

As it happens, that's just about exactly how old Franklin Richards is at this point. He habitually wears a shirt that reads "4 1/2" in the style of the Fantastic Four's circular "4" logo, and he *really* needs some peers. Here, he encounters Power Pack for the first time. Naturally, they immediately befriend him and invite him to join the team: it's as if he made them up himself. He becomes a full-time member of *Power Pack*'s cast for the next year, and intermittently thereafter.

Fantastic Four #1 (November 1961)
STAN LEE, JACK KIRBY, GEORGE KLEIN (?)*

Some new readers' impulse to begin exploring Marvel's comics with the Fantastic Four's origin story, the first Kirby and Lee superhero comic book, is understandably strong. I encourage you to do so if and only if you somehow find yourself in the fall of 1961, ten years old, standing at a newsstand with a dime in your hand. Otherwise, it's much more enjoyable for a contemporary reader after you've got a sense of where its creators were going and where they'd been.

The earliest issues of *Fantastic Four* are crude and cramped, but they're wonderfully energetic, with plots that rush along like children's improvised play. Here, Reed Richards and his group try to launch a rocket to the stars, fail to get where they're going, and are transformed (by radiation)

---

*Klein's name gets a question mark because nobody is entirely sure who inked Kirby's pencils for *Fantastic Four* #1.

from humans into superhumans. In an indelible panel, they agree to stay together, and reach out to touch one another's hands and Ben Grimm's huge orange paw.

Over the next few issues, the Fantastic Four are impersonated by shape-changing aliens (the Skrulls, a throwaway idea that became one of the pillars of Marvel's cosmology), then discover that the superstrong ruler of Atlantis had lost his memory and had been living in a New York City flophouse for years, then travel back in time and accidentally create the legend of Blackbeard. They seem to spend a lot of time being taken captive too: the title of #5 is "Prisoners of Doctor Doom," #6 is "Captives of the Deadly Duo," #7 is "Prisoners of Kurrgo, Master of Planet X," #8 is "Prisoners of the Puppet Master," and #19 is "Prisoners of the Pharoah" [sic].

Fantastic Four #19 (October 1963)
STAN LEE, JACK KIRBY, DICK AYERS

That last one was cultural coattail-riding: the breathlessly anticipated movie *Cleopatra*, starring Elizabeth Taylor and Richard Burton, had opened about a month before *Fantastic Four* #19 went on sale, and the Nile was in style. "Prisoners of the Pharoah" comes on like a jugful of jitter juice—what it lacks in sense, it makes up for in Kermit-armed enthusiasm and velocity. Reed Richards looks at some hieroglyphics in the Museum of Natural History and concludes that "a radioactive herb" known to ancient Egyptians was the antidote for blindness (and could therefore cure the Thing's girlfriend, Alicia Masters), so the Fantastic Four fly to Doctor Doom's castle and commandeer his time machine to head to pharaonic times, but Rama-Tut (an ancient Egyptian pharaoh who turns out to be from the year 3000, and whose headquarters/time machine is the Great Sphinx of Giza) has a mind-controlling ray gun, and then the Thing briefly turns back to human form for no reason at all, and . . . you get the idea. Kirby's artwork is still edging toward what it would become a few years later—it's assertive rather than explosive, solid rather than visionary.

Doctor Strange #53 (June 1982)
ROGER STERN, MARSHALL ROGERS, TERRY AUSTIN, BOB SHAREN

For the generation of mainstream comics creators who grew up reading Lee and Kirby's *Fantastic Four*, though, every single issue was the crossroads of infinity. This issue is the conclusion of a serial in which Doctor Strange travels backward through time in search of a woman's previous incarnations; here, he ends up inside the Sphinx at exactly the time the Fantastic Four were Rama-Tut's prisoners. Stern and Rogers's story reworks (and dances around) images and dialogue from "Prisoners of the Pharoah," and even plugs a few of *Fantastic Four* #19's plot holes in passing.

It's worth noting that Stern wrote this issue for an audience he knew would almost certainly *not* have read—or even have access to—the Lee and Kirby comic, which had last been reprinted eight years earlier. There's not even a footnote referring to it; as far as the characters and most readers were concerned, the early Fantastic Four were in ancient Egypt for some reason, no big deal. Even so, Stern knew that the *Doctor Strange* readers who *had* seen *Fantastic Four* #19 would probably remember its every detail.

West Coast Avengers #22 (July 1987)
STEVE ENGLEHART, AL MILGROM, KIM DEMULDER, CHRISTIE SCHEELE

Five years after that, an extended time-travel storyline in *West Coast Avengers* also brought its cast to the interior of the Sphinx at the same thousands-of-years-ago moment as Doctor Strange and the Fantastic Four—although, by that point, the choreography involved in making sure the earlier participants in the story didn't notice the later ones was getting complicated.* It was writer Steve Englehart's nod to the history of *Fantastic Four*, published the same month he started writing their series. The Marvel story's components can be tied together in countless ways, Englehart suggests, but Lee and Kirby's work is the bight of the knot, the primordial fountain that makes further creation possible.

Fantastic Four #329 (August 1989)
JOHN HARKNESS [STEVE ENGLEHART], RICH BUCKLER, ROMEO TANGHAL, GEORGE ROUSSOS

Acknowledging history, though, doesn't mean repeating it. Englehart wrote *Fantastic Four* for a few years, and tried to make it evolve *past* the Richards family—he wrote out Reed and Sue for a year and a half—but eventually yielded to editorial pressure to make his changes illusory. He changed his byline first to S. F. X. Englehart,† then to John Harkness, to disavow his scripts altogether; his final storyline includes this bizarrely funny, angry issue in which stand-ins for the Fantastic Four blunder through a simulacrum of their encounter with the Mole Man from *Fantastic Four* #1, speaking only in not quite contextually appropriate dialogue from the first couple of issues. If you just want regurgitated Lee and Kirby, Englehart implies, you'll get what you deserve.

Fantastic Four #347 (December 1990)
WALT SIMONSON, ARTHUR ADAMS, ART THIBERT, STEVE BUCCELLATO

Writer/artist Walt Simonson followed Englehart, and as with his *Thor*,‡ he honored Kirby by emphasizing his own stylistic idiosyncrasies rather

---

*The 1996 miniseries *The Rise of Apocalypse*, about the early years of an X-Men villain, is also partly set during the events of *Fantastic Four* #19.
†"The standard abbreviation for simple Sound Effects," Englehart writes on his website.
‡See chapter 12.

than Kirby's. Simonson's run as writer also included a delightful three-issue story about the "New Fantastic Four," drawn gorgeously by Arthur Adams. Rather than altering the group's family structure, this sequence pretends to supplant it altogether, roping together Spider-Man, Ghost Rider, the Hulk, and Wolverine (all very popular characters at the time who had almost nothing in common), and tossing them into an archetypal Fantastic Four plot—a mash-up of the first issue's Mole-Man-and-his-island-of-monsters story and the second issue's Skrull adventure.*

Fantastic Four #54 (June 2002)
CARLOS PACHECO, RAFAEL MARIN, KARL KESEL, MARK BAGLEY, ET AL.

Still, no attempt to push *Fantastic Four* forward stuck until 2002, when a tangled storyline with four or five different writers culminated in the birth of Sue and Reed Richards's second child.† Doctor Doom manages, through his command of magic and science, to deliver their daughter alive and healthy, in return for which he demands the right to name her (Valeria, after his first love) and to become her godfather—which makes him the monster who must be accepted *into* the family.

---

*"New Fantastic Four" was presented as a self-aware piece of commercial cynicism—the Punisher even shows up for what the cover of #349 calls THE WORLD'S MOST EXPLOITATIVE CAMEO—but it was endearing enough that other creators have paid homage to it. The 2012 *Venom* storyline "Circle of Four" concerned Spider-Man stand-in Venom, the Alejandra Jones version of Ghost Rider, the red version of the Hulk, and the Wolverine clone X-23; 2017's *Ghost Rider* miniseries nominally focused on a then new version of that character, but costarred the spider-powered heroine Silk and the protagonists of *All-New Wolverine* and *The Totally Awesome Hulk*.

†How tangled? It's technically not Sue's third pregnancy, but a cosmic-powered do-over of her second.

Fantastic Four: The World's Greatest Comics Magazine! #1 (February 2001)

ERIK LARSEN, ERIC STEPHENSON, BRUCE TIMM, KEITH GIFFEN, ET AL.

By that point, the tone of Marvel's new comics had fallen so far away from Lee and Kirby's style that pastiching their work was specifically a retro gesture. The twelve-issue miniseries *Fantastic Four: The World's Greatest Comic Magazine!*, created jam-style by a horde of writers and artists led by Erik Larsen and Eric Stephenson, was an attempt to imagine what *Fantastic Four* #100 might have been if it had been Lee and Kirby's celebratory capstone on their accomplishment rather than the product of a faltering détente.

Fantastic Four #570 (October 2009)

JONATHAN HICKMAN, DALE EAGLESHAM, PAUL MOUNTS, ET AL.

Twenty-first-century issues of *Fantastic Four* itself don't look or read like issues from its first decade, but they've often concerned themselves with further mapping out the territory of the first hundred issues rather than moving past it. The exception is a 2009–2012 sequence written by Jonathan Hickman and drawn by Dale Eaglesham, Steve Epting, and others. It still plays almost exclusively with the instruments of the Kirby and Lee era—the locations and characters and power dynamics of 1961–1970— but Hickman finds a new tune: Reed Richards dealing with his own family heritage, and finding a way to bring together and teach both his children and the strange cosmic children he's encountered in the Fantastic Four's explorations.*

The emotional center of Hickman's *Fantastic Four* (and *FF*,† which briefly replaced it and then continued alongside it) shifts by degrees to-

---

*One of them is Alex Power of Power Pack, who is about the closest thing Franklin has ever had to a social peer outside his family.
†It stands for Future Foundation.

ward the Richards children, and how different their ways of being fantastic are from their parents' ways. Franklin Richards is sort of omnipotent, but can't yet understand or control his own power.* And his supergenius little sister, Valeria, has a real affinity for her Uncle Doom.

In 2015, two more brief relaunches later, *Fantastic Four* went on hiatus for three years, and (as a consequence of another long sequence written by Hickman) the Richards family vanished altogether from the Marvel Universe† and from the pages of new comic books. The rumor was that the order to stop publishing the series had come from corporate higher-ups, resentful that Marvel didn't control the film rights to the team. Fans complained, but in practice, they *wanted* to miss it more than they actually did—it felt entirely exhausted, and its sales had drooped badly. The crossroads of infinity was overshadowed by an infinite cloverleaf; the new territories to which *Fantastic Four* had provided a gateway didn't need explorers anymore. Its monsters had all been vanquished or tamed, or been warily welcomed into the family, or come to terms with themselves.

Marvel Legacy #1 (November 2017)
JASON AARON, ESAD RIBIC, STEVE MCNIVEN, MATTHEW WILSON

Even so, the moment when the Fantastic Four's return is finally foreshadowed is exquisite. It comes at the end of *Marvel Legacy*, a one-off, fifty-page teaser for forthcoming storylines: a bunch of short scenes, held together only by a narrator's rambling captions about the idea of "legacy." Just as her meditation is reaching a crescendo ("Something both real and profoundly unreal. Something mad. Something magical. Something *fantas—*"), it's cut off.

---

*Between 2005 and 2009, he also starred in a string of one-shot specials by Marc Sumerak and Chris Eliopoulos: *Franklin Richards, Son of a Genius*, a whimsical knockoff of Calvin & Hobbes.
†See chapter 18.

The narrator is Valeria Richards, and her big brother, Franklin, is interrupting her: "Dad says there's another new universe up ahead for us to explore." The brilliant girl and the all-powerful boy are a little older now. Their own adventures are just beginning, and the future belongs to them.

5

INTERLUDE:
MONSTERS

There's a different pathway that intersects with *Fantastic Four* #1: not through the superhero comics that appeared in that issue's wake, but from its publisher's beginning, twenty-two years earlier, moving toward and through the monster comics that were its precursors. Here's a brief timeline of Marvel as seen through that lens.*

October 1939: *Marvel Comics* #1 appears, during the initial American comics boom, as the first comic book published by a company that was then called Timely Publications, run by Martin Goodman. It features a few characters whose names and appearances are still familiar (the Human Torch, the Sub-Mariner), others whose names were later recycled

---

*This is, of course, a drastically abridged and skewed version of that period. For an entertaining, extensively reported look at Marvel's complete history, see Sean Howe's excellent 2012 book, *Marvel Comics: The Untold Story*.

The Gool rises from Bikini Atoll in *Marvel Tales* #93, 1949, creators uncredited; possibly penciled by Ed Winiarski.

(the Angel, Ka-Zar), and a few non-starters (the Masked Raider* and the generic characters in the one-off story "Jungle Terror"). With its second issue, it changes its title to *Marvel Mystery Comics*. Over the next decade or so, Timely cranks out genre comics of all kinds— funny animals, situation comedies, Westerns—although its biggest success is Joe Simon and Jack Kirby's *Captain America*, launched at the end of 1940.

May 1949: As superhero comics, a decade-long cultural fad that seems to have run its course, are disappearing one by one, Goodman's company† experiments with publishing horror comics. Its first horror title is *Amazing Mysteries* #32 (taking over the numbering of *Sub-Mariner Comics*). The lead stories in that issue and the next are, respectively, "The Thing at Chugamung Cove!" and "The Thing in the Vault!" With #34, *Amazing Mysteries* becomes a crime series.

August 1949: *Marvel Tales* #93 assumes the numbering of the former *Marvel Mystery Comics* and becomes a horror series. The cover of this

---

*The Masked Raider appeared in the series' first dozen issues, then vanished until 2019's *Marvel Comics* #1000 (there had been no issues #93 to #999, but never mind that).

†The company went by several different names: in early 1949, its comics had a little round logo that read MARVEL COMIC. For the sake of clarity, I mostly just refer to Timely, Atlas, and its other early incarnations as Marvel.

issue declares "Don't Miss 'The Ghoul Strikes'!" The entity that appears in one of the stories inside is not the Ghoul but the Gool, a huge, lumpy, orange monster from under the earth who commands "a great, screw-shaped vehicle." It surfaces at Bikini Atoll just as the second atomic test there is conducted.

A scientist named Doctor Kirby is involved in the first human encounter with the Gool, which becomes gigantic and wanders off into the sea. "Don't dare miss the 'Mark of the Gool' in the next issue of *Marvel Mystery*!" the final caption insists. No further Gool stories ever appear.

October 1949: *Captain America Comics* changes its title to *Captain America's Weird Tales*, two issues before it expires.

October 1954: To protect itself against the threat of external regulation, the Comics Magazine Association of America, a publishing organization to which Marvel belongs, adopts the original version of the Comics Code. "All scenes of horror, excessive bloodshed, gory or gruesome crimes, depravity, lust, sadism, masochism shall not be permitted," the Code declares. "Scenes dealing with, or instruments associated with walking dead, torture, vampires and vampirism, ghouls, cannibalism, and werewolfism are prohibited." Marvel's sci-fi and fantasy anthologies largely steer clear of monsters for the next five years or so.

November 1956: Martin Goodman shuts down his distribution company, Atlas, and switches to distributing its line of comics (also known as Atlas)—romance, horror, comedy, war, and Westerns—through American News Company.

June 1957: American News Company collapses. Atlas, which has been publishing upward of forty comics a month, suddenly has no way to get them to newsstands. The new distributor Martin Goodman lines up, Independent News, belongs to Harry Donenfeld, owner of National Periodical Publications, aka Atlas's competitor DC Comics; part of the deal is that Goodman can only publish eight issues a month. Stan Lee, by this point the editor of the entire line, is instructed to stop hiring freelance writers and artists. When the inventory of not-yet-published stories runs out, Lee starts writing most of the recurring character features, from *Patsy Walker* to *Two-Gun Kid*, himself. Meanwhile, artist Joe Maneely—an incredibly fast and versatile cartoonist and a close friend of Lee's—is around to draw nearly anything that still needs to be drawn.

June 1958: Just as Martin Goodman's now nameless comics line has burned off the better part of its inventory, Joe Maneely dies in a subway accident. Within days, Lee contacts three speedy, gifted artists whose work he knows well—Jack Kirby, Steve Ditko, and Don Heck—and tells them there's work for them.* Artwork by all three appears in the first issue of the science fiction/fantasy anthology series *Strange Worlds*, published a few months later, around the time an atomic weapons test ban goes into effect.

January 1959: The first issues of *Tales of Suspense* and *Tales to Astonish* join the already extant *Journey into Mystery* and *Strange Tales* in Marvel's sci-fi/fantasy/horror anthology line. Within a few months, they settle into a formula: three or four stories in each issue, with one apiece drawn by Kirby and Ditko, and usually one drawn by Heck. The writers are mostly uncredited, although some stories may have been written by Lee, and others by his brother, Larry Lieber.

Certain plots and premises get recycled on a regular basis. A greedy artist or musician, having taken possession of a magical tool that gives

---

*Dr. Michael J. Vassallo's writing about his research into Marvel's early history is hugely helpful in making sense of this chaotic moment.

him mastery of a particular craft, discovers that he can't ever stop creating until he dies of exhaustion; invaders plan to conquer Earth, but their microscopically small fleet is wiped out by a drop of water; aliens change their shape to resemble humans, or to look like *other* aliens.

January 1960: The syntax of cover blurbs on the company's horror anthologies shifts. In 1959, they'd mostly been first-person reportage ("I Was Trapped in the Tunnel to Nowhere!" "I Dared to Explore the Unknown Emptiness!"). This month, they're starting to feature monstrous creatures ("I Fought the Molten Man-Thing!" "I Spent Midnight with the Thing on Bald Mountain!" "I Brought Zog the Unbelievable Back to Life!").

From here on out, the first person will often be downplayed, at least on the covers, in favor of the creatures' names: SPORR ("The Thing That Could Not Die"), ELEKTRO ("He Held the World in His Iron Grip!"), ROMMBU ("His Very Name Made Mankind Tremble!"). The monsters may be created by scientists who know not what they do, or they may burrow up from underground, or fly in from outer space. If they're aliens, they often come from somewhere in our solar system: they're Martians, Saturnians, Venusians. (Even Kirby and Ditko and Heck devised new rubber mask–looking forms for the residents of each of those planets every time they were called on to feature them.) No matter what they are, they threaten the world. Then, someone challenges the monster's supremacy by closely interpreting the rules of the contract by which it gains its power. (Groot the tree-creature is defeated by termites, for instance.) Cleverness conquers all, and normality is restored.

February 1960: "Grottu, King of the Insects" is the cover star of *Strange Tales* #73: an ant turned monstrously huge by radiation from atomic bomb tests. The next month's "Monstro," in *Tales of Suspense* #8, concerns an octopus mutated to enormous size thanks to secret atomic tests by "the Reds." Another enormous ant, Krang, appears later the same year in *Tales to Astonish* #14, mutated by a growth serum.

May 1960: "Return of the Genie!" in *Tales to Astonish* #9, "The Return of the Living Robot!" in *Tales of Suspense* #9, and "Return of the Martian!" in *Journey into Mystery* #58 are the first of the horror anthologies' sequels to earlier stories. On the cover of that issue of *Journey into Mystery*, a gigantic monster called Rro is bursting up through the street of a city, holding a subway car in his hand. "IT'S RRO!" one of his victims shouts. "Up from the bottomless pit! Mankind is DOOMED!"

June 1960: Taboo ("The Thing from the Murky Swamp!"), in *Strange Tales* #75, is defeated by clever humans hiding an H-bomb in its space capsule.

September 1960: The flying saucer that invades Earth in *Tales of Suspense* #11 turns out to actually *be* a saucer-shaped Martian. The same month's *Journey into Mystery* #60 includes a Stan Lee and Steve Ditko story, "I Turned into a . . . Martian!" Two months later, Lee, Jack Kirby, and Dick Ayers's "A Martian Walks Among Us!" appears in *Strange Tales* #78.* Mars itself remains something of a mystery: that October, the Soviet Union's first two attempts to launch unmanned probes to study the red planet fail to achieve orbit.

November 1960: The cover of *Journey into Mystery* #62 bellows "Here comes . . . the HULK"—but this Hulk is a shaggy orange alien called Xemnu.† (Four months later, the same series features "Return of the Hulk.")

---

*In 1982, the Misfits' punk rock standard "I Turned into a Martian" appeared on their album *Walk Among Us*.
†When Xemnu the Hulk's initial appearances are reprinted a decade later, they're relettered to refer to him as "the Titan."

June 1961: A fifth monster/horror/sci-fi anthology, *Amazing Adventures*, begins; the final story in its debut issue introduces a recurring protagonist, occult investigator Dr. Droom.* The same month's *Tales to Astonish* #20—"I Was Hunted by 'X': The Thing That LIVED!!"—concerns a milquetoast writer, browbeaten by the demanding editor of *Tales to Astonish*, who discovers that his typewriter magically brings the monsters he imagines to life. Even the Western comic *Rawhide Kid* gets in on the act, as the Kid encounters the Living Totem, a hostile space alien in the form of a totem pole.

October 1961: The international moratorium on testing atomic weapons ends; the U.S.S.R. detonates a 50-megaton weapon, the *Tsar Bomba*. Meanwhile, *Strange Tales* #89 introduces a Chinese dragon, Fin Fang Foom, whose name causes "terror in the craven hearts of the Communist police," and *Journey into Mystery* #73 involves a spider that grows enormous after it's caught in atomic rays at a research lab.

November 1961: The cover star of *Amazing Adventures* #6 is "Sserpo, the Creature Who Crushed the World!!"—a rocky orange monster drawn by Jack Kirby, who is ineffectually fired upon by the military until he wanders off into the sea like the Gool, then bursts up from beneath the waves. The new series that Stan Lee and Kirby launch a week later is a throwback in some ways: *The Fantastic Four* #1 can be read as a modern monster comic disguised as an old-fashioned cape comic. As its first issue begins, another one of Kirby's rocky orange monsters, the Thing, is ineffectually fired upon by police until he takes refuge in the sewer system, then bursts up into the streets.

The second half of *Fantastic Four* #1 involves a bunch of other sub-

---

*When his stories are reprinted a decade later, they're relettered to refer to him as "Dr. Druid."

The Thing initially appears in the guise of a monster, or perhaps a Martian, in *Fantastic Four* #1, 1961, by Stan Lee and Jack Kirby.

terranean creatures and their shriveled, embittered master, the Mole Man. (It's not impossible that it could have been a touched-up version of a story that was already sitting in Marvel's inventory, something along the lines of "I Defied the Mole Man's Monsters!") The first panel of the Mole Man episode, like the cover of the issue, shows one of the monsters erupting from underground into an American street, exactly as the Thing did earlier in the issue. That's a purely symbolic image: within the story, where the monster actually bursts out of the ground is "French Equitorial Africa" [*sic*]—colonial territory, with only the colonizers in view.

January 1962: In *Fantastic Four* #2, Reed Richards convinces the shape-changing Skrulls to leave Earth alone by showing them images of *other* monsters "clipped from 'Strange Tales' and 'Journey into Mystery,'" and pretending that they depict "some of Earth's most powerful warriors." The same month, "The Man in the Ant Hill!" in *Tales to Astonish* #27 is a seemingly one-off story about inventor Henry Pym, who creates a shrinking serum and encounters ants that have become comparatively enormous to him.

May 1962: In *Fantastic Four* #4, the Sub-Mariner leads an undersea monster called Giganto to attack New York when he discovers that his aquatic kingdom has been destroyed: "The *humans* did it, unthinkingly, with their accursed atomic tests!" That issue, like many others published that month, has a series of messages printed at the margins of its pages: "The Hulk is coming!" "Who is the Hulk??" "You've never seen anyone like the Hulk!" *The Incredible Hulk* #1, on newsstands at the same time, concerns a test of a new kind of bomb whose radiation turns its inventor into a raging monster.*

July 1962: "The Monster in the Iron Mask!" from Kirby and Lee's story in *Tales of Suspense* #31, has a nearly identical mask design to that of Doctor Doom, who first appears in Kirby and Lee's *Fantastic Four* #5, released the same day.

September 1962: Henry Pym returns in *Tales to Astonish* #35, now in a superhero costume and calling himself Ant-Man; he becomes a monthly feature of the series.

February 1963: With Thor now appearing monthly in *Journey into Mystery*, the Human Torch in *Strange Tales*, and Ant-Man in *Tales to Astonish*, *Tales of Suspense* #38 is the last of Marvel's sci-fi/monster anthologies without a superhero on its cover. Iron Man debuts in the following

---

*The centerpiece of the first Hulk story is one of the most effective sequences Jack Kirby ever drew. The image of gangly Bruce Banner being hit by the gamma bomb's radiation—standing behind the trench he's just pushed Rick Jones into, arms and tie flung out to his sides, lab coat billowing open, while the explosion appears as a puff of smoke and force behind him—has been redrawn nearly every time his story has been told. It's followed by a panel in which Banner's body is seen only as negative space with the lines of the explosion passing through it, then a close-up of his screaming face with impossible illumination that makes it look almost like a photographic negative or an X-ray, and finally a "normal" image of his face, still screaming, "hours later," as Rick shakes him back to awareness. The moment the bomb goes off, everything is too late; the monster has arrived in the world, the horror will never end, and we will be judged by the very last thing we did before that instant.

issue. By that fall, Dr. Strange, the X-Men, and the Avengers are all up and running too.

January 1971: The Comics Code is rewritten, lifting the prohibition on several staples of horror comics: "vampires, ghouls and werewolves shall be permitted to be used when handled in the classic tradition such as Frankenstein, Dracula, and other high calibre literary works written by Edgar Allen [*sic*] Poe, Saki, Conan Doyle and other respected authors whose works are read in schools around the world." Over the next few years, Marvel launches a fusillade of single-character-focused horror series. The monsters of a decade earlier eventually reappear, too—first as reprints, then as nostalgic references, then as goofy reminders of the sort of things people used to fear.

October 1971: Stan Lee takes a few months off from comics to work on a script for French filmmaker Alain Resnais. *The Monster Maker* concerns a horror film producer who tries to branch out beyond cheap genre entertainment; it is never filmed.

April 2013: In *Journey into Mystery* #649—now a series devoted to Thor's supporting cast, its title a sort of historical joke for longtime Thor fans—Rro (the "monster from the bottomless pit" who had appeared in the same series fifty-three years earlier) bursts up through a Tokyo street. "Oh, look. It's Rro," says one salaryman waiting at a crosswalk nearby. "Mm-hmm," says his friend, without looking up from his phone.

6

SPINNING IN CIRCLES

The Spider-Man story is about growing up, and failing, and growing up some more, and failing again, and clawing one's way back up again. The rudiments of it are the same across close to a dozen movies, several TV shows, a stage musical, and over four thousand comic books: that Peter Parker was bitten by a radioactive spider and gained its powers, that he's sort of a born-loser type, that he feels eternally guilty about his beloved uncle Ben's death, that there's a newspaper editor named J. Jonah Jameson who can't stand Spider-Man but commands Peter to produce photos of him, and so on. Marvel's recent movies, in which Peter is played by Tom Holland, don't even bother to explain his origin, because *everyone knows it already*.

It's the story of a young man who's leading a double life—who has a secret that he can't reveal to anyone. A question it keeps asking is who Peter Parker can be if he can't be himself, and it keeps answering that question by giving him *other* selves: uncanny doubles, alternate versions, and terrible inversions of his two identities. The biggest difference between Spider-Man and every other well-known superhero, though, is the specific genre to which his story belongs. It's a *bildungsroman*, the story of how a youth becomes an adult. In the comics, it's a very *long* story, and it comes in observable cycles; it's "The Itsy-Bitsy Spider." Peter is not yet—never yet—the person he needs to become.

Even so, some of his readers want him to get on with it and finish growing up already. I occasionally see demands for instruction on how to read Spider-Man comics as efficiently as possible. Just the essential stories, no filler, please. Just the high points, the best stuff, the important stuff. That is a terrible, boring, frustrating way to experience them. It's not that there aren't consensus "classic" Spider-Man moments, or long, not-so-hot stretches of his comics. But the reason the "important" bits are important is that they alter the course of what comes before them. Reducing Peter Parker's story to a sizzle reel eliminates the momentum, gradual development, and theme-and-variations flourishes that are a lot of what's special about it. What matters is the journey.

The course our tour takes here, then, is not a list of the best Spider-Man comics, or a shortcut past skippable passages. Instead, it's the looping, self-intersecting shape of a web, a way to observe the repeating structure of Spider-Man's path as it's grown and expanded.

Free Comic Book Day (Spider-Man) #1 (May 2007)

DAN SLOTT, PHIL JIMENEZ, ANDY LANNING, JOHN DELL, JEROMY COX

This giveaway issue (released to coincide with Sam Raimi's *Spider-Man 3* movie), also known as "Swing Shift," isn't a particularly classic Spider-Man story. It's a deliberately and entirely formulaic one, a charming, seemingly inconsequential reassurance to its readers that they know how this works. Acrobatic action scene? Check. Peter Parker fumbling a social obligation because of his double life? Check. Aunt May fussing over him? J. Jonah Jameson ranting angrily about him? Note signed "friendly neighborhood Spider-Man"? Mysterious goings-on in the criminal underworld? Alluring redhead? "Spider-sense tingling"? Talk of responsibility? Check, check, check, check, check, check, and check.

It's also a fine place to start wandering through the labyrinth of Spider-Man comics: the beginning of one of the grand cycles of his narrative, of the long and consistently enjoyable sequence of stories called "Brand New Day," and of Dan Slott's decade-long tenure as one of the people running (or corunning) the Spidey show. Slott has written more comics about Peter Parker than anyone else;* he's described "the world of Spider-Man"—specifically as presented by Stan Lee, Steve Ditko, and John Romita Sr. between 1962 and 1972—as "my favorite place in all of fiction." His own accomplishment was using the recognizable materials of that place to build new ones.

Amazing Fantasy #15 (August 1962)
STAN LEE, STEVE DITKO

The bulk of those materials come from the forty-odd comic books about Spider-Man by Lee and Ditko that Marvel published between 1962 and 1966. They're stiff, gawky, talky, entirely unmodern; they're also incandescent and indelible.

The first Spider-Man story appeared in the final issue of a series that had started as *Amazing Adventures*. With issue #7, it changed its title to *Amazing Adult Fantasy* ("The Magazine That Respects Your Intelligence"), and became an all-Lee-and-Ditko showcase;† it dropped the *Adult* on its way out the door. "Spider-Man!"‡ is a sharp inversion of a lot of the tropes

---

*By Slott's count, he narrowly edges out Brian Michael Bendis's first 160 issues of *Ultimate Spider-Man*.

†See chapter 7 for more on Ditko and his working relationship with Lee.

‡Jack Kirby appears to have suggested the Spider-Man name, and he drew the published cover of *Amazing Fantasy* #15 after Lee rejected a version Ditko drew. The "Spiderman" [*sic*] that Kirby initially proposed to Lee, though, has nothing but the name in common with the character as we know him.

associated with what its opening caption calls "long-underwear types." Its protagonist, Peter Parker, isn't a billionaire playboy or supernatural royalty. He's a lonely, bitter teenage bookworm, a would-be scientist and inventor whose accidental acquisition of a bug's powers ruins his life. The story's final images are of Spider-Man sobbing in horror and shame at his failure. *That* was something new.

The closing line of Lee's narration—"with great power there must also come great responsibility"—has become an endlessly repeated and misquoted catchphrase, but the constant tension between what Spider-Man wants to do and what he forces himself to do is what makes him who he is. A lot of the thematic material of the next few thousand *Spider-Man* comics is already present in this first story, or has been extrapolated from it. In eleven pages, Peter is transformed from a sour misfit ("Some day I'll show them! [sob] Some day they'll be sorry!—sorry that they laughed at me!": that's not generally how a hero-to-be talks) to a shattered penitent slinking into the darkness. As the beginning of an endless serial, it's extraordinary: the first fall of a proud young man who didn't think he had anywhere to go but up.

Spider-Man's Tangled Web #14 (July 2002)
BRIAN AZZARELLO, SCOTT LEVY, GIUSEPPE CAMUNCOLI, STEVE BUCCELLATO

This is, on its surface, not a Spider-Man story at all. It's a story about a wrestler* called Crusher Hogan, whose marriage and livelihood are on the verge of collapse until he comes up with an ingenious gimmick on which he stakes everything: a cash reward for anyone who can stay in the ring with him for three minutes. The final page shows a kid with a stocking over his face swinging himself over the ropes and into the ring.

Azzarello and Levy's story balances on a weird but not unreasonable

---

*Its cowriter Scott Levy is better known as the pro wrestler Raven.

assumption, which is that anybody reading a tertiary Spider-Man title like *Spider-Man's Tangled Web* will almost certainly be familiar with *Amazing Fantasy* #15 and immediately understand that this is a tragedy (whose climax isn't even shown here): the kid is Peter Parker, and he's about to destroy Hogan's life without even realizing it. There's a fun little scene in the middle of Lee and Ditko's first Spider-Man story in which Peter has decided to use his new powers to make some money. He takes the throwaway character Hogan up on his challenge, and of course beats him handily.* But there are no throwaway characters in that story, it turns out. Everyone, and everything, ends up mattering in the long run; every detail of those eleven pages has been pored over, retold, revised, and expanded.†

The Amazing Spider-Man #1 (March 1963)
STAN LEE, STEVE DITKO

Why, for instance, does Peter live with his aunt and uncle rather than his parents—who are never even mentioned until years later? That detail grounds him, implying something painful in his past. It also doubles the impact of his uncle's death, and sets up a major theme of the first few cycles of Spider-Man's story: as devoted as he is to his frail, doting Aunt May, Peter Parker is desperately in search of a father figure.

Read in that light, the first few years of *The Amazing Spider-Man* focus on presenting Peter with one terrible new potential father after another: kind scientists who reject him (like Reed Richards of the Fantastic Four, in this first issue) and cruel scientists who try to tempt him; a friend's wealthy and seemingly benevolent father who is secretly a socio-

---

*Hogan also appears in 1985's *Amazing Spider-Man* #271, as a beaten-down janitor, spinning tall tales of his past.
†The most ridiculous example is probably *Marvel Comics Presents* #120, from 1993, in which a kid who sees Peter climbing the side of a building in a single panel of *Amazing Fantasy* #15 has *his* story told.

pathic killer; a boss who exploits his skills and despises his alter ego. The last of those, J. Jonah Jameson, debuts here, presented as a newspaper editor and as a good father, for some value of "good," before Peter has any relationship to him. And Spider-Man encounters his first supervillain, the Chameleon: a master of disguise who can assume his identity and, perhaps, act out his unconscious desires. (There will be a lot more people doing that later on.)

The villains Peter fights in the course of Ditko's Spider-Man stories are almost entirely older men who are inventors or scientists: the Vulture, the Tinkerer, Doctor Doom, the Lizard, the Beetle, and on and on. Some of them even try to mentor him. In particular, Doctor Octopus, a hilariously nasty old scientist named Otto Octavius, whose eight-limb motif echoes the spider design, represents the most horrible version of what the Peter Parker we saw in *Amazing Fantasy* #15 could have become: embittered, lonely, angry, condescending, really creepy about women. Kraven the Hunter isn't a scientist, but he's the jock-father sort, macho in a way Peter can't be, and very much a pro-wrestling type in presentation. J. Jonah Jameson, the rageful father figure who makes Peter complicit in humiliating his own alter ego, puts on a suit of technology he doesn't understand and becomes the Spider-Slayer. As for the antagonists of this period who don't fit that schema (the Looter, the Molten Man, a few others)—well, there's a reason they haven't turned up quite as much.

From his position of abject despair at the end of his first appearance, Peter slowly climbs the ladder of accomplishment across the Ditko-drawn issues, moving forward toward maturity. He gets a girlfriend briefly, graduates from high school, and wins a science scholarship to college. And Spider-Man becomes a durable character, in ways that turned out to be exceptionally useful for the purpose of adventure stories. He can pull off extraordinary feats, but he's vulnerable enough that he can often seem to be legitimately in danger. He's fun to look at (Ditko, like the artists who followed him, poses him in ways that defy normal human anatomy), and his presence makes almost any situation more interesting (the constant nervous wisecracks of Lee's dialogue for him keep his stories lively). He's hugely flawed but incredibly brave, and his overcompensatory sense of responsibility can draw him into conflicts of any scale; what keeps tripping him up is that he's *too* interested in doing right.

The Amazing Spider-Man #38 (July 1966)
STAN LEE, STEVE DITKO

It's not a secret that Ditko plotted his later Spider-Man stories independently of Lee, although there's a persistent myth that Lee tried to pretend otherwise. The letter column of *Amazing Spider-Man* #17 announces that the next issue's "whole plot was dreamed up by Sunny Steve and it was just nutty enough for Stan to okay it!" In issue #24, Lee was credited with "script" rather than as the "writer"; #25's first page notes that "Sturdy Steve Ditko dreamed up the plot of this tantalizing tale"; #26 announces that it's "painstakingly plotted and drawn by Steve Ditko"; #27 is "plotted and drawn by scowlin' Steve Ditko"; #28 is "plotted and drawn with talent rare by Steve Ditko"; and so on.

The Amazing Spider-Man had become Marvel's bestselling title, so it was a surprise when Ditko abruptly left it. At the end of #38, Ditko's final issue, the frustrated Peter Parker punches a clothing store dummy who looks like his former girlfriend's suitor Ned Leeds, goes home, watches a little television (an echo of his own TV appearances in his first story), and sullenly walks up the stairs to his bedroom. He's ascending for sure, but he knows he's got a long way to go.

The Amazing Spider-Man #50 (July 1967)
STAN LEE, JOHN ROMITA SR., MICKEY DEMEO [MIKE ESPOSITO]

John Romita was Ditko's replacement as *Amazing Spider-Man*'s artist and, frequently, plotter. A few years earlier, he had mostly been drawing romance comics—from 1959 to 1963, his work had appeared in nearly every issue of DC Comics' *Heart Throbs* and *Secret Hearts*. Before that, he'd drawn war and Western comics, as well as the short-lived 1954 revival of *Captain America*. With Romita's arrival, *Amazing Spider-Man* lost Ditko's luminous eccentricity, but it suddenly looked glamorous and limber, like a former teen prodigy who's gotten a flattering new wardrobe over the summer. It became more of a romance comic itself, too, as Lee and Romita's Peter Parker moved from being a high-school social outcast to settling into college, enjoying the company of his peers, and exploring the possibilities of his own identity.

Over the course of the late 1960s, Peter Parker redefines his relationship to some of the failed father figures from the Ditko period as he's working out who he's going to become. The new nemeses that Lee and Romita created for him are mostly not scientists or other kinds of surrogate fathers: they're characters like the Kingpin or the Rhino or Man-Mountain Marko, who move through space very differently from Spider-Man and are generally mobsters or mob enforcers of some kind.

Peter Parker walks away from his costume in *Amazing Spider-Man* #50, 1967. Art by John Romita Sr. and Mike Esposito (as Mickey Demeo), script by Stan Lee.

This issue, though, is the first instance of a kind of shift that would go on to be repeated in each cycle of the Spider-Man story. "Spider-Man No More!" declares the cover of *Amazing Spider-Man* #50. Midway through the issue is one of the most quoted and homaged images in the character's history: a full-page scene of Peter walking away from a trash can with his costume hanging out of it, thinking, "Every boy... sooner or later... must put away his toys... and become... a man!"

That's a shock, and it's got a vague hint of truthiness about it—the trash can was likely to be the final destination of readers' outgrown *Spider-Man* comics—but it's not a dramatically satisfying ending. Peter realizes within a few pages that being Spider-Man isn't what's keeping him moored to his youth, it's what's allowing him to grow up. At the end of the issue, he tells J. Jonah Jameson that he's been "out recruiting—!... I'm signing up volunteers! I'm gonna fill the whole city with Spider-Men!" It's a joke that was more serious than anyone realized.

The Amazing Spider-Man #99 (August 1971)
STAN LEE, GIL KANE, FRANK GIACOIA

The coming-of-age story is one whose rough outlines and ending we know from its outset. A bildungsroman concerns a young person who's not yet fully formed and has some kind of conflict with society; its protagonist tries to figure out how to become part of the grown-up world. Eventually that happens, and the story ends.

If Peter Parker's story could conclude, *Amazing Spider-Man* #99 might have been a happy ending.* He's on salary at the *Daily Bugle* now; he appears on TV, just as he did in his first story; his attitude toward crime has changed enough that he's talking about prison reform; and he's thinking about proposing to his girlfriend, Gwen Stacy—although she doesn't know his secret and unfairly blames Spider-Man for *her* father's death.

In any case, the following issue was the last of Lee's unbroken run writing *Amazing Spider-Man*'s scripts. (On the last page of #99, #100 is advertised as "The Summing Up," which it's not, despite brief dream-sequence

---

*Thanks to the pseudonymous creator of the invaluable SuperMegaMonkey site for pointing this out.

appearances of various villains Spider-Man has fought. It ends on a ludicrous cliffhanger, as Peter wakes up having grown four extra arms.) Lee returned for half a dozen issues early in 1972, and a few short backup stories for old times' sake much later on,* but he'd taken Peter Parker as far as they would travel together.

The Amazing Spider-Man #121 (June 1973)
GERRY CONWAY, GIL KANE, JOHN ROMITA SR., TONY MORTELLARO

Bestselling superhero franchises don't end, though, and a Spider-Man who's confident and secure in his place in the world and has lived up to what he sees as his responsibility would be a painfully boring Spider-Man. Peter Parker's story repeatedly gives him a moment in which his conflicts are more or less reconciled, followed by a catastrophic failure that knocks him back down—not to where he began, but to a point where there's nothing for him to do but learn to crawl again.

The real conclusion to the first grand cycle of the Spider-Man story involves his longtime nemesis Norman Osborn: the cackling Green Goblin, another one of Ditko's unsettling inventions. Norman is another one of the horrible father figures who's been hovering around Spider-Man since his earliest days; he presents himself as a wealthy, successful industrialist, and his son Harry (who looks just like him) is Peter Parker's closest male friend. But his legacy to Harry is violence, addiction, and mental illness, and here Norman takes his revenge on Spider-Man by murdering Gwen Stacy.

Gwen's death also plays directly into the "responsibility" strain of the Spider-Man story: Norman throws her off a bridge, but she dies an instant before she otherwise would have, when Peter's desperate attempt to rescue her breaks her neck. In the next issue, Norman dies when a piece

---

*Lee also wrote the *Amazing Spider-Man* newspaper strip that began in 1977, at least initially: when it ended in 2019, Roy Thomas noted that he had been ghostwriting it since 2000.

of his own equipment impales him. Crushed by his failure and loss, shut off from the possibility of the future happiness he'd imagined, and unable even to take revenge, Peter is ready to begin the second cycle of his story.

Amazing Spider-Man #151 (December 1975)
LEN WEIN, ROSS ANDRU, JOHN ROMITA SR., GLYNIS WEIN

Almost immediately after Gwen's and Norman's deaths, Spider-Man starts running through most of his past conflicts again—literally fighting the same villains, in a jumbled order. For the next fourteen years, the Spider-Man story is a vague, bland paraphrase of its first decade, with artwork by a handful of git-'er-done professionals. A few more Spider-Man series turn up on newsstands to keep *Amazing* company. Peter graduates from college, thirteen years' worth of issues after he graduated from high school. There's a "Crisis on Campus" in *Amazing* #221, just as there was in #68.

A pivotal moment in this period—although it took a while to look like one—is a 1975 storyline involving clones of Gwen and Peter. There's a question, at one point, about which of two Spider-Men is the clone. Then one of them dies; in this issue, in order to avoid tricky questions, the Peter Parker who's still alive dumps the dead one's body down a smokestack and swings away. His physical double is the trash he abandons this time, just as he tried to escape his double life by throwing his costume in the garbage in "Spider-Man No More."

Amazing Spider-Man Annual #21 (September 1987)
DAVID MICHELINIE, JIM SHOOTER, PAUL RYAN, VINCE COLLETTA, BOB SHAREN

In 1987, the story's slow, directionless drift suddenly becomes a dash to the end of its second cycle, as Peter prepares to marry his longtime girlfriend, Mary Jane Watson. Their wedding appeared that summer in both

Amazing Spider-Man Annual #21 and the *Spider-Man* newspaper strip—
the classical-comedy ending the series might have been building toward
for a while. The hero gets the girl, they'd been right for each other all
along, and now he's a grown-up man who's reconciled his relationship
with death and love and can have a family of his own.

Web of Spider-Man #32 (November 1987)
J. M. DeMATTEIS, MIKE ZECK, BOB MCLEOD, JANET JACKSON

It's another fake ending, and the real ending of the second phase comes
almost immediately after it. In writer J. M. DeMatteis and artist Mike
Zeck's celebrated story "Kraven's Last Hunt,"* Kraven the Hunter—Peter's
long-absent nemesis/would-be father figure who's macho and animalis-
tic rather than brainy and scientific—buries Spider-Man alive, briefly
assumes his identity, and then kills himself. Our hero has gotten his
classical-tragedy ending; in this issue, he literally has to dig his way out of
his grave.

Amazing Spider-Man #300 (May 1988)
DAVID MICHELINIE, TODD McFARLANE, BOB SHAREN

Having reached what had looked like, from his starting point, a place of
maturity, Peter Parker has died and been reborn. Now he's ready to begin
the third cycle of his story, in which he needs to defend his identity where
he once only had to build it.

Once again, the first year of the cycle that follows "Kraven's Last Hunt"
replays the conflicts of the first year of *Amazing Spider-Man*: there's another Vulture story, another Electro story, another Doctor Octopus story
(in which Otto Octavius dreams about a Manhattan filled with "Spider-

---

*It was serialized across *Web of Spider-Man* #31–32, *Amazing Spider-Man* #293–294, and
Peter Parker, The Spectacular Spider-Man #131–132.

people! A-all over the place!"—just like Peter's joke at the end of "Spider-Man No More!"). A few months into it, we meet Peter's most enduring new nemesis: Venom, a malevolent alien creature that had disguised itself as the all-black costume Spider-Man had been wearing on and off since the mid-1980s. Venom's debut also introduced the third great Spider-Man artist, Todd McFarlane, whose work had an enormous impact on superhero comics throughout the '90s.

McFarlane drew Spider-Man with the body of a human gymnast but the body language of a spider, limbs folded over and under one another midair in impossible poses. He drew Venom as Spider-Man's hideously backlit shadow self, the nightmare id to Peter Parker's all-repressing superego, oozing in from off panel, an engulfing mass with a dripping corkscrew tongue.* His covers, borrowing a trick from Al Hirschfeld's *New York Times* illustrations, had a little number next to his signature: the number of spiders he'd hidden somewhere in the image. By 1990, McFarlane was popular enough that Marvel launched a fourth simultaneous monthly *Spider-Man* series, this one without an adjective in its title, as a vehicle for his artwork (and his rather less impressive writing, but that wasn't the point).†

The Amazing Spider-Man #400 (April 1995)
J. M. DeMATTEIS, MARK BAGLEY, LARRY MAHLSTEDT, RANDY EMBERLIN, ET AL.

The new look and the new antagonist gave the third Spider-Man cycle real momentum at its start, which obscured its central storytelling problem: it wasn't clear what goal Peter Parker still needed, or hoped, to

---

*Venom was so popular that he soon got a shadow self of his own, Carnage—another alien "symbiote" that was basically his offspring—and starred in a continuous string of miniseries for five years, beginning with 1993's *Venom: Lethal Protector*.

†McFarlane stuck around for fifteen issues, then left to cofound Image Comics; the adjectiveless *Spider-Man* puttered onward for another seven years after that.

attain. For most of its first three hundred issues, *Amazing Spider-Man* had been, in part, a romance comic; with Peter married to Mary Jane, that angle of his story was sealed off. It had been a long time since he had been wanted by the police or shunned by his peers. So, instead of bad father figures—people he might have grown into becoming but chose to resist—the *Spider-Man* comics of the 1990s are full of his alternate selves, characters who represented the parts of his own identity that he'd cast off or repressed.*

The cycle's turning point, in the middle of the decade, was another return and another shadow-self plot: the painfully long "Clone Saga," as it came to be known, in which the discarded clone of Peter Parker from twenty years earlier returns from his apparent death. Its planned resolution, at first, was that Ben Reilly, as the double was calling himself, would turn out to be the original Peter Parker,† and that he would take over the Spider-Man role, while the Peter we'd been following since 1975 would get his happy ending, retiring to Portland, Oregon, with Mary Jane.

The big tombstone on the front cover of 1995's *Amazing Spider-Man* #400 signals the guess-we're-gonna-wrap-things-up-now tone of its story, in which Aunt May finally dies after three decades of persistent health scares. A few days before the end, she tells Peter that she knows that he's Spider-Man—that, in fact, she's known for years but denied it at first, that she's proud of him, and that Uncle Ben would have been proud of him too. Peter no longer has to keep his secret for fear of hurting her; he has her forgiveness and her blessing, and the two parts of his identity (and Ben Reilly's) are reconciled. In the same issue, we learn that Mary Jane is pregnant. Now Peter's really ready to complete his story of overcoming the loss of his two fathers by becoming a father himself.

---

*Peter Parker's actual parents appeared to return from the dead in 1992's *Amazing Spider-Man* #365; they eventually turned out to be killer robots, naturally.

†Gerry Conway, the writer who had come up with the original clone plot in the 1970s and then left *Amazing* shortly before it ended, joked: "When I did find out the gist of the story, that the previous [twenty] years of Spider-Man stories didn't happen, I thought, this is a wonderful thing for a writer, because it means when I left the title, the book stopped."

In theory, Ben Reilly replacing Peter was a solid idea. It would have been a concrete and timely end to the third Spider-Man cycle, and the fourth cycle would have been free to begin with Ben assuming an identity that he'd lost years before, and trying to figure out who he was and what his place in the world might be.

But the necessities of serial comics meant that couldn't happen. Shelving the guy who'd been in the past 250 issues of *Amazing Spider-Man*, readers made it clear, was unacceptable. So Peter was declared to have been the real Spider-Man all along, Ben was killed off, and Peter and Mary Jane's child was stillborn (although that was presented in a way ambiguous enough that she might turn up alive somewhere down the line*). Instead of serving as the third cycle's conclusion, this sequence ends up acting as its "Spider-Man No More" moment—the point at which Peter believes he's ready to change his life, but is not.[†]

The Amazing Spider-Man #545 (January 2008)
J. MICHAEL STRACZYNSKI, JOE QUESADA, DANNY MIKI, RICHARD ISANOVE, ET AL.

The urgent needs that drove Spider-Man, as Ditko and Lee had developed him—to make amends for his uncle's death, to protect his aunt, to find love, to create a mature identity for himself—had all been resolved. His enemies had long since lost any claim to a paternal place in his psyche, and the three who had been the greatest threats to him, Kraven, Dr. Octopus, and Norman Osborn, were all dead. A happily married superhero was no kind of protagonist for a coming-of-age story. There were new

---

*"Peter and Mary Jane had a kid and..." was a plot point in which some readers were already invested. They were rewarded with the *Spider-Girl* series, set in an alternate future in which their child had survived and developed spider powers of her own, which ran for twelve years in various incarnations.

†A jokey 1997 one-shot, *Spider-Man: 101 Ways to End the Clone Saga*, is one of the sourest things Marvel has ever published: it's about the Spider-Man creative and editorial team's inability to come up with a satisfactory way to resolve the clone story.

Spider-Man comics coming out almost every week, and they were *flailing*.

So one by one, most of those changes were awkwardly walked back. Dr. Octopus was mystically returned to life. Aunt May, it turned out, was still alive, too—the one who had died, knew Peter's secret, and forgave him, had actually been an actress hired by Norman Osborn (*also* alive again), who had kidnapped the real May—and as for the false May's heartstring-tugging reconciliation with Peter's dual identity, well, let us never speak of that again. Peter and Mary Jane's marriage was trickier to undo. For a while, MJ was presumed dead in an airplane explosion, then turned out to be alive; subsequently, she and Peter were estranged, then reunited. (A widowed or divorced Spider-Man would have been even worse than a married one.)

In 2001, the TV show *Babylon 5*'s creator J. Michael Straczynski began a seven-year run as *Amazing Spider-Man*'s writer, working with a couple of excellent pencilers, especially John Romita Jr., whose artwork had the solidity of his father's but a very different, appealingly ragged line. Straczynski's storylines incorporated a few intriguing ideas, as well as some very bad ones.* He did, however, come up with a thematically appropriate climax to the protracted third Spider-Man cycle: Tony Stark, aka Iron Man, a seemingly benign older male scientist/inventor, takes Peter Parker under his wing and gives him a fancy new costume. For reasons having to do with Marvel's big *Civil War* event of 2006, Stark eventually convinces Peter to unmask on live television. At last, the two parts of Peter's identity are *publicly* reconciled; he no longer needs to lead a double life.

Cue the inevitable fall. Before long, Peter's an outlaw again, his allies have turned on him, his privacy is lost, and his loved ones are in danger. His latest life-destroying failure, it's clear in retrospect, has come from his longing for the father figure he no longer needed. That catastrophe is

---

*The worst was "Sins Past," in which it turns out that Gwen Stacy had given birth to magically aged-quickly-to-adulthood twins secretly fathered by Norman Osborn before he killed her.

repaired by a worse surrender in Straczynski's final Spider-Man story, "One More Day,"* which concluded in *Amazing Spider-Man* #545. Mephisto, the demonic figure who's been around since a 1968 *Silver Surfer* story, appears to Peter and Mary Jane and offers to make everybody forget that Peter is Spider-Man again, in exchange for making their marriage retroactively never have happened. They agree, and thus the true ending of the third Spider-Man cycle is the undoing of the second cycle's false ending, through a deal with a devil.

Spider-Man: House of M #1 (August 2005)
MARK WAID, TOM PEYER, SALVADOR LARROCA, DANNY MIKI, LIQUID!

Could things have gone worse? Sure: Peter Parker could have gotten what he *really* wanted instead. The 2005 event *House of M*† concerns an alternate reality in which superheroes' deepest desires have come true, and its spin-off miniseries devoted to that reality's Spider-Man is a clever assessment of how poisonous Peter's idea of happiness could be. Here, Spider-Man is a universally loved, wealthy superhero *and* pro wrestler, whose miserable, put-upon publicist is J. Jonah Jameson; his uncle Ben is his trusted adviser; he's married to Gwen Stacy, who's alive and well, too, and they have a young son—and Peter is a contemptible jerk whose life is built on lies.

The Amazing Spider-Man #546 (February 2008)
DAN SLOTT, STEVE MCNIVEN, DEXTER VINES, MORRY HOLLOWELL

Back in Marvel's main universe, our spiderweb path is intersecting with itself—that *Free Comic Book Day* special from 2007 was covertly a prologue to "Brand New Day," the three-year-long, three-issues-a-month

---

*As far as I can tell, nobody, including its creators, likes "One More Day." Straczynski briefly intended to have his name removed from it.
†See chapter 10.

sequence that began with this issue.* "Brand New Day" was the first time that *Amazing Spider-Man* had *not* had a single regular writer or penciler, and the most deliberately it had ever been planned in advance. A brain trust of five writers collectively plotted it and took turns writing short storylines; artists with distinctly different approaches rotated in for usually just an issue or two at a time. Marvel editor Tom Brevoort had written a manifesto for the new direction: "Part of going forward is to cease the unending homages to the same three great Spidey stories of the past. So, please, no girl-falling-from-the-bridge, and no lift-the-big-heavy-thing-off-his-back-to-save-Aunt-May.† Let's stop repeating the story iconography of the past and come up with some new images to stick in the readers' minds."

"Going forward" is a tougher sell than "back to basics," though, and as of the beginning of "Brand New Day," Peter is once again single, broke, and living in Aunt May's house in Queens, just like he had been more than forty years' worth of comics earlier. His friend Harry Osborn is back (from the grave), too, and everyone hangs out at a café called the Coffee Bean just like they did back then, and at first it reads like a witty, nicely drawn exercise in nostalgia. But the brain trust was very clearly aware of the recurrences within Spider-Man's story and took pains to extend its themes without letting its events fall into dull redundancy. Those endless imitations of the Ditko and Romita Sr. eras had been a weakness of most of the previous thirty-five years' worth of *Spider-Man* comics: the nudging reminders of how *we used to have such a good time together, don't you remember when* _____? "Brand New Day" treats the past as a force that weighs upon the present, not as an idyll to reconstruct.

---

*At the same time, the *Spider-Man* publishing schedule shifted from three different monthly series to one series published three times a month. (Before long, the new *Amazing* got some auxiliary series of its own anyway—*Amazing Spider-Man Extra!*, followed by a new *Web of Spider-Man*.)
†The "big heavy thing"—initially a magnificently paced sequence from Ditko and Lee's *Amazing Spider-Man* #33—had been reprised in so many stories that it had become Spider-Man visual cliché #1.

The early issues of "Brand New Day" deliberately avoid most of the "classic" Spider-Man rogues' gallery. Twenty issues pass before the brain trust brings in a Ditko-era villain, and even that is a story about Kraven the Hunter's absence rather than his presence. The new master manipulator of this period is Mr. Negative, who can turn people into their antitheses or shadow selves (his real identity is businessman Martin Li, whose name slyly conflates the names of Stan Lee and Martin Goodman). That, in turn, leads to the creation of Anti-Venom, the inverted double of Spider-Man's own inverted double. Meanwhile, a new red-haired heroine called Jackpot* is running around and is so blatantly signaled to be Mary Jane in disguise that it's a welcome surprise when she turns out not to be.[†]

The Amazing Spider-Man #600 (September 2009)
DAN SLOTT, JOHN ROMITA JR., KLAUS JANSON, DEAN WHITE, ET AL.

The "Brand New Day" brain trust kept an eye on the fathers-and-sons theme of Spider-Man's story and brought it to the fore in the fall of 2009. One of Peter Parker's two great enemies/rejected father figures, Norman Osborn, had become a central character in the larger Marvel story throughout that year;[‡] his appearances in *Amazing Spider-Man* at the time focused on his return to grooming his son, Harry, to become *his* double.

The other one, Dr. Octopus, had been entirely absent for the first fifty issues of "Brand New Day" and finally turns up here, in a story that begins a slow crescendo that extends for the next hundred issues. At the

---

*The first line of dialogue Mary Jane spoke to Peter, back in 1966's *Amazing Spider-Man* #42, had been: "Face it, tiger, you just hit the jackpot"—another moment that's been subjected to innumerable homages.

†Jackpot gets her star turn as the protagonist of the lightweight late-2008 miniseries *Secret Invasion: The Amazing Spider-Man*, in which Spider-Man never actually appears until the last few pages of its final issue. In less than a year, "Brand New Day" had established its look and feel and supporting cast so clearly that Peter Parker himself didn't need to show up—a preview, in its way, of what was to come a few years later.

‡See chapter 16.

same time, it resolves another long arc, as Aunt May marries J. Jonah Jameson's father—effectively making Jonah and Peter brothers, and switching up their long-stagnant relationship.

Amazing Spider-Man #600 is an extra-long anniversary issue, with a bunch of backup features. One of them is a short, silly piece written by Stan Lee, in which Spider-Man takes his troubles to psychiatrist "Dr. Gray Madder," drawn by Marcos Martin to look exactly like Lee circa 1970. Of all the artists who drew bits of "Brand New Day," Martin was the most interesting stylist: he's a witty, ingenious page designer, and his Spider-Man stories take advantage of the character's peculiar acrobatics to show scenes from improbable perspectives. He's only drawn ten complete issues of *Amazing Spider-Man* (and parts of about a dozen more), but he's one of the very few artists who's figured out how to build on Ditko's innovations.

The Amazing Spider-Man #642 (November 2010)
MARK WAID, PAUL AZACETA, JAVIER RODRIGUEZ

The third and final year of "Brand New Day" turns, at last, to the mass of Spider-Man's history: the anxieties about fathers and sons and fathers devouring sons that have rippled through the whole thing; the specific opponents he faced in the hundred issues Stan Lee wrote; and Peter Parker's inability to move beyond the patterns of his past. It's mostly taken up by four extended sequences, each of which directly echoes the corresponding iteration of the Spider-Man cycle. The last of those, "Origin of the Species," which begins in this issue, centers on Spider-Man fighting nearly every major antagonist of his career *while carrying a newborn boy whose paternity is uncertain.**

"Origin of the Species" presents itself as a conclusion to the fourth cycle, but it's actually another false ending. It effectively leaves Peter where he

---

*The baby's name, in an almost-but-not-quite-too-cute touch, is Stanley.

SPINNING IN CIRCLES / 99

was at the peak of the first cycle—pretty much content with his life—and he has to climb higher so he can fall harder.

The Amazing Spider-Man #655 (April 2011)
DAN SLOTT, MARCOS MARTIN, MUNTSA VICENTE

Dan Slott, who'd been part of the "Brand New Day" brain trust, took over as *Amazing Spider-Man*'s main writer for "Big Time," the umbrella title for the two years and fifty-three issues that began with issue #648, again drawn by a rotating lineup of artists. He immediately made a big change in the series: Peter Parker finally lives up to his long-neglected potential by getting a lucrative, rewarding job as an inventor with a scientific think tank.*

That sounds like the culmination of a character's rise. Slott, ingeniously, made it the beginning of his fall. Death continues to follow where Spider-Man goes, and most of this issue is Peter dreaming about everyone he's ever known who has died: an accusatory procession of his parents, his uncle, his friends and enemies, his lover, his other selves. (It's exquisitely drawn by Marcos Martin—dry, surreal, terrifying.) He wakes from it in horror, then makes a declaration as the sun rises over Manhattan: "I swear to you... from now on... whenever I'm around, wherever I am... no one dies!"

There had been an inverted "Spider-Man No More" moment a year or so into "Brand New Day," when Peter briefly decides he needs to be "Spider-Man 24/7." That was mostly a joke, though; this is a real turning point, another one of Peter's impossible vows. Death is his new nemesis, and defying it is a new way for him to fail, and fail, and fail again.

---

*Lee and Ditko's first few Spider-Man stories established Peter as an engineering wizard—he invented his web-shooters and their fluid at the age of fifteen!—before they started treating him as merely very bright.

Ultimate Spider-Man #153 (April 2011)

BRIAN MICHAEL BENDIS, SARA PICHELLI, DAVID LAFUENTE, LAN MEDINA, ED TADEO, JUSTIN PONSOR

Another Peter Parker was about to defy death and lose altogether. The same month as *Amazing Spider-Man* #655, the Ultimate Comics line, set in a parallel Marvel universe,* began a storyline called "Death of Spider-Man," which does what it says on the package. The story of the Ultimate universe's teenage Peter Parker concludes as a tragedy: he saves *his* aunt May but perishes in a fight with the Green Goblin, finally having redeemed himself in his own mind for his uncle's death.

Ultimate Comics Spider-Man #4 (January 2012)

BRIAN MICHAEL BENDIS, SARA PICHELLI, JUSTIN PONSOR

Ultimate Spider-Man continued (under a slightly different title), by posing a question clever enough to keep its Spider-Man from spinning in circles forever: *What if "Spider-Man" didn't have to be Peter Parker's story? What if it didn't have anything to do with Peter Parker at all?* Here, Miles Morales, a Black and Latino teenager who's also gotten powers from a spider bite, decides to honor the dead Spider-Man by taking on his costumed identity.

Miles is exactly what was needed: a way to tell Spider-Man stories about a present-day kid—an outsider, struggling to figure out who he is in multiple ways—who finds himself with power he never asked for, takes on a responsibility that seems like more than he can handle, and rises to the challenge anyway.

*See chapter 1.

Miles Morales, clinging to the ceiling, considers taking on the Spider-Man identity in *Ultimate Comics Spider-Man* #3, 2011, written by Brian Michael Bendis and drawn by Sara Pichelli.

The Amazing Spider-Man #700 (February 2013)
DAN SLOTT, HUMBERTO RAMOS, VICTOR OLAZABA, ET AL.

Back in the main Marvel universe, over the course of the hundred issues leading up to this point, Slott had counterposed Peter Parker's newfound ambitions with Dr. Octopus's collapse. Otto Octavius is dying, his robotic prosthetics the only thing he can still control as his body falls apart on him. Peter refuses to let anyone around him die; Otto will stop at nothing to survive.

In the final three issues of "Big Time," *Amazing Spider-Man* #698–700, Otto switches minds with Peter, devouring from within the surrogate child who rejected him. Ultimately, Otto-in-Peter's-body kills Peter-in-Otto's-body. The latter, with his dying breath, makes the villain who has stolen his identity promise to keep his loved ones safe, and Otto makes his own impossible vow: to be a "superior Spider-Man."

This is presented as the "final issue" of *Amazing Spider-Man* (of course it couldn't be... *could it?*), and the last page of Slott's story reads "The End" in huge letters, in the typeface the series has been using for display text since the beginning of "Brand New Day." Just to bang the point in a little harder, the sun rises at precisely the moment Peter expires. There could scarcely be a firmer declaration that the cycle is complete, and the hero's loss absolute.

Superior Spider-Man #1 (March 2013)
DAN SLOTT, RYAN STEGMAN, EDGAR DELGADO

Superior Spider-Man, which immediately replaced *Amazing* on Marvel's publishing schedule (while *Superior Spider-Man Team-Up* replaced the secondary title *Avenging Spider-Man*), was again written by Slott, sometimes with Christos Gage, and mostly drawn by three artists with swooping, cartoony styles, Humberto Ramos, Ryan Stegman, and Giuseppe Camuncoli. It was a fantastically clever move: the fifth Spider-Man cycle as an inversion of everything that had come before it. Otto Octavius isn't a good son being tempted by bad fathers and rejecting them; he's the bad father trying to be the good son he's consumed, and his utter inability to do that is *his* failure. He doesn't want to be morally righteous so much as he wants to be understood as the greatest hero of all, and even as he schemes about how to do good in the most efficient way, he can't stop thinking like a supervillain.* "Doctor Octopus is Spider-Man now" seemed like the sort of thing that would be reversed at the end of a brief story arc; instead, it went on for thirty-one issues, long enough to become the new normal.

Superior is essentially one joke, but it's a delicious joke. It presents Otto with a string of familiar Spider-Man plots, from academic trouble to a crime spree by the Vulture to medical problems for Aunt May, and he responds to them all radically differently than Peter used to, "fixing" the

---

*It's obvious to him that any self-respecting hero should have a lair and minions, for instance.

ways the old Spider-Man had held himself back from success (i.e., self-doubt and ethical compunctions). Even in this incarnation, *Spider-Man* is a romance, and Otto is also better at that than Peter ever was; he lets go of Mary Jane at last and gets a new girlfriend, Anna Maria Marconi, with whom he builds the kind of stable, mature relationship Peter always managed to screw up (well, aside from the fact that it's based on the grotesque lie of his triple identity).

Superior Spider-Man #31 (June 2014)
DAN SLOTT, CHRISTOS GAGE, GIUSEPPE CAMUNCOLI, JOHN DELL, ET AL.

The conclusion of *Superior* is a new kind of "Spider-Man No More" moment, cutting off the cycle at what's usually its midpoint: to save Anna Maria's life, Otto throws *himself* away, sacrificing his own consciousness and reinstating Peter's mind in his body. Otto also leaves Peter a legacy: Parker Industries, a burgeoning technology empire, built on both of their innovations. (He had constructed it for his own gain, but accidentally acted as a good father to the surrogate son he tried to destroy.) Every previous cycle has ended with Peter knocked down from the heights he'd achieved. The *Superior* cycle ends with Peter having been raised up in his absence.*

And then the story goes on, of course. Slott continued on as head *Spider-Man* writer for another four years, which included some good stuff. Peter Parker becomes a global technology magnate in an armored suit (taking after Iron Man, the father figure who led him to his fall near the end of the third cycle), but eventually destroys Parker Industries in a fit of irresponsible responsibility.† "Dead No More: The Clone Conspiracy," another multiple-threaded sequence, forces Peter to face what a disaster

---

*Naturally, Otto wasn't gone for good: a not-yet-humbled version of his consciousness survived and returned within a year.

†He keeps the company's technology from falling into the hands of a fascist junta, at the cost of putting thousands of employees out of work and bricking millions of customers' phones.

his denial of death could be. Another highlight of those years is "Spider-Verse,"* a team-up of "every Spider-Man ever," up to and including the Spider-Men who had appeared in cupcake ads and a Broadway musical, as well as (of course) Otto Octavius and Miles Morales.

Ultimate End #5 (February 2016)
BRIAN MICHAEL BENDIS, MARK BAGLEY, SCOTT HANNA, JUSTIN PONSOR

Inversions and recapitulations have become the primary substance of Peter Parker's comics stories. The sixth cycle, following *Superior Spider-Man*, may still be going on, or it may have given way to a seventh—it's hard to tell without some distance. Peter Parker, by now, knows very well who he is, and so do we. That's okay: Miles Morales doesn't entirely know yet who he's going to be.

The Ultimate Comics line that had introduced Miles ended in 2015;† the *Ultimate End* miniseries was its postscript.‡ It mostly concerns a version of Marvel's New York City locked in apocalyptic conflict with its own uncanny double, a cycle that ends in mutual destruction again and again. Here, Miles's arrival on the scene breaks that loop (just as his initial appearance had broken the loop of a version of Spider-Man's story), and his kindness and bravery earn him an inestimable reward.

Part of that reward is that Miles and his friends and family survive the end of the Ultimate world (and the end of its fifteen-year-long story), and move over to Marvel's main world, where he and Peter Parker are now *both* Spider-Men. Peter continued as the star of *Amazing Spider-Man*, but when

---

*It was the conceptual basis for the 2018 film *Spider-Man: Into the Spider-Verse*, although its plot is entirely different.

†See chapter 18.

‡*Ultimate End* was one of the most vilified comics Marvel had published in years—based largely, I suspect, on misreadings of its complicated premise and timeline. Its first four issues look like they take place during the "final incursion" in *Secret Wars* #1 (see chapter 18), and the plot would be nonsensical if that were the case. The key to the story is that, on careful reading, what's actually going on is something entirely different.

Miles's next solo series began a few months later, it was simply called *Spider-Man*.

Amazing Spider-Man #801 (August 2018)
DAN SLOTT, MARCOS MARTIN, MUNTSA VICENTE

Dan Slott made his exit from Peter's story with this jewel of an issue, drawn once again by Marcos Martin. It's about a man whose path intersects with Spider-Man's a few times, over the course of many years; it looks at Spider-Man from a distance, as a reliable presence whose never-ending cycle is a blessing. (A couple of details suggest that its final scene takes place immediately before *Amazing Spider-Man* #546, looping the end of Slott's part of the story back around to its beginning.) "Every day, Spider-Man saves somebody's uncle," its protagonist tells his niece, as Peter Parker swings away, past the water towers of Manhattan.

7

INTERLUDE:
LEE, KIRBY, DITKO

hree names are central to discussions of Marvel Comics' early years: writer/editor Stan Lee and artists Jack Kirby and Steve Ditko. I've brought them up a lot already on our tour, and they're going to continue to come up, so it's worth spending a bit more time observing who they were, what they did, and how they worked together.

By the early 1960s, all three of them had a substantial body of work in the comics industry. Kirby and his former partner Joe Simon had co-created some successful characters—notably Captain America, as well as National Comics' Boy Commandos—and their 1947 collaboration, *Young Romance*, had originated the entire romance-comics genre. Had Kirby left comics in 1960, he'd probably be remembered only among aficionados, as an interesting figure who was fairly important to the form's early history, a Gardner Fox or Sheldon Mayer. Lee had been the editor in chief of Martin Goodman's various comics imprints since his return from military service in 1945; he'd written an enormous number of stories for them in that time, mostly humor and Westerns. Had he left the business in 1960, he might be remembered only among comics scholars, as a journeyman professional with some interesting connections, a Joe Gill or Bob Montana. Ditko had a lower profile than either Lee or Kirby at the time of *Amazing Adult Fantasy* #7, his first full-issue collaboration with Lee, published a month after *Fantastic Four* #1; his comics career had begun in 1953 but had been interrupted by a long bout with tuberculosis.

Kirby was unbelievably productive and versatile. Before superheroes took over most of the Marvel line, he drew sci-fi, horror, romance, war, Westerns, you name it. From 1961 to 1969, not a month went by without at least forty pages of new Kirby artwork in Marvel's comics, and sometimes three times that much. Ditko was also prolific, although he wasn't a company man like Kirby: during his peak years at Marvel, he also kept his hand in with their cut-rate competitor Charlton Comics, drawing short sci-fi stories, the monster series *Konga* and *Gorgo*, and the forgettable superhero feature *Captain Atom*. The characters Ditko drew were always unpretty and a little bit grotesque: he didn't do much in the way of Westerns or war comics, and he was hopeless at romance stories. Still, he was a naturally graceful storyteller and a master of communicating the uncanny. To glance at one of his pages is to understand *exactly* what's happening on it, through framing and pacing and characters' body language.

Lee, who died in 2018, was the last survivor of the three, and the only one who was really a public figure. More than one reputation precedes him: he's sometimes (falsely) understood as Marvel's creative mastermind, or (just as falsely) as a hack who did nothing but steal credit. But the question of his actual accomplishments is connected to one that often comes up when Marvel's comics of the 1960s, in particular, are being discussed: *Who actually made this?*

It's a deceptive question, and it hinges partly on the incorrect assumptions that "writing" is how comics get made, that it works the same way for comics that it does for prose, and that only one person can be the true "author." For a lot of people who spend more time with prose than with comics, a story is created when it's *written*, which means language, which means what Stan Lee did. People who make comics rarely use "illustrator" to refer to artists, or "author" to refer to writers: both imply that images are subordinate to words, which is not how the medium works.*

Before digital workflows became common in the late 1990s, the order of operations for mainstream comics usually began with a writer, who would write a full script describing the action in each panel, along with dialogue and captions. A penciler would then draw it in pencil; a letterer would write in the text; an inker would finalize the drawings with ink lines;† a colorist would indicate which hues went where; and then it would be printed on a four-color printing press.

Marvel did things a bit differently. In the early 1960s, Lee developed what he later called the "Marvel method": instead of writing a script at the outset, he would write a loose plot for whichever artist was going to draw a particular story (or act it out for them, or chat with them about a few ideas he'd like to see realized, or very often just leave it up to them altogether), then add dialogue and captions to the artwork at the pencil stage. That saved Lee a lot of time, and gave pencilers a lot more creative latitude to tell a story visually—or a lot more unpaid work to do, depending on your perspective.‡ The "Marvel method" meant that Lee made his contributions to plots in his capacity *as an editor*, and sometimes he didn't have to.

Lee wasn't the visionary creative powerhouse that Kirby and Ditko were, but he was the gab-gifted communicator who could amplify and clarify their singular visions, and other artists', like no one else. Throughout the 1960s, Lee was Marvel's editor, talent scout, art director, and pub-

*To be fair, Lee was known to use both terms in the 1960s!
†Another division of artistic labor that's often seen in older comics is "layouts" and "finishes"—respectively drawing rough sketches of the action, and fleshing out those images more fully at the inking stage.
‡The plot > pencils > script technique was favored by some comics writers and artists for decades, and it's never entirely disappeared, although it's less common now.

Steve Ditko and Stan Lee poke fun at their working relationship in *Amazing Spider-Man Annual* #1, 1964.

lic relations person, and wrote an astonishing number of scripts—as many as a dozen a month, with language that bounced and sang and snapped and rattled on like it couldn't get enough of itself. His persona was perpetually enthusiastic about Marvel's readers, too: he addressed them as "effendi," "frantic ones," "true believers." Readers who caught an apparent error and came up with an explanation for why it wasn't *really* an error would win a "no prize"—a fancy decorated envelope with nothing inside it.

The put-on chumminess of Lee's voice wasn't *just* flimflammery, though: if the "bullpen" where Marvel's creators all hung out together didn't really exist, the obviously fake promise of looping eager readers into that community turned out to be legitimate. One familiar name after another jumps out from the letter columns of 1960s and early '70s Marvel comics—names that showed up in later comics' credits, or elsewhere in popular culture.* And Lee constantly waved the flag for his cocreators, making their names selling points even as he did the same for his own.

---

*The first published work by young George R. Martin—who had yet to add the second *R* to his initials—was a fan letter in *Fantastic Four* #20 ("I cannot fathom how you could fit so much action into so few pages").

Ditko, who had no love for the spotlight Lee tried to pull him into, was the first of the triumvirate to quit, in 1966. He became a devotee of Ayn Rand–style objectivism,* and famously made no public appearances and did no press in the later decades of his life. That gave him the reputation of being a recluse, which he absolutely was not: he continued to write, draw, and publish new comics regularly for more than fifty years afterward, his studio number was in the phone book, and he appears to have answered virtually every letter anyone sent him. He was simply unwilling to be interviewed or photographed, or (after 1966) to draw Spider-Man or Dr. Strange anymore.†

Kirby left abruptly in 1970.‡ Lee never left, exactly. After 1972, though, he largely gave up writing and editing monthly comics and spent the rest of his life as the smiling, avuncular, public face of Marvel. The title page of every Marvel comic said "Stan Lee Presents" for decades, though he famously didn't even read most of them. Later on, he appeared in the fine print of the comics as "Chairman Emeritus," and he got an executive-producer credit on every Marvel movie, as well as corny cameo appearances in most of them. Outside the comics business, he was popularly regarded as the central force behind Marvel's characters and style; within

---

*Peter Bagge's 2002 one-shot *Startling Stories: The Megalomaniacal Spider-Man* entertainingly imagines what might have happened if teenage Peter Parker had become obsessed with Rand.

†Lots of people have propounded theories about why Ditko quit; Ditko himself wrote in 2001, "I know why I left Marvel but no one else in this universe knew or knows why," and I'll take him at his word on that. (Lee, for one, claimed he didn't know. A 2015 essay by Ditko with the characteristically odd title "Why I Quit S-M, Marvel" implies that it was because of a breakdown in communications with Lee.) Ditko returned to Marvel in 1979 and worked for the company fairly regularly for another twelve years, and intermittently thereafter. His final work with Lee was a few pages of 1996's *Heroes and Legends* special.

‡See chapter 4. Kirby spent the early 1970s under exclusive contract to DC Comics, where he wrote and drew series including *Kamandi* and *Mister Miracle*. He returned to Marvel from 1975 to 1978, again writing almost everything he drew, except for a *Silver Surfer* book written by Lee (see chapters 13 and 14). Then he left again, for good. In the mid-'80s, he feuded bitterly with Marvel over the company's demand that he sign an extra long release form to get back a small fraction of the thousands of pages he'd drawn in the '60s. (He eventually got about 1,900 pages—roughly a quarter of his artwork, much of the rest of which had gone missing.)

comics, it's a truism that the only character Stan Lee created all by him-self was "Stan Lee." Lee, who thought it was hilarious to pretend to be an egomaniac and kind of was one anyway, didn't always correct people who gave him more credit than he deserved.

Jack Kirby and Stan Lee try and fail to crash Reed Richards and Sue Storm's wedding in *Fantastic Four Annual #3*, 1965. Inks by Vince Colletta.

The perception that Lee was Marvel's prime maker sat especially poorly with Kirby, who later insisted that everything important in the comics credited to "Lee and Kirby" had been his own doing. In a 1989 interview with Gary Groth for *The Comics Journal*, Kirby de-clared: "Stan Lee and I never collaborated on anything! I've never seen Stan Lee write anything. . . . Stan didn't know what the heck the stories were about." To this day, there are Lee partisans and Kirby partisans, and it doesn't help that the two men had very different conceptions of what "writing"* meant. To simplify it a bit, for Lee, "writing" meant the specific language that appeared on the page, which was his territory; for Kirby, it meant the construction of the narrative, which was much more his territory than it was Lee's.†

Even so, it's hard to dispute that Kirby and Ditko, like most of Marvel's artists between 1961 and 1971, had their biggest creative breakthroughs while working with Lee. From the way Lee's collaborators talked about him later on, you'd think he was half a dozen different people: the man who plucked them from obscurity and put their name in lights, who stole the glory that was rightfully theirs, who misconstrued and muffled their voices, who polished their work until it shined and sang. Gene Colan, a veteran comics artist whose style grew vastly more fluid and distinctive as he worked with Lee on *Daredevil*, *Sub-Mariner*, and *Captain America*, raved about Lee and the "Marvel method" in a 1998 interview with Kevin Hall, saying that drawing without a script "gives me a lot of freedom to do what I want.... You know, Stan couldn't draw a line, but he knew a *lot* about art. He influenced me a lot.... He was wonderful."

And John Romita Sr., who collaborated with Lee on *Amazing Spider-Man* from 1966 to 1972, described their working relationship to *Comic Book Artist* magazine in 1999: "Oh, he's a con man, but he did deliver. Anyone who says he didn't is not reading the facts. Believe me, he earned everything he gets. That's why I never begrudged him getting any of the credit, and as far as I'm concerned, he can have his name above any of my stuff, anytime he wants." A con man who delivers the goods: that's an excellent way of describing Stan Lee.

---

*John Morrow's invaluable book *Kirby & Lee: Stuf' Said!* surveys the history of their working relationship and quotes dozens of instances of one or the other of them discussing it. Morrow highlights the word "writing" whenever it appears in transcripts or quotations, just because the two of them used it so differently.
†Kirby partisans occasionally chafe at Lee getting equal credit with him. In terms of their working relationship on their direct collaborations, I like to think of Lee as John Oates to Kirby's Daryl Hall: he wasn't the primary creative genius or the star presence, but he was the one without whom the magic didn't happen.

8

RISING AND ADVANCING

hen people ask me about "hidden gems" or a "secret favorite" series I've encountered in reading all those Marvel comics, I immediately name *Master of Kung Fu*, which ran from 1973 to 1983. It had an aesthetic like no other American comic book has ever had, and a fantastic premise— approximately "Prince Hamlet as Bruce Lee as James Bond," an action hero who lives in his head (with some deeply repressed trauma) and is horrified by the culture of violence in which he and his associates thrive. It was blessed with a writer, Doug Moench, who built a story with escalating complexity and elegance for almost a hundred issues, and three superb artists who drew substantial sequences of it: Paul Gulacy, Mike Zeck, and Gene Day. Its hardcore fans discussed its themes and motifs in lengthy, thoughtful letters. It outlasted the fad that spawned it by close to a decade.

And then, after it ended its run, *Master of Kung Fu* disappeared—as much as a ten-year-long series can disappear. In the subsequent thirty-eight years, its protagonist has never again starred in his own ongoing series. For the first five of those years, he didn't appear in any story at all. When Marvel started bringing old comics back into print as books, reprinting *Master of Kung Fu* was out of the question; none of it was reprinted, in fact, until 2016.

Is that unjust? Not entirely. *Master of Kung Fu* went out of circulation for a number of reasons. One was creative: when Moench and Day left the series, they brought it to a satisfying end, and it had become so much the product of their voices that it quickly expired without them. One was, allegedly, legal: Marvel has never made an official pronouncement on the matter, but long-standing rumor has it that, at some point, they lost the rights to use most of *Master of Kung Fu*'s supporting characters, who had been licensed rather than created in-house. The biggest, though, was a matter of taste: as brilliant as the series often was, its roots were deep in poisoned soil. Randall Jarrell's definition of a novel as "a prose narrative of some length that has something wrong with it" applies to comics, too: *Master of Kung Fu* has something *really* wrong with it.

Special Marvel Edition #15 (December 1973)
STEVE ENGLEHART, JIM STARLIN, AL MILGROM

In February 1972, ABC broadcast a TV movie called *Kung Fu*, the pilot for a series that began that October, about a half-white, half-Chinese Shaolin monk named Kwai Chang Caine (played by the white actor David Carradine) in the American Old West. *Kung Fu* caught on, and American audiences wanted to see more martial-arts action. In March 1973, the Hong Kong–made film *King Boxer* was released in the U.S. as *Five Fingers of Death* and became a huge hit.

Asian kung fu movies were a staple of the U.S. box office for the rest of that year, peaking with *Enter the Dragon*, whose star, Bruce Lee, died shortly before it was released. Comics got in on the fad too. Charlton was first to the post with the *Kung Fu* knockoff *Yang*, whose first issue was cover-dated November 1973. A month later, writer Steve Englehart and artist Jim Starlin* introduced Shang-Chi, Master of Kung Fu, in *Special Marvel Edition*, a series that had previously been reprints of old issues of *Sgt. Fury and His Howling Commandos.*

Englehart came up with his new martial-artist character's name by consulting the *I Ching* with his friend Alan Weiss. (American hippies inventing a character by looking at the *I Ching* might be the epitome of comics' Orientalist decontextualization, had there not already been a *Wonder Woman* supporting character *named* I Ching.) Shang-Chi wasn't Marvel's first Asian hero,[†] but he was the first to star in his own series. Or, rather, he was half Asian: Englehart has complained that editorial pressure led to his protagonist being half white,[‡] like *Kung Fu*'s Caine. And the identity of Shang-Chi's father and archenemy was, apparently, another editorial suggestion: Fu Manchu.

This is where the problem really lands. Created by the English novelist Arthur Ward (under the pseudonym Sax Rohmer) in 1912, the "devil doctor" Fu Manchu was a Chinese criminal mastermind lurking in the Limehouse neighborhood of London. His name, like most other things about him, was fake Chinese. Rohmer wrote thirteen Fu Manchu novels, which inspired a series of movies from the 1920s to the '60s. The character is the archetypal Yellow Peril villain the personification of the racist fears projected onto Asian immigrants in Anglophone countries.

American mainstream comics have a long, nasty history of racist caricature. The cover of the 1937 debut issue of *Detective Comics*—the series after which DC Comics eventually named itself—is a close-up image of the

---

*Both of the character's creators are among Marvel's unsung MVPs. Englehart had a gift for finding fresh angles on stale characters—his three years on *Captain America* and four years on *The Avengers* pushed those series well beyond what Stan Lee and Roy Thomas had shaped them into in the previous decade. For more on Starlin, see chapter 18.

†That would be the 1950s-era character Jimmy Woo, who had resurfaced in *Nick Fury, Agent of S.H.I.E.L.D.* in 1968, along with his archenemy, the Yellow Claw.

‡Shang-Chi's blond American mother has never been given a name, although she's appeared a few times.

face of a sinister-looking Chinese man with a "Fu Manchu" mustache* and no visible eyeballs. (An adaptation of Rohmer's *The Insidious Dr. Fu Manchu* was subsequently serialized in *Detective Comics* #17–28 in 1938 and 1939; the last two of those issues also included the first two Batman stories.) Marvel already had some Yellow Peril villains of its own by 1973, notably the Mandarin and the Yellow Claw. At some point, though, they'd licensed the comics rights to the cast of Rohmer's Fu Manchu books, including the character's daughter, Fah Lo Suee, and his English archenemy, Sir Denis Nayland Smith. Presumably, attaching those familiar names to *Master of Kung Fu* was meant to give it more of a commercial hook.

Something about Englehart and Starlin's creation worked, in any case—especially in the U.K., where Marvel's British division took the Avengers off the cover of their weekly reprint series of the same name and replaced them with Shang-Chi, as of the March 30, 1974, issue. Every week, the British comic reprinted about eight pages of the American comic, which meant that they were going through two issues a month of a bimonthly series that had just barely started. Back in the U.S., *Special Marvel Edition* was retitled *Master of Kung Fu* upon Shang-Chi's third appearance, in issue #17; Marvel promoted it to monthly publication two issues later, and launched the black-and-white magazine *The Deadly Hands of Kung Fu*, as well as the quarterly *Giant-Size Master of Kung Fu*.

In this first story, Shang-Chi is sent to assassinate Dr. Petrie (the narrator of the first few Fu Manchu novels), learns of his father's evil, and begins his rebellion. (He also fights a samurai swordsman, a sumo wrestler, and a gorilla: mixed martial arts!) "'Shang-Chi' means," Englehart explains in a final caption atop a yin-and-yang symbol, "the rising and advancing of a spirit." No matter how dubious its derivation is, though, "the rising and advancing of a spirit" is a lovely idea. From its beginning to its end, *Master of Kung Fu* is a story about someone who realizes that

---

*The Fu Manchu of *Master of Kung Fu* has the long, dangling mustache associated with the character's name by way of Boris Karloff's portrayal of him in the 1932 film *The Mask of Fu Manchu*; he had no mustache in Rohmer's books.

the worldview with which he has grown up is actually unconscionable, and who comes—not immediately, but gradually—to do better.

Captain America #172 (April 1974)
STEVE ENGLEHART, MIKE FRIEDRICH, SAL BUSCEMA, VINCE COLLETTA, MICHELLE BRAND

Connecting that premise to Rohmer's familiar pop-culture characters made it easier for *Master of Kung Fu* to find an audience, but also linked it to racist tropes that underscored the series' other conceptual blunders and dubious visual shorthand. For one thing, Shang-Chi is a kung fu practitioner whose outfit is basically a karate gi. For another, some of *Master of Kung Fu*'s Asian characters were given peculiar skin tones, and Shang-Chi himself was colored a bizarre pumpkin-orange shade well into the 1990s.

That seems to have been Englehart's doing, although he tried to shift the blame to technology. In this 1974 issue of *Captain America*, a letter from reader Harvey Phillips complains about Asian characters being colored yellow. The response, apparently written by Englehart, notes that the four-color offset printing process used for comics at the time "allows only 32 possible color combinations—not nearly enough to make all the distinctions we'd like.... Oriental coloring is simply not available. The closest we can come is Caucasian."

He goes on to argue that using yellow for Asian skin tone is a convention of comics, but that "change is in the air. When Steve colored the premiere issue of MASTER OF KUNG FU himself, he used Caucasian for Shang-Chi's Oriental opponents (although Fu Manchu, the personification of the Yellow Peril myth and a man who always dressed in yellow, was given pale yellow skin as a motif—and Shang-Chi, he of mixed blood, was orange). Naturally, Marvel isn't trying to slur anyone; we're just doing what we can within the limits of the medium." The larger question Englehart's note doesn't address is why *any* Asian characters would not simply be colored with the closest available skin tone to reality—why it would be important to defy verisimilitude to differentiate them from white characters at the coloring stage.*

Giant-Size Master of Kung Fu #2 (December 1974)
DOUG MOENCH, PAUL GULACY, JACK ABEL, PETRA GOLDBERG

Unable to keep up with the demand for their creation, Englehart and Starlin quickly bailed on *Master of Kung Fu*. A new creative team settled in shortly: writer Doug Moench, who was fast enough to handle all the *Kung Fu* titles, and artist Paul Gulacy, a gifted newcomer whose sense of lighting and composition owed more to cinematography than to most of his contemporaries in comics. Gulacy used a lot of photographic references—one of his characters was clearly modeled on Marlene Dietrich, others on Marlon Brando and David Niven—but he was especially thoughtful about how he showed action on the page.

The dominant look of comics fight scenes at the time was cool poses, foreshortened lunges, midair flips, and shattering impacts, with no thought to how they might relate to actual combat. That was also the look of *Master of Kung Fu*'s covers, drawn by other artists, which usually implied that what was inside them was campy grindhouse donnybrooks. ("Eat cold steel, pajama-boy!" yells a knife-wielding assassin on the cover of issue #21.) In most comics combat, the point is to show how hard the characters are fighting; for a martial arts story, it's more important to show how, *exactly*, they're fighting. Gulacy's action scenes are choreographed, with the path of each body from each image to the next implied. His Shang-Chi moves with calculated precision and force, a thinker whose every movement is fully intentional.

---

*Marvel, at that point, was still signaling difference with a broad brush in general; in the same issue's story, the Irish character Banshee speaks with an outrageously overdone accent ("Ye'll be stoppin' *no one*, me criminal friend!").

This story, one of Moench and Gulacy's first collaborations, is the beginning of a phantom thread in the *Master of Kung Fu* story, one that is never directly addressed again but keeps *almost* being addressed. Shang-Chi meets the owner of a martial arts studio, a woman named Sandy Chen, and begins a romance—his first—with her over pizza (which he's never eaten before). A complicated espionage plot, in which Sandy turns out to be one of Sir Denis Nayland Smith's secret agents, ensues. Eventually, Fu Manchu kidnaps Sandy, drugs Shang-Chi with a hallucinogen, and makes him fight his way through a labyrinth, a sequence visually inspired by Jim Steranko's Nick Fury stories of the late 1960s. When Shang-Chi finally makes his way to Fu Manchu, he demands to know where Sandy is. "She died in the maze, you fool!" his father replies. "You killed her yourself—!" In the next panel, a fight scene begins; "I force myself to forget my father's words," Shang-Chi's caption notes. And he does—or, rather, he represses them.

Master of Kung Fu #33 (October 1975)
DOUG MOENCH, PAUL GULACY, DAN ADKINS, JANICE COHEN

Among its other virtues, *Master of Kung Fu* had an excellent letter column, which often included strongly critical responses from readers. A letter from Bill Wu in this issue addresses skin color again, in response to an earlier issue's kung fu villain with bright yellow skin and spiked flails attached to his topknot: "Which of the illustrious names on your title page determined that Shadow-Stalker would be the same hue as an overripe banana?" Doug Moench responds that it had now become Marvel's policy that, given the limitations of the colors available for comics, "with the exception of firmly established characters (Shang-Chi and Fu Manchu being obvious examples), all future Asian characters would be colored in the same flesh tones as are Caucasian characters. And then Shadow-Stalker happened, how and why we don't know. But we're pretty certain the situation has now been corrected. If it hasn't been, and it sometimes takes a while to learn these things, we'll see that it *is*."

Wu was the correspondent whose letters were most often printed in *Master of Kung Fu*.* He didn't hesitate to call out racist caricatures, coloring, and plot devices. He was also clearly enthusiastic about the series, and a devoted and careful reader whose reactions mattered a great deal to its creators. And in time, they *did* respond to some of his (and other readers') objections.

Master of Kung Fu was changing already. The early issues had been diverting if formulaic:† Shang-Chi would either run afoul of some plan of his father's, or randomly stumble into trouble, and kung fu his way out of it. But that approach got stale quickly, so Moench and Gulacy devised a cleverer one, in which Shang-Chi resolves to make up for his past by working against his father with Sir Denis Nayland Smith, in the British foreign intelligence service MI6. The new setup also provided Shang-Chi with a durable ensemble cast of fellow secret agents: his romantic and working partner, Leiko Wu (introduced here); the tough old bruiser Black Jack Tarr; and Leiko's bitter ex-boyfriend, Clive Reston, who is forever hinting, but never says outright, that his father was James Bond and his great-uncle Sherlock Holmes.

Master of Kung Fu #38 (March 1976)
DOUG MOENCH, PAUL GULACY, DAN ADKINS, PETRA GOLDBERG

To become a spy in the hope of clearing the red from one's ledger, though, is a tricky prospect; the phrase that Shang-Chi repeatedly uses to describe tradecraft is "games of death and deceit." The two-part story in *Master of Kung Fu* #38 and #39 is a highlight of the Moench and Gulacy

---

*They appeared frequently enough that Moench's comments in its letter pages occasionally mentioned Wu even when he didn't have a letter in that issue.
†The titles of four of Moench's first five issues: "Season of Vengeance, Moment of Death!" "A Fortune of Death!" "River of Death!" "Rites of Courage, Fists of Death!"

era, an atmospheric spy thriller that keeps doubling back on what it appears to be. Sir Denis has sent Shang-Chi to the back alleys of Hong Kong to steal some documents from a martial artist named Shen Kuei, or Cat, and rescue a British counteragent imperiled by their secrets—Juliette, the aforementioned Marlene Dietrich look-alike. But Juliette is Cat's lover, and the papers aren't what Shang-Chi thinks they are, and everyone's alliances shift quickly and violently.

Master of Kung Fu #39 (April 1976)

DOUG MOENCH, PAUL GULACY, DAN ADKINS, GEORGE ROUSSOS

The second half of the "Cat" story, like many of Gulacy's issues of *Master of Kung Fu*, starts with a symbolic splash page designed something like a

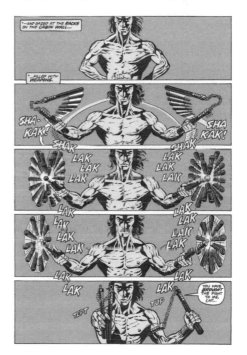

movie poster. It builds up to a climactic one-on-one martial arts duel introduced with an absolutely badass moment, a bit of visual pacing that's twenty-five years ahead of its time: a page of five horizontal panels showing Shang-Chi pulling out two pairs of nunchaku, spinning them, stopping them, and preparing to enter the battle, his face and torso focused and still, even as his weapons whirl.

But *Master of Kung Fu* never let its badass moments go unquestioned. As the fight continues, Gulacy progressively pulls readers' perspective away from the combatants, and Shang-Chi's narration becomes a meditation on the purposelessness of the violence in

Shang-Chi prepares for his showdown with Cat in *Master of Kung Fu* #39, 1976. Art by Paul Gulacy and Dan Adkins, script by Doug Moench.

which he finds himself enmeshed. The fault is the hero's; here, as everywhere, he's an outsider, as Shen Kuei underscores by perpetually, derisively calling him "Britisher."

That's a counterpart to another familiar bit of language from the series: Shang-Chi's British ally Black Jack Tarr only ever refers to him as "Chinaman." In the letter column of the same issue, Bill Wu dryly takes Moench to task for that: "While his use of the term 'Chinaman' may be more out of orneriness than hostility, I find it unlikely that Shang-Chi would give him tacit toleration indefinitely."

Master of Kung Fu #59 (December 1977)
DOUG MOENCH, MIKE ZECK, JOHN TARTAGLIONE, JANICE COHEN

In its initial ten-year run, *Master of Kung Fu* barely intersected with the rest of Marvel's world, but this issue and the next were a significant exception. Shang-Chi, drugged and hallucinating (again), imagines that he's fighting his dead nemesis Razor-Fist, and that London, Africa, and the Egyptian pyramids are covered in ice. When Sir Denis tries to calm him, he erupts in rage: "You took me away from my *father*—my *home*— tried to become my *new* father—to make this *London* my new *home!*" He imagines another of his enemies, Pavane, attacking him; when he kicks her, her head comes off, and she's revealed to be a robot. So, at first, is Clive Reston, who drugged him, but then Reston is revealed to be himself within a robot shell, and to in turn have been drugged and manipulated into drugging Shang-Chi by Doctor Doom. In the final panel, we see Doom and his robot the Prime Mover playing chess with the story's other characters as their pieces, exactly as Jim Steranko drew them in 1968's *Strange Tales* #167.

Master of Kung Fu #60 (January 1978)

DOUG MOENCH, MIKE ZECK, JOHN TARTAGLIONE, SAM KATO

Shang-Chi continues to hallucinate. Reston turns out to be a robot disguised as a person disguised as a robot disguised as a person. Shadow-Stalker, still overripe-banana-colored, attacks, and Shang-Chi kills him, whereupon Doctor Doom appears and boasts, "After all you've *experienced*, all the twisting paths of *deception* ... I have *outwitted* you, forced you to take a *human life*. ... Shadow-Stalker was *not* a robot! He was *alive*—and *you*, Shang-Chi, have just *committed murder*!" But, to paraphrase Lewis Carroll, it really was a robot, after all. In a scene recalling the final episode of *The Prisoner* (another serial about British espionage and rejected destinies), Doom's castle turns into a rocket and flies away; an epilogue establishes that nobody's sure how much of the past two issues actually happened, but that at least some of it definitely did.

Consider this story's details thematically, though: hallucinogenic drugs as tools of control, "twisting paths," the idea that manipulating Shang-Chi into unwitting murder (of someone who is not what they appear to be) would be the most crushing possible victory over him, the echoes of Steranko's comics. The entire sequence echoes the circumstances of Sandy Chen's death without once mentioning it, or her, directly. It's a repressed trauma that's *almost* bubbling up in Shang-Chi's psyche and is deforming everything around it in his consciousness.

Master of Kung Fu #71 (December 1978)

DOUG MOENCH, MIKE ZECK, BRUCE D. PATTERSON, PETRA GOLDBERG

What's compelling about Shang-Chi is less how he fights than how he thinks: he's introverted and self-questioning, perpetually looking for patterns in his personal history,* and not always finding even the ones that are there. The midpoint of the original *Master of Kung Fu* series is an issue that defied the (still prevalent) dogma that there had to be spectacular combat in every issue of an adventure comic book. It concerns Shang-Chi thinking over his recent experiences as he and Leiko Wu have a quiet evening together. They spar in a gym (the issue's only martial arts scene), listen to a Fleetwood Mac record, see *Close Encounters of the Third Kind* in a theater, make out on the couch.

Leiko gets a pizza delivered, which makes Shang-Chi briefly remember the first time he ate it, with Sandy Chen, and the first kiss that followed. Then he distracts himself by thinking of Juliette before he can remember any more about Sandy. His narration rolls onward through the issue, considering routine, loves lost and found, his pride in his art and his discomfort with that pride—and overlooking or repressing instances of his own culpability in violence, which will come back to haunt him later on.

Master of Kung Fu #82 (November 1979)
DOUG MOENCH, MIKE ZECK, GENE DAY, BOB SHAREN

The most passionate ongoing debate in *Master of Kung Fu*'s letter column concerned the presence of Fu Manchu in the series. In this issue, a long letter from Bill Wu responds to an earlier issue's letter from cat yronwode, which had argued that Sax Rohmer's bigotry was forgivable because "he lived in a different age," and that it was "about time for the return of Dr. Fu Manchu, no matter *what* Bill Wu thinks!" Wu notes that "in MOKF, Fu Manchu is *not* 'there and then' but decidedly here and

---

*On the rare occasions when other writers got to handle the character, they often had fun with his distinctive, dramatic speech patterns. Here's Shang-Chi in 1977's *Marvel Two-in-One* #29, written by Marv Wolfman: "Again my soul is in turmoil. Again I bleed. And, it seems, the wound will never be allowed to heal." The Thing's response: "Great! Ya ask for directory assistance, and ya get Robert Frost!"

now.... Fu Manchu is not 'just' an Asian villain; in Rohmer's own words, he is 'the yellow peril incarnate,' a representation of his race and the embodiment of evil at the same time."

Doug Moench's reply—in which he mentions that another long Fu Manchu storyline is about to begin—follows Wu's letter: "Bill states that Fu Manchu now appears 'without the modifications contemporary sensibilities might normally require.' This is not true. We've eliminated the pointed ears, the reptilian-like nictated eye-membranes, and—if we're lucky—the colorists will remember that the queasy yellow complexion is now *verboten*.... Finally, we've tried to stress the fact that Fu Manchu acts alone, not as 'a representation of his race.'"

(Which is to say: by this point, the series' creators have fixed the most visually egregious aspects of the character—but he's *still Fu Manchu*, and his presence or influence is still one of the axioms of this series, and there's no real way around that. Yellow peril is what he's selling.)

In 2018, I wrote to Wu and asked him what he thought of *Master of Kung Fu* from a few decades' distance. "Having a protagonist of East Asian descent was something I wanted to see in comics, but I found the early Shang-Chi disappointing in a couple of ways," he replied. "I saw potential in MOKF for a comic I'd really like from the beginning, but the presence of Fu Manchu was always going to be a limitation."

Still, he kept reading the series, and writing back to it, and his letters of commentary eventually led to private, friendly correspondence with Moench. As William F. Wu, he went on to become a Hugo and Nebula Award–nominated science fiction writer—one of many *Master of Kung Fu* letter-column contributors who subsequently had careers in the arts.*

I asked Wu why he thought *Master of Kung Fu* had drawn so many future professional writers and artists to respond to it. "I suspect there

---

*Others include cat yronwode and Dean Mullaney, whose company Eclipse Comics published Moench's subsequent series, *Aztec Ace*, as well as comics editors and creators Kim Thompson, Ralph Macchio, Robert Rodi, Peter B. Gillis, Peter Sanderson, Mike Baron, J. M. DeMatteis, Kurt Busiek, and Hilary Barta.

might have been two reasons," he replied. "One is the quality of the work; Doug Moench managed levels of characterization and plot that many other comics writers didn't reach.... The second reason... is that it was truly different from other comics for its entire run. Maybe that appealed to people leaning toward creative work."

Master of Kung Fu #103 (August 1981)
DOUG MOENCH, GENE DAY, BOB SHAREN

Master of Kung Fu's final definitive artist was Gene Day, who took over as the series' penciler after inking Mike Zeck's pencils for a few years. Day, who'd come up through the Canadian underground comics scene, had a broad experimental streak that he hadn't been able to indulge much in his Marvel work—in 1979, he'd self-published a hardcover collection of short sci-fi comics, *Future Day*—but Moench found ways to let him cut loose.

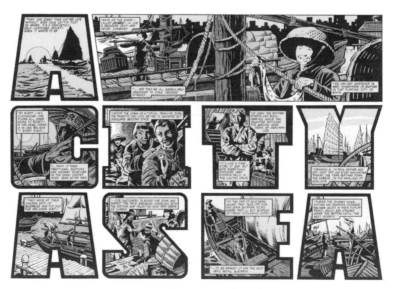

The title sequence from *Master of Kung Fu* #103, 1981, by writer Doug Moench and artist Gene Day.

This, the first full Moench and Day issue, begins with a visually spectacular sequence set in a Hong Kong harbor. The story's title, "A City Asea," covers two pages, each letter forming the outline of a panel, collectively depicting the harbor's ecosystem of junks. (It's another allusion to Jim Steranko's imagery from his Nick Fury stories of more than a decade earlier, the sort of trick that few comics artists had since dared to attempt.) Day's artwork lingers over rickety wooden houses and circling gulls, carrying the reader's focal point in acrobatic paths through the striped patterns of sunlight and shadow from slats in walls and bars in windows.

Master of Kung Fu #104 (September 1981)
DOUG MOENCH, GENE DAY, GEORGE ROUSSOS

As *Master of Kung Fu* #39 had been "Fight Without Pity," #104 is "Fight Without Reason." Juliette and Shen Kuei had appeared, on and off, since the earlier story, but their positions (and Shang-Chi's, and Leiko Wu's) had swung all the way around, as they had shifted allegiances and switched lovers. So this two-part story is not just a sequel to that one, but to its sadder reflection. Again, it ends in a showdown, and again, the fight is nominally about urgent matters of espionage that turn out to have no meaning but more genuinely about erotic betrayals. If Day's rendering of his characters didn't quite have the filmic precision of Paul Gulacy's, he had even greater command of atmosphere: the climactic battle between Shang-Chi and Shen Kuei is staged in a crumbling temple, down its Escherian staircases and past its looming statuary. (Day really, *really* liked drawing statues, apparently, and Moench was happy to oblige him.)

Master of Kung Fu #118 (November 1982)
DOUG MOENCH, GENE DAY, CHRISTIE SCHEELE

Moench and Day's *Master of Kung Fu* run encompassed something that no other Marvel title that's gone on as long has pulled off: a dramatically satisfying conclusion. Like *The Amazing Spider-Man*, it's a coming-of-age story, but the market conditions around it allowed its protagonist to reach his destination, and the story to end not long afterward. The series had begun with Shang-Chi's father sending him into a confrontation with Sir Denis Nayland Smith. Its climactic (but not final) issue, #118, concludes Shang-Chi's conflict with Fu Manchu, and severs the last of the ties between them. In its final panel, inverting his angry tirade from #59, he tells Smith, "You are the father I never had. I love you." The double-length story is also a thunderous showcase for Day, whose deliriously odd page designs incorporate scimitar-wielding assassins on horseback, a gigantic praying mantis, several quarries' worth of statuary, and Shang-Chi fighting his own clone, a shadow self who begins the fight by smashing through a mirror.

Master of Kung Fu #120 (January 1983)
DOUG MOENCH, GENE DAY, CHRISTIE SCHEELE

Marvel's editor in chief, Jim Shooter, apparently found that all to be so much frippery, and instructed Day to tone down the fancy stuff and just draw six square panels on each page. He also told Moench to change the direction of the series. Moench described Shooter's suggestions to the *Comics Buyer's Guide*: "I could kill off Shang-Chi, or replace him with a ninja, or turn him into a villain like Fu Manchu, and perhaps have a ninja hero try to bring him to justice. I tried to explain to him that a ninja is not a 'master of kung fu.' Ninjas are Japanese, and they use swords. Kung Fu is basically a Chinese form of martial arts. Jim also suggested that I kill off the entire supporting cast."

Instead, Moench wrote one more issue for Day, the elegiac *Master of Kung Fu* #120, "Dweller by the Dark Stream." It was again packed with imagery the artist could sink his brush into: even more statues, gnarled trees, a ghostly bagpiper, and a vintage Rolls-Royce whose license plate read FAREWELL. Then they both quit the series and promptly got an offer to take over *Batman* at DC. Moench went on to write more than 150

Batman stories. Day drew only one lovely Batman cover for *Detective Comics* before he died of a heart attack at thirty-one; his finest work disappeared from the public eye for thirty-five years.

Master of Kung Fu stumbled along for another five issues, the last few of which were written by Alan Zelenetz and drawn by William Johnson and Mike Mignola.* They end with Shang-Chi abandoning his old life and friends and going off to become a fisherman.

Shang-Chi next appeared five years later, still orange, in a brief serial by Moench and artists Tom Grindberg and Dave Cockrum in the anthology series *Marvel Comics Presents*. He kept a low-key schedule of one-shots and guest appearances for the next decade. By the time he turned up in *Marvel Knights* in 2000, comics had a much broader computer-colored palette, and he took on the more realistic skin tone he's had ever since.†

Domino #5 (October 2018)
GAIL SIMONE, DAVID BALDEON, MICHAEL SHELFER, JESUS ABURTOV

The vintage *Master of Kung Fu* series eventually became little more than a rumor. Nobody was demanding new appearances by Shang-Chi, although a small cult of aging nerds appreciated them. The central conflict of his story, his struggle with his father, was resolved decades ago.‡ Wearing a sleek jumpsuit instead of a gi these days, he worked with the Avengers for a little while and remains part of the texture of Marvel's shared universe. When he's appeared in recent years, it's often been as a mostly retired martial artist who now teaches others to fulfill their own potential. Comics creators still seem very fond of him: in the 2018 *Domino* series, he's

---

*Mignola subsequently became a very popular artist and the creator of *Hellboy*; his moody, statuary-heavy artwork is strongly influenced by Gene Day's.

†In a 2002 *Master of Kung Fu* miniseries for which Moench and Gulacy reunited, he often appears in scenes lit by fire—so he's orange again, but so is everything else.

‡Fu Manchu is no longer identified by that name on panel anymore, in any case. The "devil doctor" appeared in 2006 in *Black Panther*, calling himself Han (after the villain from *Enter the Dragon*), and a 2010 storyline in *Secret Avengers* renamed him Zheng Zu and suggested that he'd gone by various pseudonyms over the years.

briefly the title character's instructor, and the running joke is that he's so attractive that Domino can't even think straight around him.

/////

When I first tried to write about *Master of Kung Fu*, I began with a dramatic assertion that there would never be a Shang-Chi movie or TV show or video game. I was absolutely wrong. As of this writing, Marvel Studios is making a movie called *Shang-Chi and the Legend of the Ten Rings*, due out in 2021, with a director, screenwriter, and stars of Asian descent. Almost all of the first decade's worth of Shang-Chi stories are finally available again, in books and in digital form.

So what, then, do we do with them? For a twenty-first-century reader, there's no getting around what's wrong with *Master of Kung Fu*, from the Yellow Peril archetype baked into the series' premise to its perpetual "white people making stuff up about real-world cultures not their own" problem. It's absolutely legitimate to observe the early cover caption that reads "The Fortune Cookie Says: DEATH!" and decide that there are better ways to spend one's limited time than engaging with this mess.

To dismiss it, though, is to dismiss a genuinely special, doggedly idiosyncratic piece of art. *Master of Kung Fu* is an action-adventure series with a protagonist who questions his own actions and motivations at every turn and has a protracted crisis over his reliance on violence; an espionage series that treats the whole business of espionage as monstrous; a romance between characters with sexual agency and complicated, shifting feelings about each other. Most of it is beautifully, inventively drawn. It's a meandering but complete story, told over ten years, about a character who realizes at its outset that he's done wrong and dedicates himself to rising and advancing by way of a path that involves its own moral compromises. And it's the work of creators who came to realize—if slowly, and with some nudging from their audience—that they, too, needed to do better.

9

INTERLUDE:
THE VIETNAM YEARS

T he period when the U.S. was most heavily involved in the Vietnam War, from 1966 to 1973, coincided with a shift in Marvel's audience and creators. It gradually became clear that the readers who cared most about superhero comics weren't kids so much as college students, and that they were also gravitating toward the rising American New Left. Soon, those same readers became the second wave of Marvel's writers, artists, and editors. Over the course of those years, the anti-Communist strain of the Marvel story vanished, replaced by attentiveness—sometimes awkward, sometimes sympathetic—to young Americans' resistance to the war, as well as to the nation's own cultural and political upheavals.

August 1967: The Iron Man story in *Tales of Suspense* #92 is called "Within the Vastness of Viet Nam!" It includes a full-page image of Iron Man uprooting a tree, making three Vietnamese snipers fall out of it.

"Boy, will *this* give 'em something to talk about when they get together at their next 'Peace Through Strength' rally!" he thinks.*

January 1969: *Amazing Spider-Man* #68, "Crisis on Campus!," is substantially more sympathetic to student demonstrations than a protest sequence in Steve Ditko's final issue a few years earlier had been. The "crisis" is followed, late that year, by "Crack-Up on Campus" in *Captain America* #120 ("Either our *student committee* takes control of this college... or we smash it!").

April 1970: As Flash Thompson flies back to Vietnam in *Amazing Spider-Man* #83, Peter Parker muses, "Which is worse...? Staying behind while other guys are doing the fighting...? Or fighting in a war that nobody wants... against an enemy you don't even hate?"

October 1970: *Captain America* #130 is called "Up Against the Wall."† "I've been asked to speak to you today—to warn America about those who try to change our institutions—but, in a pig's eye I'll warn you!" Cap announces on live television. "This nation was founded by dissidents—by people who wanted something better! There's nothing sacred about the status quo—and there never will be!"

January 1971: All of Marvel's comics feature an ad for a psychedelic lamp called "Love Lite." "Invite BOYS to assemble Love Lites... and stay for a come-together Jam Session or Woodstock Festival party," it hints.

---

*"Peace through strength" was not a phrase particularly associated with the Viet Cong. It was, however, a phrase that Barry Goldwater had used in the speech with which he had announced his presidential campaign in 1964, and that Ronald Reagan had repeated in his speech on behalf of Goldwater that year. By the time "Within the Vastness of Viet Nam!" was reprinted in 1975's *Marvel Double Feature* #9, it was already a period piece: American forces had withdrawn from Vietnam in August 1973, and Saigon fell on April 30, 1975, a few months after the reprint appeared on newsstands.
†The New York City anarchist group Up Against the Wall Motherfucker, named after a line from an Amiri Baraka poem, had been active between 1967 and 1969.

August 1971: The title page of *The Incredible Hulk* #142 notes that it's "inspired by the book *Radical Chic* by Tom Wolfe." Wolfe, who had observed Ken Kesey's fondness for Doctor Strange in *The Electric Kool-Aid Acid Test* a few years earlier, had turned up as a character in *Doctor Strange* #180 and reappears in this issue, which centers on a wealthy couple hosting a fundraising party for the Hulk, populated by caricatures of that era's political activists and bandwagonhoppers.

Tom Wolfe attends a socialite's party in support of the Hulk, while a feminist protest rages outside, in *The Incredible Hulk* #142, 1971, by writer Roy Thomas and artists Herb Trimpe and John Severin.

October 1971: *Captain America* #142, entitled "Power to the People,"* begins with an image of a Black Power salute. It also includes a scene in which Sam (Falcon) Wilson argues with an armband-wearing feminist who calls him an "Uncle Tom" and a "male chauvinist"—maybe the first time multiple consecutive pages in a superhero comic had been devoted to Black characters talking to each other.

November 1971: *My Love* #14's "It Happened at Woodstock!" includes arguably the most bluntly sexual scene to appear in a Comics Code–approved romance comic, as a hippie called Flowers and the story's narrator, a young

---

*The title page quotes John Lennon's song of that name, which had been released in March of that year.

Iron Man is the target of a student demonstration on the cover of *Iron Man* #45, 1972, uncredited but probably drawn by Gil Kane, Frank Giacoia, and John Romita Sr.

woman named Jody, grope each other in a downpour at the 1969 music festival: "Oh, Flowers, the rain ... the wetness of our bodies pressed *together* like this ... it makes me feel so *close* to you!" ("This has got to be the ultimate trip!" he responds.)

March 1972: In *Iron Man* #45's "Calamity on Campus," students hold a protest rally at weapons manufacturer Tony Stark's factory. His employee the Guardsman attacks them with repulsor rays, and kills four of them. "It's another Kent State!"* announces one shocked demonstrator. The next issue walks that back: "All right, so four of the trouble-makers were hurt—were even thought dead, for a short time—!"

July 1972: *Sgt. Fury and His Howling Commandos* #100 breaks with the series' usual World War II adventures for a story set in the "present day." It concerns an event in honor of the group, emceed by Stan Lee (in his beard-and-turtleneck phase); Marvel's publisher Martin Goodman even puts in an appearance. Then someone tries to assassinate one of the commandos, "Reb" Ralston, who is now a congressman and civil rights activist but for some reason still calls himself "Reb." Stan Lee sheds a single tear, but then Ralston pulls through, and everyone listens to the New Seekers' then-recent hit single/Coca-Cola jingle, "I'd Like to Teach the World to Sing." It's weird.

---

*National Guardsmen killed four students at a protest at Kent State University on May 4, 1970.

September 1972: The barbed, satirical plot of *Captain America* #153 proceeds from a nerdy question: If Bucky Barnes had been killed and Steve Rogers frozen in ice near the end of World War II, then who was running around beating up Communists in the *Captain America* revival that had run for a few months in 1954? The answer, it turns out, is a couple of true believers whose superpatriotism and anti-Communism subsequently curdled into white supremacist violence. William Burnside, the Captain America of the '50s, explains: "Somehow we seemed to outgrow the world. We began finding Reds where others saw nothing, like in Harlem and Watts. In fact, we found that most people who weren't pure-blooded Americans were Commies!"

January 1973: Bill Everett, who had created the Sub-Mariner in 1939, centers *Sub-Mariner* #57 on a protest against the Vietnam War: "Those kids were just peaceful demonstrators until your precious 'authority' sent those pigs in to break their heads!" It's Everett's final complete issue of the series before his death that February.

June 1973: A letter from reader Bob Hartner appears in *Gunhawks* #5: "You have a cavalry troop going war-crazy and wiping out an Indian village, even the women and children, for no other reason, it seems, than racial prejudice. Right? And, on the sidelines, Kid Cassidy weeps, agonizes, and looks on in horror, unable to prevent the slaughter. And he says to himself, 'It makes me   ashamed to be... an American!'... Those were almost exactly the feelings I had when I learned about My Lai and those 'tiger pit' prisons in Vietnam! Was [writer Gary Friedrich] trying to tell us something?" The editorial response: "We think he was just trying to say that pointless slaughter is pointless slaughter, whether the perpetrators be American, Russian, Chinese, German, or, for that matter, Martian!... And if the sequence meant more than that to you... if it hit ya a little deeper... well, just think of it as a free philosophical bonus!" Genre fiction always offers plausible deniability.

10

THE MUTANT METAPHOR

For ten straight years, *The Uncanny X-Men* was the unstoppable behemoth of American mainstream comics both as a commercial enterprise and as art: a fantastically rich, inventive story about the meaning and value of group identity. Once the creative team of writer Chris Claremont, penciler/coplotter John Byrne, and inker Terry Austin set it in motion, the series' form and cast and setting constantly mutated, sometimes radically, around Claremont's assured, raconteurial voice.

Claremont and Byrne figured out how to use the protean metaphor for oppression and marginalization that was embedded in *X-Men*'s premise, and turned it into rocket fuel for their stories. They gave their characters a level of emotional depth and complexity that was unprecedented in mainstream comics, and rewarded their long-term readers with narrative arcs that developed over months or years.*

---

*The podcast *Jay and Miles X-Plain the X-Men*—a weekly commentary on mutant comics—refers to *X-Men* as "comics' greatest superhero soap opera," which is a good way of

And it sold, and sold, and sold. Other comics occasionally moved more units and often had greater artistic triumphs, but from 1978 to 1987, *X-Men* was the bestselling American comic book series, and its readership increased every year. Over the course of that decade, its average monthly sales grew from about 116,000 copies an issue to more than 430,000, now an unthinkably huge figure. People who worked at comics stores in the mid-'80s, like me, knew that the biggest sales day of each month was the third Thursday, when the new issue of *X-Men* came out.

That's a hell of a feat for any kind of popular entertainment, the equivalent of a pop band releasing a Top 10 single every month for ten years. The biggest year-to-year leap in circulation *X-Men* made occurred between 1980 and 1981, the conclusion of the era when Byrne and Austin were drawing it. And the premises of two of the stories published that year—one about personal apocalypse ("The Dark Phoenix Saga"), the other about saving the future ("Days of Future Past")—have stuck with *X-Men* and its descendants ever since, through comics and TV shows and movies.

X-Men #1 (September 1963)
STAN LEE, JACK KIRBY, PAUL REINMAN

To understand how those particular stories came to mean so much, it's useful to see how *X-Men* got to that point. Its success was a little surprising at first, since it had spent most of its first fifteen years near the bottom of Marvel's superhero line. Created in 1963 by Stan Lee and Jack Kirby, the first incarnation of *X-Men* was about a private school for teenagers with superpowers. The X-Men are mutants, an unexpected advance on their parents' genetics. At some point, they discover that they're different from other people: their bodies or minds change, and new abilities appear. "Normal" people despise them.

---

putting it, although most soap operas don't have the luxury of treating clones, interdimensional travel, and resurrection as commonplace.

In Lee and Kirby's first issue, Charles "Professor X" Xavier, a bald psychic in a wheelchair, has enrolled five teenage mutants in his academy for "gifted youngsters." (Difference is always a gift in *X-Men* comics.) He explains to his new charges that "there are many mutants walking the earth... and more are born each year! Not all of them want to help mankind!... Some hate the human race, and wish to destroy it! Some feel that the mutants should be the real rulers of Earth! It is our job to protect mankind from those... from the evil mutants!"

Stan Lee's words from early Marvel comics became the toys of the writers who followed in his path, and the premise of *X-Men* was just self-serious enough that it could be turned inside out. The charitable reading of what's going on in *X-Men* #1 is the one on its surface: Xavier is teaching his students to be superheroes. But his absolutist rhetoric there is very close to the sort offered to young people by warlords explaining why their orders must be followed without question. Read between the lines, in the light of much later parts of the story, and a grimmer interpretation presents itself: Charles Xavier has conscripted these desperate teenagers into a child army.

Still, 1960s *X-Men* is a straightforward good-guys-versus-bad-guys ensemble series.* Its archvillain, from that first issue onward, is the helmeted Magneto, who can control magnetic force. He also has a small army of his own; they're called "The Brotherhood of Evil Mutants," with sarcasm that's far more evident now than it was in the '60s.

X-Men #57 (June 1969)
ROY THOMAS, NEAL ADAMS, TOM PALMER, LINDA FITE, WERNER ROTH, SAM GRAINGER

The closest thing early *X-Men* has to a central protagonist among Xavier's students is Scott Summers, aka Cyclops, a subdued, repressed young man

---

*Both Lee and Kirby bailed out of *X-Men* before its twentieth issue. It shambled along aimlessly for most of the 1960s, punctuated by very brief runs by the excellent artists Jim Steranko and Neal Adams.

whose eyes shoot out magenta beams that destroy everything he sees unless he's wearing a special visor or glasses. (We can never see his eyes, even as readers, but perhaps we can imagine ourselves behind them.) The other four members of Xavier's team are prefab types. Hank McCoy, the Beast, has an apelike physique and a penchant for twenty-dollar words; Bobby Drake, Iceman, is a spunky, goofy youngster, a temperature-inverted Human Torch; Warren Worthington III, Angel, is a rich kid with wings; and Jean Grey, the telekinetic Marvel Girl, is *the girl*. (She and Cyclops began dating a few years into the series. *X-Men*, too, is a romance comic: the question of who's dating whom is often an important one.)

From 1967 to 1969, *X-Men*'s backup stories explained their individual origins. Marvel Girl's turn came last, in this issue: "The Female of the Species!" was dedicated to Jean demonstrating her powers rather than offering any insight into her background or personality. The first Marvel superhero story to be written by a woman (Linda Fite), it ends with two men in the background leering at Jean while she looks at the reader, noting that "part of being normal—is to turn men's heads without really trying!"

X-Men #94 (August 1975)
CHRIS CLAREMONI, LEN WEIN, DAVE COCKRUM, BOB MCIFOD, PHIL RACHELSON

At the beginning of the 1970s, *X-Men* went into reruns—like a few of Marvel's long-running war and Western series, it switched from featuring a new story every issue to reprinting older material—before expiring altogether in early 1975.

As with every *X-Men* death, it was followed by a resurrection. In late 1975, writer Len Wein and artist Dave Cockrum revived the series, replacing most of its cast with a big, international group. They included a bunch of nicely designed new characters from Cockrum's sketchbooks, as well as Wolverine, a compact, pugnacious Canadian with metal claws who had first appeared the year before in a Wein-written *Incredible Hulk* story. But Wein had his hands full at the time: besides *Hulk*, he was writing *Amazing Spider-Man*, *Fantastic Four*, and *Thor*, and was briefly Marvel's editor in chief. So after a single issue introducing the new team, *Giant-Size X-Men* #1, he turned the project over to fledgling writer Chris Claremont with *X-Men* #94.

In those days, Marvel's second-tier titles were subject to constant creative shuffling: *Super-Villain Team-Up*, for instance, debuted in August 1975, the same month as *X-Men* returned, and burned through five writers and five pencilers in its first six issues. Claremont had worked as a gofer in Marvel's office six years earlier and had written a few fill-in scripts, but his most substantial body of work at that point was a short run on the horror series *War Is Hell*. He scripted the first two issues of the revived *X-Men* from Wein's plots. Then, defying all expectations, he stuck around for sixteen years and 186 consecutive issues (as well as a tall stack of other *X-Men*-related projects), a record that remained unbroken for decades in American comics.

X-Men #101 (October 1976)
CHRIS CLAREMONT, DAVE COCKRUM, FRANK CHIARAMONTE, BONNIE WILFORD

The first few years of "the all-new, all-different *X-Men*," as its covers billed it, were awkward but promising. Claremont already had a knack for the interpersonal dynamics of the huge cast he'd been handed. In particular, he started making the long-neglected Jean Grey's personal evolution one of the emotional pillars of the series. That came to the foreground in a 1976 storyline in which the X-Men find themselves on a space shuttle that's going to crash unless someone can fly it to safety through radiation that's certain to kill its pilot; Jean decides to sacrifice herself to save her beloved Cyclops and the rest of her teammates.

At the beginning of this issue, the shuttle plunges into Jamaica Bay, and Jean flies out of the water, alive and well and wearing a new costume.

"Hear me, X-Men!" she declares. "No longer am I the woman you knew! I am fire! And life incarnate! Now and forever—I am PHOENIX!" (Rhetorical flourishes and self-introductions were catnip to Claremont, who repeated the galloping rhythm of that one until it became an incantation.) The following few issues suggested that a lot more about Jean than her superhero name had changed, but the extent of her transformation wasn't clear until after Dave Cockrum left *X-Men* a year later.*

X-Men #108 (December 1977)
CHRIS CLAREMONT, JOHN BYRNE, TERRY AUSTIN, ANDY YANCHUS

X-Men's golden decade started right here, in the middle of a story. Cockrum's replacement, as of this issue, was the young Canadian artist John Byrne, with whom Claremont had been working since 1975; along with him came two other members of the creative team that made *X-Men* a hit, inker Terry Austin and letterer Tom Orzechowski.† The final issue of Cockrum's initial run, *X-Men* #107, had ended with a cliffhanger in which the entire universe blinks out of existence for a moment, then returns. The effect of the change of artists wasn't dissimilar.‡ In a flash, *X-Men* went from "clever and intriguing" to "overwhelming and immersive."

Ask anyone who was reading the series in the late 1970s and '80s who *the* definitive *X-Men* artist was, and they'll say Byrne. Or, perhaps, they'll praise Paul Smith and John Romita Jr. and mention the several gorgeous

---

*There's a lot of very smart analysis of the Phoenix story, and Claremont's *X-Men* in general, in Ramzi Fawaz's book *The New Mutants: Superheroes and the Radical Imagination of American Comics*.

†Claremont and Byrne collaborated first on the kung fu series *Iron Fist*, which they subsequently merged with the blaxploitation series *Luke Cage, Power Man* into the durable buddy-act comic *Power Man and Iron Fist*. From 1977 to 1978, until *X-Men* went monthly, they also worked together on the Spider-Man-and-somebody-else-each-month series *Marvel Team-Up*; in mid-1977, Austin and Orzechowski joined them for a lengthy Star-Lord story in the black-and-white magazine *Marvel Preview*.

‡This issue concludes with two notes. "This book is dedicated with respect and admiration to Dave Cockrum—who helped make the dream a reality," reads the first one. The second, right below it: "I'm not dead—Dave Cockrum."

issues drawn by Barry Windsor-Smith and the handful of breathtaking annuals drawn by Arthur Adams, before coming back to the Byrne and Austin team as the obvious choice. Of all the 1970s comics artists who took obvious inspiration from Jack Kirby, Byrne had the freshest, most aestheticized take. His images had the spring-loaded force and assured flow of Kirby's *Fantastic Four*, but they were also smooth and pretty, rippling rather than jagged.

Terry Austin had worked with Continuity Associates, the illustration studio founded by former *X-Men* artist Neal Adams and the veteran inker-editor Dick Giordano, and took the sharply varied weight of those artists' brushstrokes even further, adding craggy contours and rough, feathered shading to the curving paths of Byrne's pencils. Tom Orzechowski's assured, nearly square letter forms had the same sort of solidity as Byrne's figures and echoed Austin's lines in the panels around them. Inkers and letterers, in those days, were even more likely than writers and pencilers to be swapped out as deadlines dictated, but it was obvious how well Austin and Orzechowski's peculiar styles harmonized with Byrne's on the page. Austin ended up inking all but one of Byrne's *X-Men* issues, and Orzechowski stayed with *X-Men* (with a few breaks) even longer than Claremont.

From the first page of *X-Men* #108—an alien landscape, with a gigantic crystal at its center emitting beams that reverse the darkness and light in half of the sky—to the last page of 1981's *Uncanny X-Men* #143,* Claremont, Byrne, and company set the template for thousands of subsequent X-Men comics.† Their stories juggled psychological complexity and spec-

---

*"Uncanny" officially became part of the title with #142. *The Uncanny X-Men* is often retroactively used as the title for the entire series that started in 1963.
†Since the end of Claremont and Byrne's collaboration, there have been about 500 more issues of *Uncanny X-Men*, another 350 of *X-Men*, 150 or so apiece of *New Mutants* and *Excalibur*, 270 of *X-Factor*, 250 of *X-Force*, about 100 of *Astonishing X-Men*, and 700 or so other mutant team comics. Then there are the solo series: well over 400 *Wolverine* comics, 150-plus of *Cable*, and a pile of others.

tacular imagery, intricate plots and explosive action, despair and delight, with seemingly effortless grace.

By all reports, it actually took a great deal of effort. Byrne and Claremont clashed constantly: the sweet spot was where they could find compromise. "I've always said we had kind of a 'Gilbert and Sullivan' relationship," Byrne told interviewer Brian Lamken in 2000.* "We came at the whole storytelling problem from very different directions, and such sparks as there were came about largely from us banging into each other." The two of them plotted *X-Men* together, and it's hard to tell where their respective ideas began and ended. But they went on to write hundreds of comics without each other, so it's fair to guess at the impulses that were battling it out in their collaboration.

Byrne is a meat-and-potatoes storyteller, a craftsman with the technique of a showman. He pleases the eye before he does anything else. His characters are posed to display their presence and weight and distinctive ways of moving through space. In his *X-Men* years, his most prominent flaw as an artist was that almost all the women he drew had approximately the same pretty face; to his credit, he later fixed that. He knows when to hold back and let blankness or silence do his work for him—his X-Men villain Proteus is unforgettably represented as negative space, a person-shaped absence in the middle of an image. He keeps pacing on track, showing readers exactly what they need to see.

Claremont's writing, conversely, is all fantastic tics. He focuses on characters' particular drives, their personal linguistic quirks, their hidden dimensions, their unconscious urges. He sets stories in interesting places around the world, real and invented. He lets his characters splash around in the pools of their emotions, exploring their feelings at length in dialogue or thought balloons. Then he explains in garrulous captions whatever won't fit into their mouths or minds. He scatters potential plot

---

*The librettist W. S. Gilbert and composer Sir Arthur Sullivan, collaborators on a string of enormously successful nineteenth-century comic operas, squabbled endlessly over the plots and tone of their work.

threads everywhere, picking them up later, or not, at his convenience. If Byrne draws a pistol on a wall, it will be fired by the end of the issue; if Claremont has a character mention a pistol on a wall, it might never be mentioned again, or it might turn out, sixty issues later, to have been cursed by an eighteenth-century warlock.

Both Claremont and Byrne are devotees of Stan-and-Jack-and-Steve; the first ten years of Marvel are the foundation of both of their individual work. For Byrne, that often means refurbishing particular Lee and Kirby or Lee and Ditko stories and characters, or steering the tone of a series back toward something like what it was in that era.* Claremont's homages to early Marvel, conversely, take the form of trying to make series evolve as quickly as *Fantastic Four* or *Amazing Spider-Man* did in the 1960s.

X-Men #124 (August 1979)

CHRIS CLAREMONT, JOHN BYRNE, TERRY AUSTIN, GLYNIS WEIN

Claremont's *X-Men*—with Byrne, and then for much longer without him— can be alarming or off-putting to readers picking it up forty years later. On its surface, it looks more like contemporary comics than anything else of its era does, but it's distinctly unlike them. It's wordy and plotty. Its tone is overripe, like a stone fruit dripping juices with a hint of rot. Half of its characters speak in some kind of dialect. It has the ectoplasm of an old era of superhero comics clinging to it—everyone is forever explaining their powers and motivations, dropping their catchphrases, erupting in exclamations.

---

*Byrne's most recent officially published X-Men project to date is the 1999–2001 series *X-Men: The Hidden Years*, which he both wrote and drew. It stars the 1960s X-Men team in a story that's set immediately after the last of their original appearances and overlaps with the plot of Lee and Kirby's final few issues of *Fantastic Four*. Since 2019, Byrne has been writing and drawing the monthly series *X-Men: Elsewhen*, set near the end of his own original tenure on *Uncanny X-Men* and presented as "just for fun" fan fiction on his personal site—Marvel's not involved with it.

To extend the Gilbert and Sullivan analogy, Claremont's equivalent of Gilbert's "magic lozenge," the plot device for which he always reaches first, is mind control. Charles Xavier can psychically alter people's perceptions and memories; that had been true since the Lee and Kirby days. Mastermind, Mesmero, and Sauron, all mind-controlling baddies, had appeared in 1960s *X-Men* stories, so they were fair game too. But then there are the mind-controlling White Queen, the psyche-possessing Brood, the emotion-manipulating Empath, the thought-commanding Selene, the consciousness-overtaking Malice, the will-enslaving Genegineer, the mental-"software"-rewriting Pretty Boy, and the brain-beguiling Shadow King, among many others. When Dracula turns up in *X-Men*, Claremont focuses on the vampire's ability to bend his victims to his will. In *X-Men* #124, Arcade, the most ridiculous villain of the 1970s—he kidnaps his victims to a putatively lethal amusement park called Murderworld—somehow brainwashes the X-Men's Russian member Colossus into becoming "The Proletarian, workers' hero of the Soviet Union!"

Uncanny X-Men #221 (September 1987)
CHRIS CLAREMONT, MARC SILVESTRI, DAN GREEN, GLYNIS OLIVER

X-Men fans also get used to "Claremontisms," the Homeric formulae with which he salts his dialogue and captions. Quarter is neither asked nor given. Everything happens inexorably. Psylocke's psychic knife is "the focused totality" of her powers. People experience things "with all their heart," or are given over to things "body and soul." Any situation can be described as a "caper." An answer is "as quick as it is painful," a destiny is "as glorious as it is tragic," a trance is "as refreshing as it is harmless," a psychic bond is "as unbreakable as it is permanent." (There are a lot of psychic bonds in Claremont's stories, but they're less like mind control than like having access to someone else's GPS.) Characters adjust and intensify what they're expressing midsentence: "We must not—dare not—harm him." "Ah can't—ah won't—walk out on 'em." "I must—I shall—destroy him." "Who—what—*are* you?!?"*

Claremont has a distinct narrative voice, which isn't jocular like Stan Lee's or poetic like Alan Moore's or folkloric like Neil Gaiman's. It's that of a yarn-spinner who's already worked up a head of steam: "But those days, that role, that dream are long gone—possibly, she fears, lost forever. She is an X-Man now, her fate bound to that team of outcast, too often outlaw heroes—standing alone like the Spartans at Thermopylae against the modern equivalent of Xerxes' Persian horde, Mr. Sinister's Marauders. And now as then, the future of the world hanging in the balance." (That's just one of five captions in a single panel of *Uncanny X-Men* #221.)

Poring over a page of vintage Claremont takes as long as navigating four or five pages of an average new comic book. And no melodramatic inversion or emphasis is too much *too-muchness* for him. Three consecutive lines of dialogue from issue #135:

"Yours was an admirable ploy, Storm. But escaping me won't be that easy."

"Why are you attacking us? For pity's sake, Jean—why?!"

"Ask not for pity from *Dark Phoenix*, my love. There is none in her."

Readers can either buy into this stuff or roll their eyes at it hard, but it's more fun to do both. It's very easy to mock Claremont by quoting him out of context; all his biggest fans do it. Of course his work is emotionally oversized—that's the whole idea. (The same could be said of Freddie Mercury or Maria Callas or Otis Redding.) And, my God, do his stories *move*. Claremont's *X-Men* bolts along at incredible speed, with perpetually escalating drama. Every overstuffed word balloon fleshes out something

---

*Some Claremontisms live in the memory more than they do on the page. The rocket-powered Kentuckian mutant Cannonball from the *X-Men* spin-off *New Mutants* is remembered as constantly noting that he's "nigh-invulnerable when ah'm blastin'"—which Claremont doesn't seem to have written him saying. Claremont did give Cannonball lines including "Good thing ah'm invulnerable when ah'm blastin'," "Ah'm pretty near invulnerable when ah'm blastin'," "My own power makes me invulnerable when ah blast," "practically invulnerable when ah'm blastin'," and so on, but that specific way of putting it didn't turn up within the Marvel canon until 2016, in an Al Ewing–written issue of *New Avengers*.

about its speaker, and allows readers to linger over what's happening before the next hairpin turn in the plot; every issue has grand spectacles and intensely emotional moments to look at.

The golden decade of *X-Men* soars and roars. Superhero comics are still grappling with its most potent moments and images.* For all his quirks and tropes, Claremont mastered the storyteller's greatest trick, Scheherazade's imperative of making the audience need to find out *what happens next.*

Uncanny X-Men #149 (September 1981)
CHRIS CLAREMONT, DAVE COCKRUM, JOSEF RUBINSTEIN, DON WARFIELD

Still, the other comics that Claremont was writing before mutants became his full-time gig (*Spider-Woman, Man-Thing, Ms. Marvel,* and a few others) are intermittently enjoyable while his *X-Men* is thrilling, and it wasn't just Byrne's presence that made the difference. The Claremont-Byrne team's smartest innovation on *X-Men* was that they began to take proper advantage of the metaphor that had been built into the series all along: mutants as the despised and oppressed Other. The X-Men are "feared and hated by the world they have sworn to protect," the world of *Homo sapiens.* That hate and fear is directed toward them as a group and binds them as a group. What either the X-Men or their enemies do is inseparable in the public eye from what mutants do.

The particular genius of that metaphor is that it applies to a whole lot of people in a very general way—enough to permit readers' identification with the X-Men as a group—without applying completely and directly to anyone. And its sly corollary is that mutants' oppressors are humans, a group to which every reader (and creator) of X-Men comics *does* belong; violence against mutants is committed by us, or at least in our name.

---

*Variations on the final panel of 1980's *X-Men* #133, for instance—Wolverine waist-deep in sewer water, rearing up to take his revenge—turn up in some series or other every couple of years, because it's still bracing even as an ironic quotation.

Mutation is, in effect, any way that someone can be different from people in power, or anything for which someone can be unjustly oppressed. The characters who get the least sympathy in Claremont's stories are the ones who exploit real-world power structures the most: xenophobic demagogues and the vicious rich. Sometimes the mutant metaphor is spelled out a bit more. Magneto is a Roma survivor of the Holocaust (although he was earlier implied to be a Jewish Holocaust survivor); Professor X (usually) uses a wheelchair. Even so, *X-Men* helpfully resists attempts to map it directly onto real-world analogues. Anyone who starts thinking of Magneto and Xavier as equivalents to Malcolm X and Martin Luther King Jr., or Lee Kuan Yew and Lim Chin Siong, or Betty Friedan and Valerie Solanas, will not get very far before realizing what a terrible idea that is—the fictional mutants' ideologies are their own, and can change over time without doing a disservice to real people's histories and evolving ideologies. And the clunkiest X-Men storylines are often the ones that try to draw direct connections to real-world issues, like a 1990s sequence involving a mutant-killing AIDS stand-in called the Legacy Virus.

Mutants are *sort of* every marginalized group, but they're also none of them, or at least not one that exists in the real world. Is *X-Men* a story about race, or perhaps class? Metaphorically, for sure, but not literally. Mutants are Others to their parents and to their original communities: mutation is a kind of difference that a birth family often can't understand, or even accept.

The mutant metaphor applies a bit more directly to sexuality—if you're a mutant, you're born that way, although your difference/gift might not reveal itself until puberty or thereabouts—even if it's still not entirely on the mark. LGBTQ readers have embraced *X-Men* like few other comics, although its plots have often hinged on straight romances. It definitely has more characters who are canonically not cis-hetero than most superhero comics, if still relatively few of them. Iceman came out as gay in 2015, after decades of intentional and accidental hints about his being closeted;* Mystique, who generally presents as a woman but is a gender-and-everything-else-fluid shape-changer, refers to the cis woman Destiny as "my wife"; Karma of *New Mutants* self-identifies as a lesbian in 2002's *Mekanix* miniseries; Shatterstar and Rictor of the spin-off series *X-Force* were implied to be a couple as early as 1995, although that wasn't confirmed on panel until 2009.† Beyond that, it's mostly implication and suggestion—but those implications and suggestions are everywhere.

In the 1970s, '80s, and '90s, when the heroes of popular culture were even more monotonously straight, white, able-bodied American cis-male types than they are now, *X-Men* declared that there were other possibilities. There are lots of mutant characters who can legitimately be read *as* queer in some way, or as neurodiverse, or disabled, or a number of other things a reader might imagine or desire them to be. Claremont and many of the writers who followed him don't always explicitly confirm those readings, but they take pains not to contradict them either.

A long and eloquent letter from reader Carolyn Amos in 1981's *Uncanny X-Men* #149, for instance, singles out the team's Kurt Wagner, aka Nightcrawler, for praise: "I may not be pointy-eared and blue or able to go 'bamf,' but because my hands and feet are mis-shaped and I wear an artificial limb I can no more pass for 'normal' than Kurt. So it is that his and my life experience and outlook most interlock; and he becomes both a mirror and a self-portrait of sorts, as well as a role model. Like Kurt, and

---

*Reading Iceman's appearances in mid-1980s issues of *The New Defenders*, in which he's shocked to have developed a crush on the gender-fluid Cloud, briefly pretends to be Warren Worthington's boyfriend, and scrubs his male teammate Gargoyle's back in the bathtub, with that later revelation in mind, it's hard to imagine him having taken another thirty years' worth of comics to come to terms with his sexuality—not that it would have been possible for a mainstream superhero series to have an openly gay protagonist in 1983.

†The first Marvel superhero to be directly identified as gay was Northstar, a mutant introduced in *X-Men* in 1979 but mostly seen in the Canadian superteam series *Alpha Flight*. After a decade of very broad hints, he finally declared "I am gay" in 1992's *Alpha Flight* #106; he married his boyfriend in 2012's *Astonishing X-Men* #51, another first for the Marvel story.

sometimes with or through him, I discover that it truly is better to be a whole 'me' than 'normal.'"

Amos's word "self-portrait" is worth lingering over: she's not the person who's writing or drawing *X-Men*, she's the one whose reading of the story renders it into her portrait of herself. Did Claremont and Byrne and Cockrum ever present Nightcrawler as disabled? Not in so many words, but the way they portrayed him is absolutely open *to* being understood that way, as *X-Men* in general is open to being read as a story about disability. (It's not an unproblematic reading, but what is?)

Mutant bodies can do things that human bodies can't; many mutant bodies also can't do things that most human bodies can do. Rogue can't touch anyone without injuring them and absorbing their memories. Cyclops doesn't dare to take off his special glasses. Wolverine is in pain all the time because of his powers. And Charles Xavier's academy is nominally for "gifted youngsters," but in practice it's a school for young people who need special training to manage their unique bodies or minds.

X-Men is a history of a (fictional) community with a shared identity, seen through a small cross-section of the group that's heterogeneous in every other way. Claremont and his collaborators were ahead of their time in making *X-Men*'s mutants look much more like the real world than superhero comics had tended to be, in terms of race and gender and nationality. Legend has it that any time a new Marvel character was proposed, Claremont would ask, "Is there any reason this character can't be a woman?"

In *X-Men* and its spin-offs *New Mutants* and *Excalibur*, Claremont gradually assembled a huge ensemble of characters in whom readers could, perhaps, see themselves, or possibilities for themselves. His difference from his contemporaries, and his gift, was that he wrote each of those characters as an individual with a distinctive history and agenda and worldview. That's become one of the defining features of *X-Men* ever since. Each of the hundreds of Marvel's mutants who have ever been identified on panel, from A-listers who've starred in their own series (Gambit, Nightcrawler, Storm) on down to one-off curios (ForgetMeNot, Stringfellow, Tremolo), is more than a costume and a code name—and has *some-one* who loves them beyond reason.* *X-Men* fans, more than any other superhero comics readers, are passionately invested in the fates and relationships of their personal favorite characters. They feel proprietary about them; they need *X-Men* comics and TV shows and movies to *do right* by them.

X-Men #109 (February 1978)
CHRIS CLAREMONT, JOHN BYRNE, TERRY AUSTIN, ANDY YANCHUS

To loop back around to Byrne's arrival in 1977: The work that made that investment possible started in earnest then, as Byrne and Claremont started to pay special attention to a few members of their cast. One was Jean Grey, Phoenix, who could now do all sorts of things more or less by willing them to happen. The other was Wolverine. Claremont famously disliked the violent upstart with the metal claws at first, and was going to get rid of him until Byrne, in his words, "stamped my little foot and said there is no way you're writing out the only Canadian character." The first sign of real depth for him comes here, in Byrne's second issue of *X-Men*: an ingenious character beat in which Wolverine announces that he's going hunting, then clarifies what his idea of "hunting" is. "It takes *no* skill t' kill," he sneers. "What takes *skill* is sneakin' up *close* enough to a skittish doe t' *touch* her."

Over the next few years, Claremont and Byrne continued to parcel out (or rather, invent) bits of Wolverine's history slowly and cagily, suggesting that he had a self-healing power, that he was a lot older than he looked, that he spoke fluent Japanese, and so on. (His civilian name, Logan, was mentioned only once in Claremont's first forty issues of *X-Men*—by a

---

*The extremely minor mutant I love way too much is No-Girl, aka Martha Johansson, a brain in a floating glass jar who can only communicate via telepathy. She's appeared in a handful of issues of *New X-Men* and *Spider-Man and the X-Men* and even had her own solo story once, in 2010's *Nation X* #2.

leprechaun!—and the question of whether that was his first or last name remained unanswered until 2001.*) They also found a way to make his violent streak heartbreaking rather than simply nasty. Wolverine is quick to anger, but his relationship with violence is less that he's eager for it than that he's resigned to it, they suggested; he understands that he's already damned, so he might as well be the one who does terrible things when they need to be done.[†]

X-Men #137 (September 1980)

CHRIS CLAREMONT, JOHN BYRNE, TERRY AUSTIN, GLYNIS WEIN

The first of Claremont and Byrne's two most enduring X-Men stories, the accidental tragedy known as "The Dark Phoenix Saga," focused squarely on Jean Grey. "Dark Phoenix" was a landmark when it appeared in 1980's X-Men #129–137, and through the weird, occasionally retroactive way serial superhero stories are constructed, it became both more and less dramatically powerful over the following decade.

It escalates from another instance of Claremontian mind control: a no-goodnik called Mastermind psychically gaslights Jean into believing she's in a sort of Regency-romance-by-way-of-Histoire d'O scenario,[‡] and consequently into attacking the X-Men. When Jean breaks free of the illusion, her fury and confusion explode into ravenous cruelty. Now calling herself Dark Phoenix, she goes off on an interstellar rampage, devouring

---

*A trick question, it turned out: "Logan" is a nickname.
†The 2011–2014 Wolverine and the X-Men series once again revived the "school for super-heroes" concept and provided an elegant if impermanent end point to Logan's forty-year narrative arc: having first appeared as a desperate, isolated killer who turns to a school as his unlikely final hope for redemption, he ends up running a school of his own. (That series concluded alongside 2014's Death of Wolverine miniseries, which was inevitably followed by the Return of Wolverine miniseries a few years later.)
‡Kink and fetish-inspired imagery perpetually turns up in Claremont's comics, usually in the context of a trial a character has to go through to be strengthened. If somebody is wearing a slave collar in X-Men, as happens surprisingly often, their mind or body or both are being controlled by someone else—or were once, and now they're keeping it as a symbol of their autonomy. Leather underwear tends to accompany it, perhaps for the sake of coordination.

a sun and dooming the inhabitants of a planet that orbits it. By the time the X-Men are able to help her regain stability, it's too late: there's a space empire that's convinced she's a threat to all of existence and intends to execute her. In a battle on the moon, her teammates fight for her (as always; if you identify as part of a group in Claremont's *X-Men*, the group will support you even when you're in the wrong), but as her dark side is once again emerging, Jean kills herself.

Claremont and Byrne hadn't planned for Jean to die. Their initial version of "Dark Phoenix" ended with Jean simply being depowered, and Byrne had already drawn most of the following issue before Jim Shooter pointed out that their resolution to the story would let her off the hook for genocide. In the few days before *X-Men* #137 had to go to press, they whipped up its new—and much more compelling—ending.

It was a shocking turn for 1980. A few minor superheroes and supporting cast members had died in earlier comics, but never a character as high profile and well-loved as Phoenix. The meaning of Jean Grey's fate, at the time, might have been that she was an individual who had been overwhelmed and corrupted by power, and chose death to protect her loved ones; it might also have been that the empowerment of women is so dangerous to patriarchal culture that it will systematically destroy a woman who claims power for herself.

X-Men's readers fell into stunned mourning for Jean*—who, as much as Claremont and Byrne had developed her character around her frustrated longing for self determination, still remained mysterious in some respects. Her origin had never been seen, for instance; she'd just turned up in the first issue, as *the girl*.

---

*A letter from reader Kurt Busiek in 1981's *Uncanny X-Men* #143 complains: "I've watched the book degenerate, watched the X-Men become a perversion of what they once were, watched you twist and mangle characters you virtually created.... I can no longer justify buying the X-MEN, not even to keep my collection complete. Each issue hurts too much." Two years later, Busiek was writing *Power Man and Iron Fist* for Marvel; he's gone on to write some very good X-Men stories, mostly set either in the past or in alternate universes.

The new girl who enrolled at the Xavier School just after the end of "Dark Phoenix" (having first appeared early in that story) fit that role in a much more deliberate way. Kitty Pryde was an actual, not yet fully formed personality: a spunky kid, passionate about justice and still unsure of how best to heal the world, who could turn immaterial and walk through walls.

X-Men #141 (January 1981)
CHRIS CLAREMONT, JOHN BYRNE, TERRY AUSTIN, GLYNIS WEIN

Kitty has slowly aged across four decades of comics, but the version of her who lives in memory is forever thirteen or fourteen years old, hopeful and wide-eyed (Byrne drew her eyes extra-large). She's had a few official super-hero names—Sprite, then Ariel, and later Shadowcat—but mostly she just goes by her given name. "Welcome to the X-Men, Kitty Pryde," read the cover of 1981's X-Men #139. "Hope you survive the experience!" She provided something X-Men had needed for a while: a character who had just come to understand that she belonged to the culture of mutants (or whatever they might stand in for), and a fresh point of identification for readers.

The last few issues of the Claremont and Byrne X-Men all feature Kitty prominently, and "Days of Future Past," which appeared in issues #141 and #142, juxtaposes the new girl with the woman she might grow up to be: "Kate Pryde," a fragile-looking, sunken-faced adult, maneuvering through the demolished landscape of Manhattan in the terrible future of 2013. Byrne and Austin's cover for #141 has been the subject of countless homages: the future Kate and Logan, bracing for a fight with somebody who's shining a spotlight on them, in front of a wall on which a dilapidated poster of their comrades' faces is covered with stickers reading SLAIN or APPREHENDED.*

---

*That image also establishes the relationship between the two of them that would develop over the next few years of X-Men: the angry, violent old loner Logan finds himself pushed into becoming a mentor to a teenage girl who has nothing in common with him but a desire to make the world less awful, and he turns out to have a gift for it.

Claremont and Byrne lay out the premise in just six pages: gigantic robotic Sentinels oversee the ruins of the world, and the few mutants they haven't yet killed are in concentration camps. A small cluster of survivors—including Magneto (who has assumed his old enemy Charles Xavier's role, to the point of being in a wheelchair) and Franklin Richards (Reed and Sue Richards's son from *Fantastic Four*, connecting this vision to the broader Marvel story)—have devised a plan to send Kate's consciousness back in time to her teenage self's body, to prevent a political assassination that started everything going wrong. It's mind control yet again, but benign mind control this time.

Wolverine and Kate Pryde in the dystopian "Days of Future Past" era on the cover of *X-Men* #141, 1981, drawn by John Byrne and Terry Austin.

The rest of the densely compressed story cuts back and forth between that dystopian future, as Sentinels slaughter the last few rebellious X-Men, and the present day, where Kate-as-Kitty leads the X-Men to fight a new version of the Brotherhood of Evil Mutants, who are gunning for an anti-mutant U.S. senator. She does manage to save the senator, just before her consciousness is called back to its own time. But the plan for which all her friends have died is a failure: the political machinations that led to Kate's future are still happening. "This issue—EVERYBODY DIES!" reads the caption on the cover of #142, overlaid on an image of Wolverine being eviscerated midair. It's a fakeout, of course, but it's also real, not just a nightmare but a premonition.

"Days of Future Past" was a conceptual turning point for *X-Men* as a series. Even an individual act of heroism, Claremont and Byrne suggest, can't avert the tide of history, and the post-1981 *X-Men* has almost always been, in part, a story about defense against dystopian possibilities. It's no longer enough for the X-Men to deal with immediate threats (as often as they present themselves), or to stand up for mutants' rights for their own sake. They have a systemic catastrophe to stave off, the nightmare point in the distance at which all of the roads they might follow converge. The world in which mutants live is always threatening to become unlivable to them; the stakes of their struggle are their survival as a species.

With "Days of Future Past" finished, Byrne was nearly out the door. The next issue, *Uncanny X-Men* #143's frantic horror story "Demon," was his last.* Dave Cockrum returned as the regular penciler for a while, followed by Paul Smith, then John Romita Jr., then others. Claremont kept pushing forward with all of them, playing to their particular strengths as artists, refusing to let the series settle into a formula. He also (temporarily) got rid of the nominal premise of *X-Men*, the "school for superheroes" business that it had outgrown: a year after Byrne's departure, Claremont wrote a story in which Charles Xavier's mansion/school is demolished by an alien attack.

Bizarre Adventures #27 (July 1981)
CHRIS CLAREMONT, JOHN BUSCEMA, KLAUS JANSON

Over the course of that year, Jean Grey's shadow had fallen over nearly everything in *X-Men*. Her grief-stricken lover, Scott (Cyclops) Summers, had encountered the reification of despair itself (a demon named D'Spayre; subtlety wasn't really the point). A story in which her teammate Storm appeared to lose control had borne the cover caption "We did it before... dare we do it again? ROGUE STORM!" And Claremont had finally expanded Jean's personal history.

---

*When the word went out in 2018 that there was a Kitty Pryde–focused movie in development, *X-Men* enthusiasts understood its code name "143" as a cue that the people behind it knew whereof they spoke.

In a Phoenix story that appeared in the black-and-white magazine *Bizarre Adventures* #27, Claremont explained that Jean's psychic abilities had first appeared when she was eleven years old, at the moment when her best friend, Annie, was hit by a car. Jean had experienced Annie's death through a mental link and then became overwhelmed by the thoughts of everyone around her, until Charles Xavier helped her control her own mind.

That single episode changed the meaning of her fate. Now, readers understood that Jean had been marked by death ever since the moment when she became fully herself, and that her great ongoing battle was to keep the rest of the world *out* of her head. Mastermind's control of her, then, represented a fatal failure in that struggle. Her relationship with the eternally repressed Scott Summers looked different, too: his ability to hold back the dark parts of his own mind, Claremont implied, might have been something she valued in him.

Uncanny X-Men #168 (April 1983)
CHRIS CLAREMONT, PAUL SMITH, BOB WIACEK, GLYNIS WEIN

Claremont's characters grappled with the difficulties of adult life—trauma and desire and loss—in the context of gaudy, violent superhero entertainment, which is an impressive feat. He was also great at addressing adolescent angst in the same context: the indelible opening page of this issue is Kitty Pryde whirling around to point a finger at the reader and declaring, "Professor Xavier is a *jerk!*" X-Men's young people learn to experience their difference as a gift, but they also always experience it as difference.

Still, if you're a kid growing up in a place where people hate and fear you for what you are—no matter what that is—then *X-Men* is the story that tells you that *you can be yourself, and it's going to be hard, but there is hope.* Once Claremont and Byrne started playing with the mutant metaphor, *X-Men* became to comics approximately what David Bowie was to music: the signal to every misfit out there that they weren't alone and that things might be okay after all. To identify (or be identified) as a mutant means that you will be hated, but it also means that you will be loved—that you'll have a community that will have your back and take you seriously.

Uncanny X-Men #170 (June 1983)
CHRIS CLAREMONT, PAUL SMITH, BOB WIACEK, PAUL BECTON, JANINE CASEY

The metaphor wouldn't work as well as it does if X-Men stories functioned like Avengers or Iron Man or Fantastic Four stories, with antagonists and conflicts drawn from Marvel's common pool. But even more than most contemporary superheroes, the X-Men don't tend to fight "criminals." They don't represent police or a government (if anything, they have to beware of those). Nor do they go on patrol for cat burglars, or get into punch-ups with the Wrecking Crew or Electro.

X-Men, both in Claremont's time and afterward, does involve monsters who are to be slain without compunction (the Brood, the N'Garai); it also involves literal devils (Mephisto, Belasco) and the occasional necessity of making deals with them. Mostly, though, it's just about mutants. In practice, X-Men stories most often have to do with political attacks on the mutant population, or somebody trying to engineer mutant genes for sinister purposes, or, as here, factional conflicts within the mutant community.

This issue is an inflection point for one of those conflicts, the long-simmering enmity between the X-Men and the bitter, literally underground mutant group called the Morlocks (after the subterranean society in H. G. Wells's *The Time Machine*). It's also a stellar example of Claremont's gift for developing characters through action. Up to this point, Claremont has written the X-Men's weather-controlling Ororo Munroe, aka Storm, as having a deep aversion to violence and a reverence for life, as well as an intense, near-maternal love for Kitty Pryde. With Kitty's life at stake, the X-Men and Morlocks' conflict comes down to a knife fight between Ororo and the Morlocks' leader Callisto; Ororo shanks Callisto through the heart and walks away without a word. (Then she spends the next few issues drastically changing her life in a way that looks, from a distance, like a mental-health crisis.)

More broadly, though, *X-Men*'s divisions between mutants are generally shown as less important than solidarity among them. Almost no (mutant) villain is entirely irredeemable, no matter how terrible their actions in the past have been (by 1986, Magneto is running the Xavier School, for instance). Almost no hero is entirely incorruptible, or doesn't have some blood on their hands. Marvel's tradition of heel-face turns had started much earlier—Quicksilver and the Scarlet Witch had been part of Magneto's original Brotherhood of Evil Mutants before they joined the Avengers in 1965.* But virtually all of the X-Men's adversaries eventually become their allies, if sometimes uneasy ones. Even Ororo and Callisto gradually come to trust and rely on each other.†

Wolverine #1 (September 1982)
CHRIS CLAREMONT, FRANK MILLER, JOSEF RUBINSTEIN

In 1982, *X-Men* began to multiply itself like a cell in mitosis. Its first spin-off was that year's *Wolverine* miniseries, a stark, gorgeous, violent thing that indulged *Daredevil* artist Frank Miller's enthusiasm for drawing Japanese landscapes (and ninja attacks). "I'm the best there is at what I do. But what I do isn't very nice," Logan announces at its outset, as he has countless times in the ensuing decades.

---

*See chapter 17.
†Or more: by 2004's Claremont-written *X-Treme X-Men* #39, they're hanging out in a hot tub together. (Yes, of course Callisto survived being stabbed through the heart.)

The key to the way Wolverine functions in that story, though—and the way in which he makes adventure stories in which he appears more interesting in general—isn't the mayhem he can dish out, but the torment he can withstand. His "healing factor" makes him capable of taking almost limitless amounts of physical abuse. What actually *has* damaged him, and made him a more interesting character, is the psychological abuse he's also had to absorb from being used as an instrument of violence.*

Wolverine was a hit, and more *X-Men*-related comics followed. *The New Mutants*, an ongoing series launched by Claremont and artist Bob McLeod in late 1982, focused on the inner lives and identity-building struggles of its teenage cast. (The school was rebuilt for it.) Claremont wrote more miniseries, too: *Storm and Illyana: Magik* in 1983, *X-Men and the Micronauts* and *Kitty Pryde and Wolverine* in 1984.

New Mutants #18 (August 1984)
CHRIS CLAREMONT, BILL SIENKIEWICZ, GLYNIS WEIN

Could Claremont's mutants support all those comics? They could, it turned out; they could get away with anything at that point. The X-Men line's editor, Ann Nocenti, brought in Bill Sienkiewicz to draw a 1984–1985 stretch of *New Mutants* that was as visually radical as anything that had ever appeared in pulp comics. Frequently veering into impressionistic ab-

---

*As with every other major Marvel character, Wolverine has been subject to endless doubles and shadow selves and what-if-we-changed-one-thing versions. The most compelling X-Men-related series of the mid-2010s was *All-New Wolverine*, written by Tom Taylor, which ran between 2015 and 2018, while Logan was presumed dead. In it, his role and costume are assumed by Laura Kinney, his teenage, gender-switched clone (who had initially appeared in 2003, as X-23, not in comics but in the animated series *X-Men: Evolution*). Laura has been trained from birth to be a subservient killing machine but has rebelled against her creators' control; *All-New Wolverine* concerns her struggles to hold on to her autonomy and create her own family of choice. The ways in which young women fight for self-possession and are expected to endure limitless abuse are very different from the way those struggles are experienced by men like Logan, and Taylor's story focuses on that difference.

straction, it was anchored to the familiar look of *X-Men* only by Tom Orzechowski's foursquare lettering.

The first image of Sienkiewicz's *New Mutants* is one of the team's young members, Dani Moonstar, hiding in terror beneath a checkerboard quilt, whose pattern resolves by degrees into the form of what she describes as "the *demon bear* that murdered my parents." In the rest of the story, Sienkiewicz draws the bear not as a realistic animal but as a terrifying, amorphous mass— enormous claws, tiny red eyes, sharp teeth, and almost nothing else but hulking negative space. Sienkiewicz occasionally anchors a page with a photorealistic rendering of a face or a bit of architecture, but more often shows action as smears or spatters or scratches. He draws scenes the way they *feel*, rather than the way they would appear to the eye.

Dani Moonstar and the demon bear: the opening image of 1984's *New Mutants* #18, the first issue of Bill Sienkiewicz's run as the series' artist. Script by Chris Claremont

This issue also introduces Sienkiewicz's signature piece of character design, the mechanical alien Warlock, who looks like a circuit board mashed onto the page in a vaguely humanoid shape. Sienkiewicz has described him as "a character that you can't draw incorrectly, one where you ... don't worry about anatomy, or get a specific costume right. Just emotion. Jazz."

The Claremont and Sienkiewicz *New Mutants* was the sort of thing that Marvel might have aimed at a smaller, experimentation-friendly audience, like Sienkiewicz's previous work on *Moon Knight* and subsequent work on *Elektra: Assassin*, but any mutant comic in those years was automatically a big deal. Even knockoffs and parodies of *X-Men* became hits: DC Comics' biggest success of that era was the very similar superteam soap opera *The New Teen Titans*; and Kevin Eastman and Peter Laird's self-published 1984 comic *Teenage Mutant Ninja Turtles* was a homemade spoof of *X-Men* (and of Frank Miller's *Daredevil* and *Rōnin*) that unexpectedly grew into a media empire of its own.

Fantastic Four #286 (January 1986)
JOHN BYRNE, CHRIS CLAREMONT, JACKSON GUICE, TERRY AUSTIN

The peak of *X-Men*'s world-beating phase was the autumn of 1985. In a single month, Marvel published the double-sized *Uncanny X-Men* #200; another Claremont-written story in four oversized episodes (the two-part *X-Men/Alpha Flight*,* an *X-Men Annual*, and a *New Mutants Special Edition*); and, in keeping with the vibe of that year of Live Aid and "We Are the World," *Heroes for Hope*, a one-off X-Men fundraiser for African famine relief, by Claremont and an all-star group of writers and artists.† It didn't seem like too much at all, just as Bruce Springsteen's quintuple live album the next year seemed reasonable.

There was another X-series on the way, though, and it brought with it another retroactive change in Jean Grey's history—a change that came about over Claremont's objections, although with his participation. The 1986 *X-Factor* series, initially by writer Bob Layton and artists Jackson Guice and Josef Rubinstein, was devised as a marketing scheme‡ reuniting the five original X-Men. That meant, though, that Jean somehow had to be alive and available for it. Marvel's editorial solution to that problem was declaring that the "Jean" who had died had never been the real Jean

---

*See chapter 12.
†They included Stan Lee, Stephen King, Alan Moore, George R. R. Martin, and many other marquee names. As Christopher Priest (then a Marvel editor) pointed out, they did not, however, include any African American contributors.
‡Not that there's anything intrinsically wrong with comics devised as marketing schemes. Really, they sort of all are.

in the first place; that the Phoenix was a cosmic force that had replaced and impersonated Jean, and believed it *was* Jean; and that all this time the real Jean had been healing in a cocoon the Phoenix had created for her at the bottom of Jamaica Bay.*

That explanation didn't appear in *X-Men*, but in a 1986 issue of *Fantastic Four*. It was credited cryptically to "You-Know-Who," and mostly written and penciled by John Byrne, who was *Fantastic Four*'s regular writer/artist at the time, although the crucial flashback to Jean bargaining with the Phoenix in the irradiated space shuttle's cockpit was ghostwritten by Claremont and penciled by Guice—an editorial emendation that replaced Byrne's version of that scene.

Jean's return made the meaning of her story change *again*. The entity that had died on the moon in *X-Men* hadn't been her at all, but some kind of reincarnation-prone space creature. Jean's sacrifice had come earlier, and it's a different kind of tragedy. Having spent her entire adult life struggling to define her own identity and destiny, she had finally achieved her goal by choosing to die for her teammates' sake—and then the Phoenix appeared and told her that what she actually needed to do to save them was to turn over control of her body and give up her identity. And with that, her single flickering moment of self-determination had ended.

Or, rather, it *would* have ended, had she stayed dead. The negation of Jean's death opened up a new kind of story for her, one in which she gets to have agency and to live. The revised story undermined the dramatic force of her death, but what mutant comics' readers long for isn't enduring tragedy but improbable hope.†

---

*The "Phoenix wasn't really Jean" scenario had been conceived by none other than Kurt Busiek—see * on p. 153—some years earlier.
†Also, come on: if any character gets to come back from the dead repeatedly, it's one whose identity is literally "Phoenix."

X-Men #3 (December 1991)
CHRIS CLAREMONT, JIM LEE, SCOTT WILLIAMS

The end of a pop-culture reign like *X-Men*'s isn't necessarily a plunge from glory. It can be signaled by a little dip in commercial fortunes, or by a star letting it be known that the hit-parade game no longer interests them. In 1987, Claremont handed off writing *New Mutants* to his former editor Louise Simonson. A few months later, he all but announced that *X-Men* was veering off the pavement with a sequence called "The Fall of the Mutants," in which the team fakes their deaths and relocates to Australia. By the end of 1989, there was no actual group called the X-Men anymore. Instead, for more than a year, the focus of *Uncanny X-Men* bounced between characters who had previously been in the team's orbit.

It was an original, smartly executed idea, but not quite a crowd-pleaser, and even though *Uncanny X-Men* remained the bestselling American comic book, its sales were flagging for the first time.* In mid-1991, Claremont quit the series halfway through issue #279 over a dispute with editor Bob Harras, just as a second, adjectiveless *X-Men* series was about to debut as a showcase for artist Jim Lee. Claremont wrote the new series' first three issues as a sort of golden parachute, and took the opportunity to tie up some of the themes of his sixteen-year run, if not many of its open plot threads.

Claremont has referred to his 1975–1991 *X-Men* run as "a novel," which doesn't seem quite right. It's a distinct body of work, but it's an improvisation more than a composition. One of the most rewarding things about it is that it's *not* especially consistent in any way other than its central metaphor and Claremont's unmistakable voice. At any given point, it's very different from what it had been two years earlier.

---

*That's where I initially got off the bus, too, after being one of those third-Thursday-of-the-month readers for close to ten years.

X-Men: Grand Design #1 (February 2018)
ED PISKOR

Even so, the superhero-comics reader's instinct to make everything flow together can find a shape to it. Writer/artist Ed Piskor's miniseries *X-Men: Grand Design* is an attempt to condense everything from the beginning of *X-Men* to Claremont's 1991 departure into a single story, tweaking its plot and twisting loose ends together. But the premise of *Grand Design* is entirely contrary to how *Uncanny X-Men* worked in practice. Everything Claremont and his collaborators did was extemporaneous, free-styled, subject to revision by creative whim or editorial fiat, the product of plans derailed and salvaged much more than plans executed as they were conceived.

Reading *X-Men* comics from the first few years after Claremont's departure is like listening to one saxophonist after another attempting to play "Chasin' the Trane": whether they can convincingly imitate John Coltrane's sheets of sound or not, they're tribute acts, repeating a spontaneous invention without the spontaneity that gave it life. It took a solid decade for post-Claremont *X-Men* writers to figure out how to stop recapitulating his work and start responding to it. (Devising an approach to *X-Men* that doesn't owe much to Claremont one way or another has never been a realistic option.)

For most of the 1990s, everybody tried to crack the formula that had made *X-Men* a hit, resulting in a lot of the worst tendencies of that decade's American comics. The artistic path from John Byrne to Jim Lee went on to extend over the abyss of hypertrophied anatomical impossibilities overrendered with fussy feathering; Claremont's fondness for leather-and-lace imagery and mind-control themes opened the gates for a wave of hideous fetish-porn comics; the complexity of *X-Men*'s long-term plots metastasized into incoherent billion-part superhero crossovers.

As the X-Men went adrift without Claremont, he did the same without them. For a while, he wrote *Sovereign Seven* for DC Comics—a series best described in fan fiction terms as "an X-Men coffee shop AU."* And still the empire rolled onward. The *X-Men* animated TV series that ran from 1992 to 1997 created a new generation of fans and adapted a cluster of Claremont's stories, including both "Dark Phoenix" and "Days of Future Past." The mutant-focused comics kept selling, too, if not quite as well as they had in the '80s, and at some point they became effectively a line within Marvel's line, their internal narrative growing ever more baroque. By the beginning of 1995, there were eight monthly X-titles.

X-Men: Alpha #1 (February 1995)

SCOTT LOBDELL, MARK WAID, ROGER CRUZ, STEVE EPTING, TIM TOWNSEND, DAN PANOSIAN

That sprawl brought about the centerpiece of that decade's mutant comics, "The Age of Apocalypse," a gigantic story about a catastrophic shift in reality created by a well-meaning attempt to repair history. The change was signaled by a metafictional gesture: for four months, following the introductory one-shot *X-Men: Alpha*, all of the X-Men-related series were replaced by retitled substitutes—*Excalibur* became *X-Calibre*, *Generation X* became *Generation Next*, and so on—set in a nightmarish alternate timeline.

"The Age of Apocalypse" is a hugely clever exercise in worldbuilding (and world-wrecking). Its setting, a mangled, bloodstained version of the

---

*Claremont has occasionally returned to *X-Men* and related series from 1998 onward, with mixed results. In the first decade of the 2000s, he was usually writing at least one series for his hardcore fans, most of which were more or less walled off from the rest of X-continuity. *X-Treme X-Men* (2001–2004) focused on a small cluster of characters; *X-Men: The End* (2004–2006) and *GeNext* (2008–2009) took place in an alternate future; the two "seasons" of *X-Men Forever* (2009–2011) were allegedly Claremont's vision for where he might have taken the original series after his 1991 departure, had he had his druthers. As of 2020, he remains under exclusive contract to Marvel for writing comics in America, but aside from a 2014 stint on *Nightcrawler*, he's only been called on to write one-off X-stories, once or twice a year, since the 2011 conclusion of *X-Men Forever 2*—putting him in the odd position of getting paid to *not* write comics.

familiar Marvel landscape, is fertile enough that a string of sequels and prequels have returned to it; some of its variations on already extant characters were intriguing enough that they stuck around once it was over.* Its only significant flaw is that it ignores the mutant metaphor almost entirely. (It could just as well have been an Avengers story, had there been as many Avengers series in 1995 as there were a couple of decades later.) At its heart, though, it's a souped-up version of an old favorite: "Days of Future Past" again, run upside down and played out over thirty-four issues instead of two.

New X-Men #150 (February 2004)
GRANT MORRISON, PHIL JIMENEZ, ANDY LANNING, SIMON COLEBY, CHRIS CHUCKRY

After all the effort invested in bringing her back to life in 1986, Jean didn't get to do anything especially interesting until she died again in this issue of *New X-Men*. Death returned her to her position of eminence: 2006's brutal *Uncanny X-Men* sequence "End of Greys," the gargantuan 2012 crossover *Avengers vs. X-Men*, and 2014's "The Trial of Jean Grey" were all driven by the fact that Jean, or at least that version of her, was no longer around. Her role in the broad X-Men story as well as the broader Marvel story, it appears, is to be *the one who died*. She shapes the narrative much more by her absence than by her presence.

New X-Men #154 (May 2004)
GRANT MORRISON, MARC SILVESTRI, JOE WEEMS, STEVE FIRCHOW, ET AL.

"Here Comes Tomorrow," the storyline that immediately followed Jean Grey's second death and concluded writer Grant Morrison's superb

---

*One of them, the confusingly named X-Man, got a series of his own that lasted seventy-five issues.

2001–2004 run on *New X-Men*, is a sort of "Days of Future Past"/"Dark Phoenix" mash-up beneath its tricky, sparkly surface. It's a catastrophic, hypercompressed fever dream, set 150 years in the future, as humans, mutants, and Sentinels unite for a doomed final stand against an enemy of mutation, or progress, itself. Everybody dies, of course. Jean, revived in a burst of white-hot flame, sacrifices the thing that meant the most to her—Scott Summers's devotion—to make sure that timeline never comes to be. (*X-Men* is a romance comic, and sometimes a tragic one.) It's implied that the whole future sequence is Jean's vision at the moment of her death.

A lot of the biggest and most notable *X-Men* stories after 1991—not all, but a lot—take one of two basic forms: either they're cousins to "Dark Phoenix" or they're cousins to "Days of Future Past." Marvel's 2005 crossover event "House of M" is an inside-out "Age of Apocalypse," making it "Days of Future Past" at two removes: this time, the false reality that has to be torn away is not dystopian but utopian for mutants. The "Messiah Complex"/"Messiah War" sequence that followed it in the *X-Men* line is another avert-the-terrible-future time-travel tzimmes. The 2019 "Age of X-Man" is "Age of Apocalypse" inside out, upside down, and backward: a cluster of miniseries set in another false reality, in which *everyone* is a mutant but love and sex are forbidden. (All desire, then, is queer, and of course it saves the day.)

Various *X-Men* series continue to pump out new issues every month, some of them very good. Someone going into a store in the spring of 2018 looking for a new *X-Men* comic book would have their choice of *X-Men Blue*, *X-Men Gold*, *X-Men Red*, *Astonishing X-Men*, *Weapon X*, *Rogue & Gambit*, *Generation X*, and solo series starring Iceman, Legion, and (two alternate versions of) Wolverine. The old guard of X-Men have almost all taken their turn at being dead for a while; Jean Grey concluded her most recent tenure in the grave with 2018's *Phoenix Resurrection: The Return of Jean Grey*. Mutant comics' 2018 ended with *Extermination*, in which the present-day X-Men are attacked by a time-traveling nemesis from Kate Pryde's future dystopia.*

House of X #1 (September 2019)
JONATHAN HICKMAN, PEPE LARRAZ, MARTE GRACIA

The most recent overhaul of the mutant line began with *House of X* and *Powers of X*, a pair of interconnected 2019 miniseries written by Jonathan Hickman and drawn, respectively, by Pepe Larraz and R. B. Silva. Both of them gracefully integrate allusions, both conceptual and visual, to the history of X-comics. Larraz's cover image for *House of X* #1, for instance, subtly hybridizes the cover compositions of two earlier relaunch issues—Gil Kane's art for 1975's *Giant-Size X-Men* #1 and Frank Quitely's art for 2001's *New X-Men* #114—to show the team pacing calmly forward, seeming to emerge through a hole in the picture plane.

Hickman's story reframes the history and future of mutants, but "Dark Phoenix" and "Days of Future Past" are still central to his vision. (So is those stories' earlier hybrid, "Here Comes Tomorrow," whose imagery is reprised in *Powers of X*.) Jean Grey appears in the late-1960s costume to which she had returned for her final battle in the "Dark Phoenix" sequence. There's a new mutant homeland, an idea that *X-Men*'s characters had tried to make real twice before with disastrous results; this time, though, it's built on the (meaningful, questionable) idea that unity among mutants is more important than *any* conflict between them. There are visions of a horrible future ruled by genocidal machines, and a desperate scheme to keep it from coming to pass.† Everybody dies, and everybody is

---

*Its ad slogan echoed the cover blurb from Kitty's first appearance as an X-Man: "No one survives the experience."
†As of the beginning of the 2019 *Marauders* series that followed *House* and *Powers*, the former Kitty Pryde starts going by "Kate," the name used by her older self in "Days of Future Past."

resurrected. And rebirth after self-sacrifice takes on a new role in *X-Men* comics: no longer an overused deus ex machina, it becomes the uncanny centerpiece of the mutants' story.

Both of *X-Men*'s master plots have endured because they're evergreen, adaptable settings for the mutant metaphor. "Dark Phoenix" says: this world is terrible to my people; what might happen if it pushed one of us too far? "Days of Future Past" says: this world is terrible to my people; what might we have to do, or sacrifice, to make it right? Those are questions that haven't gone away in the past forty years, and it's not a flaw in *X-Men* that it continues to find new ways to ask them. That's what sets it apart, and its difference is its gift.

11

INTERLUDE:
DIAMONDS MADE OF SOUND

The mutant who's most famous *within* the Marvel story didn't become famous for being a mutant: she's a pop star, Alison Blaire, aka Dazzler.* Her powers are turning sound into colored light (useful for a stage performer) and, it was eventually revealed, returning from the dead in under two hours (useful in general). Most of the first few years of the *Dazzler* series that ran from 1981 to 1986 involve her attempts to establish her career as a disco singer, although her gigs are often canceled due to superhero battles. In 1982's *Dazzler* #21, she scores a gig at Carnegie Hall, where she sings her composition "A Little Girl's Dream." At last, she gets to record, and within a year her album, *Sounds of Light and Fury*, has made her a star.

---

*Dazzler was originally going to be a collaboration between Marvel and disco label Casablanca Records—the part of the plan that never came to fruition was having a singer record and tour under that name. The concept was revisited in 1991, when Marvel published a single issue of *Nightcat*, a superhero comic whose protagonist was a real-world singer, Jacqueline Tavarez. The *Nightcat* album stiffed, and that was that.

Sadly, Dazzler's career is soon derailed when she's outed as a mutant and blacklisted. She briefly becomes a gladiator, then joins the X-Men; in 1987's *Uncanny X-Men* #217, the Juggernaut initially refuses to fight her because he's such a big fan. Dazzler doesn't go back to performing under her own name until 2006's *New Excalibur* #1, by which point she's on the oldies circuit. She seems to have remained a cult favorite, though. Wiccan, Pixie, Cyclops, Squirrel Girl, Carol Danvers, and Jessica Jones have all been seen wearing Dazzler T-shirts over the years. When a group of teenage superheroes in 2017's *Secret Empire: Uprising* #1 are figuring out which of them will infiltrate the Hydra youth choir, Ironheart starts singing "A Little Girl's Dream," and the Wasp joins in, belting it out along with her.*

Riri Williams sings an old Dazzler favorite in *Secret Empire: Uprising* #1, 2017, written by Derek Landy and drawn by Joshua Cassara.

Pop music, within the Marvel story, seems to work pretty much the same way it does in our world, and involves a lot of the same people. The Beatles, for instance, turn up in the flesh in *Strange Tales* #130.† The climax of *Nick Fury, Agent of S.H.I.E.L.D.* #15 takes place at a Country Joe & the

---

*It's not even identified in that issue as a Dazzler song: that's just an Easter egg for readers who recognize the lyrics from an unreprinted issue published thirty-five years earlier.
†In the home universe of Nocturne from *Exiles*, they stayed together and alive long enough to make a fortieth-anniversary album.

Fish concert. Michael Jackson was a big deal on Earth-616, although so was the very similar Teddy Lingard (from *Dazzler* #33 and *X-Men Unlimited* #32), who made a zombie-themed video for his hit song "Chiller." Even *Rolling Stone* magazine's founding editor Jann Wenner has a prominent role in *Daredevil* #100.

A few real-world musicians' lives have taken different paths in comics. The Long Island garage-rock quartet Hypnolovewheel kept a fairly low profile in our universe, but they're superstars in Marvel's, packing a club in *Spider-Man* #4 and scoring radio hits in *Darkhawk* #16. (In *Amazing Spider-Man* #347, Flash Thompson complains that "it took me *weeks* to get these Hypnolovewheel tickets!")* The long-running metal group KISS have superpowers—they fought Mephisto and Doctor Doom in 1977's *Marvel Comics Super Special* #1, and they also appeared in the same year's *Howard the Duck* #12 and #13. And the late-1970s punk band the Plasmatics are revered as "classical music" in the far-flung year of 2020, according to 1984's *Machine Man* #1.

Then there are a handful of musicians who, like Dazzler, have become marquee names within the Marvel story without even existing in our world. Lila Cheney, for instance, is a British-born teleporter who lives in a Dyson sphere and spends most of her time in the far reaches of outer space when she's not being a Pat Benatar-ish touring performer on Earth. (Dazzler briefly played keyboards in her band.) In her first appearance, she attempted to sell the Earth's residents into slavery. She subsequently dated Cannonball of the New Mutants for a while; according to 1984's *New Mutants Annual* #1, a song she wrote about him "rocket[ed] to the top of the charts."

The Marvel-Universe-only pop star who's had the most interesting life is, inarguably, Rick Jones. In his first appearance, in 1962's *Incredible Hulk* #1, he's playing his harmonica at an atomic test site where a gamma

---

*It can't have hurt that Hypnolovewheel bassist Dan Cuddy was an assistant editor at Marvel.

bomb is about to go off; Bruce Banner turns into the Hulk as a consequence of rescuing Rick, who becomes his sidekick and occasional jailer.

Rick subsequently becomes affiliated with the Avengers, goes back to hanging around with the Hulk, then briefly takes over as a replacement for Captain America's dead sidekick Bucky. Shortly after becoming psychically bonded with the first Captain Marvel, the alien warrior Mar-Vell, Rick starts to pursue a career in folk-rock. We get to see bits of the lyrics to a few of his songs, including a nuclear-protest number he performs in 1970's *Sub-Mariner* #30:

> *One day the power that we've released*
> *Is gonna light up west and east...*
> *And there's no place to retreat*
> *'Cause we've all got a seat...*
> *At the feast of the A-tomic beast...!*

Rick Jones sings about nuclear terror in *Sub-Mariner* #30, 1970, by writer Roy Thomas and artists Sal Buscema and Joe Gaudioso.

After saving the world during the Kree-Skrull War, Rick is convinced by his manager to form a short-lived duo, Rick 'n' Dandy. By 1978's *Marvel Team-Up* #74, he's once again a solo act, and a big enough deal that he's the musical guest on *Saturday Night Live* (the same week that Spider-Man and the cast of *SNL* fight the Silver Samurai*).

---

*I'm not making this up.

Rick's career seems to have gone into decline over the next decade or so. In a couple of 1991 issues of *Incredible Hulk*, he's playing in a bar band that also includes real-world actors Bill Mumy and Miguel Ferrer. An impostor, in a 2002 *Alias* storyline, has convinced everyone that he's the real Rick Jones, even playing gigs around New York. The real Rick, by that point, has another body-swap situation going on, this time with Mar-Vell's son—the third Captain Marvel, Genis-Vell—which leads to his being stranded for a while in the Microverse (a universe that can only be reached by shrinking to subatomic size). His music becomes wildly popular across thousands of Microverse planets; his fans call themselves "Jonesys."

After his return to Earth, Rick has one last pop hit in 2004's *Captain Marvel* #19: a love song to his ex-wife, Marlo, who's dating the superheroine Moondragon at the time. Rick's subsequent adventures have included work as a hacktivist under the name the Whisperer, death by firing squad during the Hydra occupation of the U.S., and resurrection as the monster Subject B, but not much in the way of music.

Why would so many aliens be so interested in Earth musicians, though? That question may have been answered by still another alien Captain Marvel, the Kree warrior Noh-Varr. In the 2013 *Young Avengers* series, Noh-Varr is often shown to be an obsessive fan of Earth pop music—he's rhapsodizing over the Ronettes' "Be My Baby" in its first issue. When we see him again in 2018's *Royals* #12, he's thousands of years in the future, confronting Earth's conquerors and suggesting that music is, in fact, what's most special about this world: "There was *music* here, once. Diamonds made of *sound*, created in thoughtspace. A form of magic *unique* to this planet. You *destroyed* the planet. Destroyed the *music*. But *I* remember. I remember the *drums*." With that, he opens fire.

12

THUNDER AND LIES

T he present-day Marvel series that's been running the longest, under one title or another, is *Thor*. That's a deceptive way of putting it—*Thor* began its existence as a horror anthology series called *Journey into Mystery* in 1952, and Thor himself didn't show up in it for ten years—but deceptions are an important part of what it became.

So is mystery—not in the sense of a puzzle with a solution, but in the older theological sense of secret ritual and religious revelation. The publication that gave Marvel Comics its name quickly changed its own name to *Marvel Mystery Comics*,* and it's not entirely false to say that all Marvel comics are mystery comics—that there's hidden knowledge to be found in them, for those who take the time to look deeply.

That's especially the case for *Journey into Mystery* and its offspring. They're something different from their peers, hiding in plain sight. The

*See chapter 5.

comic books about Thor and Loki look and behave like superhero comics, but they're not exactly that. They're an elaboration on a set of stories that have been told for more than a millennium, the body of Norse mythology. They're only tangentially about *people*; more often, they're about gods and how they fall, through sacrifice and apocalypse. They give us thunder, and they give us lies.

Journey into Mystery #83 (August 1962)
STAN LEE, LARRY LIEBER, JACK KIRBY, JOE SINNOTT

The story of the hammer-wielding thunder god Thor comes to us through the Eddas: Snorri Sturluson's *Prose Edda*, a thirteenth-century overview of Norse myths, and the *Poetic Edda*, a collection of poems from the Icelandic oral tradition, written down sometime around 1300 but probably significantly older. (Attestations of Thor go back much further.) In 1962, as Marvel started to convert its sci-fi and fantasy anthology comics to superhero stories, Thor—or rather, Jack Kirby, Stan Lee, and Larry Lieber's modified version of him*—took over the front section of *Journey into Mystery*.

In place of the death-dealing, red-bearded god described in the Eddas, Marvel's Thor was awkwardly retrofitted to the contemporary superhero template. He had blond hair and a human secret identity as an American doctor, Donald Blake, who could strike his walking stick on the ground to transform himself into Thor, and the stick into his hammer, Mjolnir.

His first appearance, in this issue, is even more watered down than that suggests. It's a superhero story grafted onto an alien-invasion story: a bunch of "Stone Men from Saturn" invade Earth and sic a robot on Thor,

---

*The first time a Kirby-drawn comic mentioned Thor had been more than twenty years earlier: in 1941's *Captain America Comics* #1, the "Hurricane" feature by Kirby and Joe Simon begins with the caption "Hurricane, son of Thor, god of thunder, and the last descendent of the ancient Greek immortals, returns to Earth to fight his ancestral enemy, Pluto, the devil." As *Peanuts'* Linus Van Pelt put it, "the theological implications alone are staggering."

until his prowess with his hammer convinces them to go away. The one piece of it that's remained important to *Thor* as a series is the inscription on Mjolnir: "Whosoever holds this hammer, if he be worthy, shall possess the power of Thor."*

Part of its resonance is the archaic formality of its language, which is otherwise absent from this first story but would become one of the series' signature elements. The other aspect of the inscription that's echoed through Thor's stories ever since is the idea of "worthiness." Other Marvel characters have their power thrust upon them or create it themselves; in Thor's comics, the question of who *deserves* power is almost always open. If you don't deserve to hold Mjolnir, you can't even pick it up.

Journey into Mystery #85 (October 1962)
STAN LEE, LARRY LIEBER, JACK KIRBY, DICK AYERS

Most of the first year and a half of the Thor feature is throat clearing: unthrilling superhero adventures, written by Larry Lieber or Robert Bernstein, and only occasionally drawn by Kirby. The third episode, though, introduces another character from Norse myth who became one of the broader Marvel story's pillars: Thor's half brother, Loki.

From this point onward, *Journey into Mystery*, in its various incarnations, is really the twined stories of two characters: Thor and Loki, the hard hitter and the slick talker, the maker of thunder and the teller of lies, the restorer of order and the instigator of chaos. Those two narrative threads aren't equally weighted. Thor is louder, of course, and much more reliable, and he overwhelmingly dominates the story most of the time. But Loki is persistent and clever, and he can appear in many guises. He's a game player, and he's partial to the long game.

From the start, the Loki of the comics is reasonably close to the version

---

*Recent manifestations of the hammer make the inscription slightly more egalitarian: "if they be worthy."

portrayed in the Eddas: a demivillain, cruel and vengeful at times, but more interested in seeing what he can get away with than in doing real harm. Identified as "the god of mischief" in this first appearance, Loki can do magic, which leads to ongoing vacillation about the limits of his capabilities. (Here, his powers don't work when he's wet.) Jack Kirby's design for him is part warrior, part jester: a green bodysuit with yellow accessories, including a jagged collar, a sort of dragon-shaped helmet with long horns, and armor that suggests serpentine scales.

The Avengers #1 (September 1963)
STAN LEE, JACK KIRBY, DICK AYERS

Through Marvel's first few decades, Loki appeared almost exclusively in Thor's stories, but one of the only exceptions was a big one. "The Avengers... *Bah!* I'll destroy you *all!*" Loki declares on the cover of *Avengers* #1.* We know it's him, even though we can only see the side of his head and a bit of a shoulder and arm, from behind: Kirby was such a gifted designer that his characters are identifiable from fragmentary details. At the end of the story, Loki can't escape from a lead-lined tank, because... There's no real reason, actually, but okay.

Journey into Mystery #97 (October 1963)
STAN LEE, JACK KIRBY, DON HECK, C. BELL [GEORGE ROUSSOS]

A month after *The Avengers* debuted, Kirby and Lee introduced a new feature to the back pages of *Journey into Mystery*. "Tales of Asgard" ("Home of the Mighty Norse Gods") was adapted much more directly than "Thor" from Norse mythology, at least at first. Freed from the confines of (relative) realism, Kirby cut loose on it, with fantastical designs and just three

---

*Much later, in *Avengers* #300, he blames himself for bringing the Avengers together in the first place, which is a sidelong way of giving himself credit for it; he effectively serves the same purpose in the 2012 *Avengers* movie.

or four huge panels on most pages. For the next four years, "Tales of Asgard" occupied the last five pages of each issue. The squat, smoldering demon Surtur* makes his first appearance here, a single panel that's been the basis for how he's looked in comics ever since.

The "Thor" feature itself was still fairly weak sauce at this point: "I claim all the dry surface of Earth for the *lava people*!" declares this issue's villain, while Thor's milquetoast alter ego Donald Blake spends interminable pages pining for his nurse, Jane Foster.

Journey into Mystery #104 (May 1964)
STAN LEE, JACK KIRBY, CHIC STONE, DON HECK

A few months after Kirby became the full-time artist on the "Thor" feature, he and Lee appear to have figured out that "Tales of Asgard" was so much more exciting that they might as well extend its tone to the rest of *Journey into Mystery*. With this issue, the series' title shrank to small type at the top of its cover, and THOR appeared in huge, rough-edged letters beneath it. Thor began to spend more time in the Norse gods' realm of Asgard than in New York City. The doomed warrior-god Balder, who had earlier been seen briefly in *Journey into Mystery*, became a recurring member of its cast. And in general, Lee and Kirby dialed down the long-underwear heroes-and-villains stuff (and the tedious presence of Donald Blake) in favor of mythological and cod-mythological spectacle.

That gave them both license to play triple fortissimo almost all the time. Of the two series Kirby drew the most of in the 1960s, *Fantastic Four* is richer—its characters have a sense of interiority in a way that Thor and Odin and Loki don't—but *Journey into Mystery/Thor* is bigger and more operatic. Lee seized on the opportunity to belt out arias of his own: "Nothing you have ever seen before can equal the breath-taking spectacle

---

*He's Surtr in the Eddas, but Marvel's version of mythological characters usually had more standard-looking English orthography; see also Balder and Baldr.

of 'GIANTS WALK THE EARTH!'" declares this issue's cover. His blurb for the story's first page hedges its bets only slightly more: "Possibly one of the ten all-time epics you will never ever forget!!"

Thor #126 (March 1966)
STAN LEE, JACK KIRBY, VINCE COLLETTA

There was no pretending that *Journey into Mystery* was anything other than Thor's comic book anymore, so it changed its title with this issue. On its cover, Thor is fighting with a hero from a different body of mythology: the Greek demigod Hercules,* who had substantially more cultural currency than Thor did at that point. (There had been a string of Italian *Hercules* B movies between 1957 and 1965, and other sword-and-sandal films were syndicated on American TV as *The Sons of Hercules.*†)

Lee, by this point, had developed "archaic," mock-Shakespearean speech patterns for the gods—not quite historically or geographically accurate, but they got the point across. Here's a bit of midfight banter between Hercules and Thor: "By the cloven hooves of Pan!! What doth it *take* to defeat the son of Odin??!" "A stronger arm! A stouter heart! A nobler soul! And none doth Hercules possess, thou blabbering, blustering, boastful buffoon!"

"Tales of Asgard," meanwhile, had veered slightly off the territory of the Eddas. At this point, it was a serial adventure prominently featuring Fandral, Hogun, and Volstagg, aka the Warriors Three, all of whom had recently been invented for the comics. It's not clear whose idea it was to recast Shakespeare's Sir John Falstaff, by way of the Three Musketeers' Porthos,

---

*The first-century Roman historian Tacitus's comments on Germanic peoples' worship of "Hercules" have sometimes been taken to be references to Thor.

†Hercules has been a recurring Marvel character ever since: a jovial, self-glorifying strongman with painful memories that he often tries to drink away. The orthography of his name is in line with his presence elsewhere in pop culture, which is why he's not "Herakles."

as a Norse god—Lee and Kirby both claimed that honor*—but Volstagg the Voluminous is, in any case, a magnificent supporting character, an enormous, over-the-hill warrior who talks a bold game despite his blatant cowardice, and manages to keep coming out on top by sheer accident.

At this episode's very end, Odin, the king of the gods, summons the cast home to Asgard to explain what the blurb for the next issue calls "the meaning of Ragnarok!" That word's meaning within the Marvel story is pretty much the same as the meaning of "Ragnarök" in "Völuspá," the first poem in the *Poetic Edda*†—a cataclysm in which the gods die, followed by a rebirth—and the story Odin relates in the following episode is clearly derived from that text.

What Ragnarok means *to* the Marvel story, though, is that Thor's story (unlike Spider-Man's, or Iron Man's, or the Fantastic Four's) has a *specific* ending: he will someday fight Jormungand the Midgard Serpent, take nine steps backward, and fall. Odin's initial retelling of that prophecy in "Tales of Asgard" doesn't get into the details of Thor's demise, but it does indicate that Jormungand's parent, Loki, will be responsible for Ragnarok. Death is coming.

Thor #190 (July 1971)
STAN LEE, JOHN BUSCEMA, JOE SINNOTT

Death, in fact, became a recurring character in *Thor*, in the person of the goddess Hela. (In Norse mythology, she's Hel; in both traditional sources and Marvel's comics, Hel is also the name of her realm.) She made only a

---

*Lee, talking to Roy Thomas about the Warriors Three in 1998: "I made those up. I specifically remember that I did them because I wanted a Falstaff-type guy, a guy like Errol Flynn, and then I wanted a guy like Charles Bronson who was dire and gloomy, riddled with angst. Those three were mine." Kirby, interviewed by Gary Groth in 1989: "I even threw in the Three Musketeers. I drew them from Shakespearean figures. I combined Shakespearean figures with the Three Musketeers and came up with these three friends who supplemented Thor and his company."
†The earliest extant copy of "Völuspá" dates from the thirteenth century, but it was probably composed a few hundred years earlier.

few brief appearances in Kirby-era *Thor*, which was generally high stakes in a way that suggested that, even when the universe was threatened, no character we cared about was particularly endangered. But after Kirby left the series in mid-1970, she appeared with increasing frequency, and in recent years she's rarely gone more than a few months without showing up somewhere.

This sequence—one of Stan Lee's last *Thor* stories—is about death as a necessity and sacrifice as a virtue, both of which would be themes of *Thor* and its spin-offs ever after. Thor offers to sacrifice himself to spare a group of mortals from death at Hela's hands. When Odin rescues Thor by killing Hela, Thor envisions the disastrous consequences of an end to all death and convinces Odin to resurrect her. As Thor ages to a horrified, withered shell, his lover, Sif, appears and offers her life in his place; Hela, moved, restores him. (Meanwhile, as usual, Loki is sneakily trying to take over Asgard.)

Lee's writing was going through an odd phase at this point: for some reason, he omitted punctuation from the end of most word balloons for three months in mid-1971. He was also clearly having a blast with the gods' dialogue, occasionally slipping into full-on iambic pentameter. One brief exchange:

> "Karnilla! Thou must cast another spell
> Mayhap if Odin sees what we have seen—"

> "Too late, alas! The thunder god is doomed"

> "I say thee nay! The mighty Thor shall live!"

Thor #337 (November 1983)
WALTER SIMONSON, GEORGE ROUSSOS

As with *Fantastic Four*, *Thor* spent a decade or so after Kirby's and Lee's departures sticking cautiously to the template of their work. About as big a change as it dared was Odin sacrificing one of his eyes for knowledge (the better to conform to myth).

Then, with this issue, Walter Simonson took over the series as writer and artist, and was not subtle about breaking with convention. On its cover, instead of Thor himself, Simonson drew his own creation, Beta Ray Bill, an alien with a head like a horse's skull, wearing a modified version of Thor's costume and smashing the comic's logo, which had gone unchanged for nearly twenty years.

Simonson's four-year run on *Thor* is still the series' most fondly remembered era. He'd been brewing it up for a while, having conceived of the basic plot of its first year as a college student in 1967. That year, he'd also had a letter published in *Tales of Suspense* #93, complaining about Gene Colan's artwork on the Iron Man feature being "a little too stylized."

He evidently got over his objection to stylized imagery at some point. By the time *Thor* #337 appeared, Simonson had been drawing comics professionally for ten years,* and he'd gradually developed an insistent, original visual style built on crackling angles, geometrical precision, and the weight of negative space. Any curve in his drawings that wasn't a compass-ruled circle seemed to have been bent by brute force. That even extended to his signature, a sort of brontosaurus shape with the first "O" in "Simonson"— another perfect circle—as its hump.†

American mainstream comics have never had many writer/artists— the demands of producing twenty or so pages a month has usually led to division of labor—but at the time of this issue, Simonson was sharing an art studio with two other creators who both wrote and drew: Frank Miller, who had recently concluded a hugely successful run on *Daredevil*,

---

*Simonson had also drawn, but not written, a year's worth of *Thor* in 1977–1978; it's much more timid looking, a second-tier imitation of John Buscema's approach to its Kirby-designed characters.

†One of the best-loved panels of Simonson's run—Odin, Thor, and Loki preparing to attack in *Thor* #353, respectively yelling "For Asgard!" "For Midgard!" and "For myself!"—includes a pile of rubble shaped more or less like his signature.

and Howard Chaykin, whose *American Flagg!* (published by the independent First Comics) had debuted a month earlier. All three of them took pains to establish a distinctive look and feel for their work, and Simonson's *Thor* foregrounds its style and its imagery more than anything else Marvel was publishing at the time.

It begins with the kind of flourish that suggests a single creator at the controls of both language and images: a crackle of unknown light and a crash of unfamiliar thunder. In place of Thor's hammer, we see the tongs of a shadowy cosmic blacksmith, "beyond the fields we know."* Over the course of a three-page prologue, he captures "a molten ingot of star-stuff" and smashes it onto an anvil, with a sound effect— "DOOM!"—that spans the width of the page, in lettering that resembles Celtic letterforms more than anything that ordinarily appeared in American comics.

Like almost all of Simonson's *Thor*, that sound effect was lettered by John Workman, who also made deliberate, unusual visual gestures: most of his word balloons were extensions of panel borders rather than intersecting with them, for instance. For too long, *Thor* had looked like just another comic that Jack Kirby used to draw. Now, it had an aesthetic of its own.

Thor #338 (December 1983)
WALTER SIMONSON, GEORGE ROUSSOS

Simonson repudiated the *Thor* tradition of following in Kirby's footsteps, but that wasn't a rejection of Kirby. His run included two loving, direct salutes to the master, this one as Simonson's tenure on the series began and the other just before it ended. This issue's cover shows Thor and Beta Ray Bill grappling over Mjolnir and exchanging blows; their pose is, almost

---

*That phrase is a refrain in Lord Dunsany's 1924 fantasy novel, *The King of Elfland's Daughter*.

exactly, the pose in which Kirby had drawn Thor and Hercules on the cover of *Thor* #126.

Jack Kirby and Vince Colletta's cover for *Thor* #126, 1966, is echoed by Walter Simonson's cover for *Thor* #338, 1983.

There's a new *Thor* logo above their heads—designed by Alex Jay, with further influence from Celtic manuscripts—replacing the one that Bill had destroyed the month before. *We're doing things very differently now,* the cover indicates, *but that doesn't mean we don't care a lot about where we came from.*

Thor #352 (February 1985)
WALTER SIMONSON, CHRISTIE SCHEELE

The most welcome change in *Thor* was that absolutely everything about what Simonson was doing seemed to be deliberate. For its first twenty years, *Thor* had mostly been improvised issue to issue. Kirby and Lee, in particular, had been winging it, to the point where Marvel eventually started sending Kirby photostats of each issue so he'd have some reference for what he'd drawn the previous month.

Simonson, conversely, planned *way* ahead. The crash of "DOOM!" from his first episode recurs in every issue for a year, and is eventually revealed to be Surtur the fire demon forging a sword called Twilight. That year is a gradual, steady crescendo toward this frenzied sequence, in which Surtur attempts to bring about Ragnarok (literally "twilight of the gods").

Another part of that crescendo involves the opening of a magical box called the Casket of Ancient Winters, which causes a worldwide blizzard in the middle of American summer. Simonson gave other creators enough advance notice that it also snowed unexpectedly in concurrent issues of *Avengers, Amazing Spider-Man, ROM, West Coast Avengers, Peter Parker, Uncanny X-Men,* and the *Kitty Pryde and Wolverine* miniseries. The snow didn't much affect any of those stories, but it sure gave the impression that what was happening in *Thor* was a big deal.

And Simonson had also figured out how to use the quotidian elements of *Thor* to make the mythological elements even more dramatic by contrast, without letting them drag the story down. (He had written the tedious Donald Blake out of the series almost immediately.*) The centerpiece of this issue pits two otherworldly armies against each other, but sets their clash amid the specific architecture of Lower Manhattan, a trick that several of Marvel's movies would later reprise.

Characters in Simonson's *Thor* spend a lot of time patiently explaining the plot—a style of comics writing that was already beginning to seem a little dated in the mid-1980s. Still, his language is often lovely, especially when he revs it up toward the bombastic, scenery-chewing archaisms of Stan Lee at his best. At the climax of this issue, Surtur gets a King-Lear-in-the-storm moment: "Come, ye hoary winters, cold as death! Come, ice!

---

*The remaining plot threads about Blake's medical practice were dispatched in a brief backup feature in *Thor* #354: "Tales of Midgard, Home of the Amazing Human Race!"

Come, hail! Come, sleet! Come, ye chill and frosty rimes of white! Before the nine worlds were! Before Odin was! Then were the *lands of fire and ice* alone in being! From the beginnings of the world, I call the ancient breath of winter, brother of the fire! *Heed my call and come!*"

Thor #356 (June 1985)
BOB HARRAS, JACKSON GUICE, BOB LAYTON, CHRISTIE SCHEELE

Marvel was not yet in the habit of typesetting creators' names on the front of its comics—that wouldn't happen until around 1997—but it was no secret that Simonson was the chief selling point of *Thor*. Still, he couldn't *quite* produce a full issue every month, and as long as newsstand distribution was a significant part of Marvel's business, skipping a publication month was out of the question. Only two fill-in issues by other creators appeared during his four-year *Thor* run; on the cover of this one, Hercules is shoving Thor out of the way, saying, "Stand aside, thunder god— *Walt Simonson* is on vacation and so art *thou*!"

Thor #362 (December 1985)
WALTER SIMONSON, MAX SCHEELE

The second half of Simonson's *Thor* concerns its hero's response to death and deterioration. Near its beginning, Thor leads an invasion of Hel to rescue some mortal souls,* and his confrontation with Hela leaves him with a badly scarred face, which doesn't heal. Over the next twenty issues, his injuries mount up, and he's in increasingly severe pain—although Simonson balances that drama with some sly whimsy, like a sequence in which Thor has been turned into a frog.

This issue, though, is raw heavy-metal thunder. For the battle in Hel,

---

*The resemblance of this premise to Christ's Harrowing of Hell is not remarked upon by anyone in the story. Totally different theological system.

Simonson pushes his visual technique deep into abstraction (by the standards of representational storytelling), rendering everything as assemblages of shards and broad swatches of annihilated space. One scene, in particular, always comes up when aging fans boozily reminisce about how great mid-1980s *Thor* was: the sacrifice of Skurge the Executioner (one of Thor's earliest antagonists from *Journey into Mystery*), who stays behind in Hel to hold off the armies of the dead while Thor and his company escape. Simonson's signature appears on that sequence's final page, as it occasionally did on pages he realized were especially terrific. (A version of the same scene appears in the movie *Thor: Ragnarok*.)

The unsung creative hero of this issue, and of the better part of Simonson's *Thor*, is colorist Christie "Max" Scheele.* She renders Skurge's last stand in just five flat tones: a pale yellow, two oranges, and two deep reds. Those colors appear throughout the rest of the issue, along with a few sickly sea greens that are Scheele's motif for Hel, paler than the green shades of Hela's costume. The red and orange part of the palette falls away over the last few pages, as Thor's force emerges into Asgard, but the travelers are still marked by the faintest of the colors of Hel.

X-Men/Alpha Flight #1 (December 1985)
CHRIS CLAREMONT, PAUL SMITH, BOB WIACEK, GLYNIS OLIVER

At the same moment as the peak of Simonson's *Thor*, Loki's strain of their paired story begins to emerge from his brother's shadow. In this two-issue team-up between the X-Men and the Canadian superhero team Alpha Flight, Loki claims that he's trying to earn redemption; ever since *X-Men/Alpha Flight*, that's been his ostensible goal most of the time. (What he really wants, though, is not quite redemption as such, but the fruits of redemption—being let off the hook for his past actions.)

---

*Recent print editions of Simonson's *Thor*—and many of his issues' digital incarnations—have been recolored by another artist with overwrought, fussy modern techniques. If you can read the Scheele-colored versions instead, do.

But who could forgive Loki for being Loki? The entities he's petitioning are seen for the first time here, and they've subsequently appeared at a few crucial moments within his story (and Thor's). They're identified only as Those Who Sit Above in Shadow—the gods' own gods—and represented as white contours on a black background, an inversion of comics' "reality."

Loki fails to impress them, of course, but in failing, he frees himself in a small way. Up to this point, his presence within the Marvel story has been almost entirely in the pages of Thor's comics, and his fate has been tied to Thor's. Hereafter, he's got the run of the place.

Walter Simonson's text echoes the *Poetic Edda*, and John Workman letters a very big sound effect, in *Thor* #380, 1987, drawn by Simonson and Sal Buscema.

Thor #380 (June 1987)
WALTER SIMONSON, SAL BUSCEMA, MAX SCHEELE

Most of the final fifteen issues of the Simonson-written *Thor*, as well as its 1985 spin-off miniseries *Balder the Brave*, were drawn by Sal Buscema, but Simonson returned to pencil one more issue—not his last, #382, but this singular thing. It's the loudest episode of them all, an issue-length fight between Thor (now cursed by Hela with brittle bones and unhealing wounds, but unable to die) and the Midgard Serpent, Jormungand. There's a further bit of revealed mystery about this attestation of the Serpent: he's also the dragon Fin Fang Foom, a Jack Kirby cocreation who had appeared in 1961's *Strange Tales* #89, just before the Fantastic Four's debut.

Thor #380 is almost entirely full-page images.* Simonson's captions are composed in the mode of the half-lined verses of "Völuspá," and echo its refrain of "Vituð ér enn eða hvat?" (Which roughly translates to: "Would you know more, or what?") The story's sound effects, as John Workman letters them, are so thunderous that they often extend onto a second line:

BRAKAKKTH
WOOOMMM!

With his second *Thor* cover, Simonson gave us the first of his story's direct visual homages to Kirby, and now he gives us the other, as a signal that he's almost done. One page is a close-up of Thor's face that's pure Kirby, from its "camera angle" to a jagged stripe that represents a reflection of light on metal. Immediately after it, as in "Völuspá," Thor sacrifices himself: he kills the serpent, takes nine steps back, and falls. The climax of Simonson's *Thor* is the prophesied end of Thor himself: "Silent his hammer; Mjolnir's song ended, / this tale is told. Would you know more?"

Of course there's more to know—being unable to die is part of Thor's curse. Simonson's run has two more issues' worth of resolution. As she did, approximately, at the conclusion of Stan Lee's run, Hela restores both Thor's body and his mortality: "The touch of death shall be the breath of life to thee... even as 'Hela' shall become 'heal' and all thy wounds made whole!" (That's not the last time an anagram of her name has been significant.) And Thor deals with Loki's most recent deceits in a characteristically direct way, by breaking his arm with Mjolnir.

---

*Writer/artist Dan Jurgens borrowed this trick for the death of Superman in *Superman* #75, five years later.

Thor #85 (December 2004)
MICHAEL AVON OEMING, DANIEL BERMAN, ANDREA DIVITO,
LAURA VILLARI

After Simonson's story ended, *Thor* swung and whiffed for a long time. To return to the Lee and Kirby model would have been hopelessly retrograde, not that some of the series' writers and artists didn't try; but to imitate Simonson's command of form and myth was impossible. No other fresh approach was evident. Loki briefly jumped into the spotlight with the 1989 crossover "Acts of Vengeance," in which he turned up in a dozen different series, manipulating villains into fighting each other's opponents. A bit later, Thor killed him, but it didn't stick.

Following 1996's *Thor* #502, the series paused for almost two years. The relaunched *Thor* ran from 1998 to 2004, and ended with a bizarre, audacious six-issue story in which Thor deliberately brings about (what he believes to be) a final Ragnarok, blinds himself, beheads Loki, and puts an end to Asgard. Most of the last two issues, #84 and #85, are callbacks to the Simonson era that had ended seventeen years earlier— Surtur, Hela, and Beta Ray Bill all turn up to take their bows. But there's one other significant thread that gets pulled in and, apparently, severed at the end: Those Who Sit Above in Shadow, the gods' gods, who had gone unseen since 1987. Thor repudiates them, then cuts them off from their power by destroying the entire Norse cosmology, calling it his "ultimate act of sacrifice."

Nice try. After another two-year break, a new *Thor* #1 appeared in 2007, and the whole familiar cast was promptly resurrected too. By then, the 2011 *Thor* movie was in development; there is no Valhalla for active film properties.

Journey into Mystery #622 (June 2011)
KIERON GILLEN, DOUG BRAITHWAITE, ULISES ARREOLA

Loki returned shortly after Thor, in a more protean form—first as a woman, then in his more familiar body, then (following still another "death") as a young, mischievous boy. The new Kid Loki was the star of the revived *Journey into Mystery*, launched as a subsidiary tie-in to the Thor-focused crossover *Fear Itself*, which coincided with the release of the *Thor* movie in which Tom Hiddleston memorably played (adult) Loki.

Fear Itself was a noisy, cluttered thing, involving a "Serpent" who was another variation on Jormungand. This incarnation of *Journey into Mystery*, on the other hand, is a delight. It's the story of what's happening backstage during the blood and thunder of *Fear Itself* and the consequences of those machinations. Young Loki persistently insists that he's nothing like the wicked old Loki: his first line of dialogue is: "Why do people always presume I'm *lying*?" That is, of course, exactly his nature. His role in *Journey into Mystery* is to be a trickster and god of lies, which also means that he's a god of fictions.* And his adviser and familiar is the magpie Ikol, whose avowedly untrustworthy voice belongs to Loki's former self.†

This wasn't *quite* the first time Loki had headlined a comic book of his own—there had been a *Loki* miniseries in 2004 and another in 2010. Still, a few decades earlier it would have been unthinkable to present him as any kind of sympathetic protagonist. Superhero comics' versions of "good" and "evil," by this point, looked a lot more complicated than they once had.

---

*The series' focus on the particular powers of storytelling—not to mention power struggles in the underworld—mean that it's operating in much the same territory as the very popular 1989–1996 *Sandman* series that Neil Gaiman had written at DC Comics. Especially in writer Kieron Gillen's early issues, this period of *Journey into Mystery* is often a direct homage—or riposte—to Gaiman's *Sandman*.
†Ikol is not the only anagrammatic alter ego in *Journey into Mystery*; a bit later, Hela's handmaiden and kind-of other self, Leah, joins the cast.

Journey into Mystery #629 (October 2011)
KIERON GILLEN, WHILCE PORTACIO, DOUG BRAITHWAITE, ALLEN MARTINEZ, ET AL.

In the final episode of *Fear Itself,* published the same day as this issue, Thor (once again) kills the Serpent, and (once again) takes nine steps back and falls. (No one even pretended that he would not be revived almost immediately.) Meanwhile, here, Loki assures Thor's victory by literally rewriting the Serpent's past, in a book, with a magical pen created from the shadow of Surtur's sword, Twilight—which is, metonymically, the shadow of the *Thor* comics in which Walter Simonson spent a year forging that sword. "We cannot change history," Loki's narration notes. "But gods do not have history. They have story. And that is something a writer always has the prerogative to twist."

Journey into Mystery #645 (December 2012)
KIERON GILLEN, STEPHANIE HANS

Gillen avails himself of that prerogative here, at the end of his *Journey into Mystery.* The mystery of this period of *Journey* is whether Loki is capable of change: whether or not he can legitimately turn his lies and mischief-making into a force for good and redeem himself for what he's done in the past. The answer—and the sacrifice required of Loki—is not simple, but it's crushing. It's been carefully set up since the beginning of Gillen's story, and in one last twist of the metafictional knife, it implicates *Journey into Mystery*'s readers. Old Loki insists that he will change. "Of course you won't," young Loki tells him. "They won't let you." His only option to prevent Hell (with a double *l*) from overtaking everything is to "swallow the lie": devouring Ikol the magpie and letting old Loki consume *him* from within and assume his form. The final image here is Loki looking directly at us, murmuring "Damn you all."

Loki: Agent of Asgard #1 (April 2014)

AL EWING, LEE GARBETT, NOLAN WOODARD

Kid Loki—or rather, old Loki in his form—bounced straight into another Gillen-written project, *Young Avengers*, a candy-colored, formally playful, yearlong series about a team of teenage superheroes. Then, magically reshaped into a dashing young man, he reappeared in a series of his own. Its title was inspired by the 1960s series *Nick Fury, Agent of S.H.I.E.L.D.*, and its ostensible premise was that it, too, was an espionage comic—that Loki would be earning the forgiveness he craved by going on secret missions for the All-Mothers who had replaced Odin as Asgard's rulers.

That, of course, was a lie. Loki is no one's agent except Loki's, the "missions" quickly cease to be the point, and forgiveness, in this story, is not as simple as striking crimes from the record. Every aspect of *Loki: Agent of Asgard* is about deceptions and shell games and fictions—especially fictions. Of *course* it's not what it purports to be.

Thor #1 (October 2014)

JASON AARON, RUSSELL DAUTERMAN, MATTHEW WILSON

From 2012 to 2019, Jason Aaron wrote what was effectively a single gigantic Thor serial, spread across nine series and miniseries: *Thor: God of Thunder, Original Sin, Thor* (2014), *Thors, The Mighty Thor, The Unworthy Thor, Thor* (2018), *War of the Realms*, and *King Thor*. The turning point of Aaron's story occurs immediately before this, in *Original Sin*, when Nick Fury—the commando turned secret agent who's been hanging around Marvel since the 1960s, and who is now omniscient and living on the moon—whispers a secret to Thor that causes him to become "unworthy," and therefore unable to hold his hammer. At the end of this issue, the hammer is picked up by an initially unidentified woman, who immediately appears in a version of the familiar armor and is referred to as Thor for the next few years' worth of comics. ("Thor," it appears, is a role as much as it is a name; in the subsequent *Thors* miniseries, "Thor" is a collectively held job title.)

The new Thor turns out to be Jane Foster, Dr. Blake's nurse from the earliest Thor comics,* now a doctor herself. The previous Thor starts calling himself Odinson. The secret that made him unworthy (it comes out much later) is the revelation that Gorr, a "god butcher" who had appeared at the beginning of Aaron's run, was correct in his assertion that mortals would be better off without gods, who are "all unworthy." The mystery's solution is an antimystery, an assertion that the journey is meaningless.

It's a truism of fiction that characters are most interesting when there's something they want, and Odinson promptly gets a lot more interesting at this point in the story: he's been exiled from his identity, his worthiness, and his name, and he desperately wants them back. At the same time, Loki is struggling to attain exactly the opposite—to no longer be the entity he has always been.

Loki: Agent of Asgard #6 (November 2014)
AL EWING, JORGE COELHO, LEE LOUGHRIDGE

There's a popular conception among irritable mainstream comics readers that crossovers wreck the flow of ongoing series, forcing them to interrupt their natural progression to conform to whatever big event comics are coming along the same month. *Loki: Agent of Asgard* makes a solid counterargument. After its first few issues, it's almost entirely tied to crossovers—*Original Sin*, then *Avengers/X-Men: AXIS*, then "Last Days" and *Secret Wars*—all of which, rather than derailing Loki's story, push it exactly where it's meant to go.

One of its key moments, in fact, is in this *AXIS* tie-in issue, in which

---

*For Jane Foster, being a hero means sacrificing her body by degrees, as it did for the previous Thor in the final year of Walter Simonson's story: she's being treated for cancer, and the transformation to Thor makes her chemotherapy fail.

Doctor Doom lectures Loki about his role (during hand-to-hand combat, since there are still genre conventions to fulfill here): "True magic is the imposition of a narrative upon reality. It is telling a story to the world... and making the world believe it [...] To be a creature of magic... to be a god... is to be a creature of story."

Loki: Agent of Asgard #17 (October 2015)

AL EWING, LEE GARBETT, ANTONIO FABELA

The last phase of *Loki: Agent of Asgard* takes place as the universe is ending, and afterward.* It speeds up the transformations of the previous few years—Loki changes shape and gender a few times, while the question of whether this trickster can change internally remains open. It also brings in most of the usual signifiers of Marvel's Ragnaroks: the sounding of the Gjallarhorn, the return of Jormungand, narration in the rhythms of "Völuspá," and so on. (No Thor, though. She's occupied elsewhere, and so is Odinson.)

Then there's this final issue, a piece of metafiction that takes place after everything is over, in the white space outside existence. Its cover is Loki sitting cross-legged and glowering atop copies of the previous sixteen issues.

What the god of lies has saved from the void is the stories of the gods, and the final enemies that have arrived to devour those stories are Those Who Sit Above in Shadow. Loki tells them a story of a storyteller, thousands of years earlier, inventing a magnificent lie about the origin of thunder. He suggests that "some stories are... so good they're *magic*. So good they come *alive*." He implies to his own gods that they are themselves just stories. "Don't you want to know how it ends?" he asks as they rage, and then echoes the refrain of "Völuspá" one more time: *"Would you know more?"*

---

*See chapter 18 for the circumstances surrounding that.

They depart, and Loki reconciles himself to the painful possibilities of his own narrative. Then he reaches into his stylish green jacket—his latest update of the outfit he's worn ever since Jack Kirby gave it to him—and draws a door in the nothingness, à la *Harold and the Purple Crayon*. It looks like the letters he's writing above it are EXIT, but no: they say NEXT, and he opens up the door to head to the future of his story, holding the scepter he carries in the *Avengers* movie.

13

INTERLUDE: BEFORE THE MARVEL CINEMATIC UNIVERSE

December 1962: In *Fantastic Four* #9, the team's in financial trouble and gets an offer of a million dollars to appear in a movie. It's a trap, of course—"SM Studios" is run by the Sub-Mariner—but they do end up making the film, and "all America acclaims a new motion picture hit."

1978: Stan Lee and Jack Kirby's final collaboration is a book-length Silver Surfer story (the term "graphic novel" was still not in common use), published by Fireside Books rather than Marvel itself. It's effectively a treatment for a rock-opera film that had been proposed by producer Lee Kramer, introducing a character named Ardina, who was intended as a role for Kramer's girlfriend at the time, Olivia Newton-John.

January 1980: Stan Lee's "Soapbox" on the "Bullpen Bulletins" page of every Marvel comic published this month breathlessly declares that "the

Silver Surfer seems destined to become a big, bombshell Star Wars type of movie! It'll take a year or so to film, so you should be seeing it sometime in 1982." Bodybuilder Frank Zane is cast as the Surfer, but the film is never made.

May 1980: At the Cannes Film Festival, Bo Derek agrees to star in a *Dazzler* movie. As Marvel's editor in chief, Jim Shooter, later recounts the story, the project collapses when she insists that her husband, John Derek, has to direct it.

October 1984: *Marvel Graphic Novel* #12 is "Dazzler: The Movie," in which Dazzler stars in a biopic about herself; antimutant hysteria leads to the film being destroyed and Dazzler's career being ruined.

July 1985: *Marvel Age Annual* #1* reports on the status of Marvel movies in development: "DR. STRANGE is currently being worked on by the same folks who brought you the movie hit, 'All of Me,' which starred Lily Tomlin and Steve Martin. Also in the works is a CAPTAIN AMERICA film, a SPIDER-MAN film, an X-MEN film, and even one starring HOWARD THE DUCK. (Can you imagine Howard the Duck in live-action??) And last but certainly not least, a FANTASTIC FOUR live-action feature is being worked on by the same producers who did the highly acclaimed film, 'The Neverending Story.'"

August 1986: *Howard the Duck*, the only one of those movies to be made at the time, opens. Directed by Willard Huyck, it's the first feature film to be based on a Marvel comic.† It bombs.

Marvel Age was a monthly promotional magazine in comic book format, published from 1983 to 1994.
†There had been a few earlier made-for-TV movies, as well as a theatrical *Captain America* serial in 1944.

November 1986: Low-budget film company New World Pictures buys Marvel Entertainment Group, including its comics division.

October 1987: In *West Coast Avengers* #25, Wonder Man—an occasional superhero who would prefer to be known as an actor—has a professional breakthrough as the villain in the movie *Arkon IV*, which stars "Arnold Schwarzburger." Stan Lee's announcements of New World Pictures projects in Marvel Age #55 include "A spectacular *live-action* X-MEN feature film! A dazzling DR. STRANGE live-action motion picture!" and "A *LIVE-ACTION* original Marvel film called DEATH-CATHLON—soon to be a Marvel Graphic Novel, too!" (New World ends up making none of those films, and "Death-Cathlon," whatever it is, never sees print.)

January 1988: Stan Lee's "Soapbox" in *Marvel Age* #58 announces that Chris Claremont "has agreed to come up with the story for a big-budget movie starring—oh, how I wish I could see your expression when you read this—none other than . . . WOLVERINE!" Lee also mentions that Sub-Mariner, Iron Man, and Ant-Man movies are in the works. (They don't stay in the works for long.)

January 1989: New World Pictures, facing financial troubles, sells Marvel Entertainment to investor Ronald Perelman's Andrews Group.

October 1989. The only live action theatrical Marvel movie to be made by New World, *The Punisher*, starring Dolph Lundgren, premieres in Europe. In the U.S., it's released direct to video almost two years later.

December 1989: In *Marvel Age* #82, Stan Lee announces that "after all these years of false starts, agonizing delays and endless frustration, we're finally about to start production of—you guessed it!—SPIDER-MAN, THE MOVIE!" He also notes that an Iron Man film will be directed by

Stuart Gordon and written by Dan Bilson and Paul DeMeo. (Both projects turn out to be false starts.)

February 1990: In *The Sensational She-Hulk* #12, She-Hulk discovers that there's a biopic being made about her: she had signed away her rights to her own story, thinking she was signing an autograph.

June 1990: Stan Lee's column in *Marvel Age* #89 plugs a long list of allegedly forthcoming Marvel movies, two of which (*The Fantastic Four* and *Captain America*) will actually come to fruition in something like that form. The others are Spider-Man ("We hope to have it on the screen by the middle or end of 1991!"), Iron Man, Thor, Wolverine, Dr. Strange ("We're talking to Francis Ford Coppola about producing this one! He loves the character! 'Nuff said!"), Ghost Rider, Heroes for Hire, Ant-Man, Sub-Mariner, and Nick Fury, Agent of S.H.I.E.L.D.

December 1990: A *Captain America* movie starring Matt Salinger (J. D. Salinger's son) is shown in theaters only in Europe. A year and a half later, it's finally released direct to video in the U.S., along with a comics adaptation by Stan Lee and Bob Hall.

May 1991: At the Cannes Film Festival, New World Pictures distributes promotional images of Brigitte Nielsen as She-Hulk to plug a soon-to-be-filmed movie, which then becomes a never-filmed movie.

August 1991: In *Damage Control* #3, Albert Cleary—the Black comptroller of Damage Control, a firm that repairs and reconstructs buildings smashed in superhero fights—watches the premiere of a *Damage Control* movie in horror: Hollywood has portrayed him as a gold-toothed, pimp-suit-wearing caricature.

September 1992: With their *Fantastic Four* film rights due to revert to Marvel in four months if a movie hasn't begun production, Constantin Film hires Roger Corman to make one in a hurry on a $1 million budget.* Corman's *The Fantastic Four* is never officially released, although it *is* completed and circulates as a bootleg video.

January 1994: Toy Biz's Avi Arad, interviewed in *Marvel Age* #132 shortly after he became the point person for Marvel's TV and movie projects, discusses various live-action films then in development, including *Spider-Man* (to be written and directed by James Cameron, it "could be on the screen Christmas of '95"), *X-Men*, *Hulk*, *Dr. Strange*, and *Blade*. (All of those do eventually become movies, though much later and in very different forms.)

May 1994: *Daily Variety* announces that Chris Columbus will be directing a *Daredevil* movie. (That project eventually evolves into the 2003 *Daredevil* film directed by Mark Steven Johnson.)

August 1994: A "Marvel Movie Roundup" in *Marvel Age* #139 reports that Gale Ann Hurd is producing a *Hulk* movie, that Ernest Dickerson will be directing a *Blade* movie, and that *Spider-Man*, *Black Panther* (starring Wesley Snipes), *Ghost Rider*, and *Cage* are "a bit farther off." (Gale Ann Hurd does indeed coproduce both 2003's *Hulk* and 2008's *The Incredible Hulk*; the first *Ghost Rider* film appears in 2007; 2018's *Black Panther*, starring Chadwick Boseman, becomes one of the highest-grossing films of all time.)

August 1998: *Blade*, about a vampire hunter from the 1970s *Tomb of Dracula* series (his 1994 solo series had lasted ten issues), is the first

---

*In 2017, the TV series *Arrested Development* had a subplot about a Fantastic Four musical whipped up to maintain the rights to the property.

successful movie about a Marvel character. Directed by Stephen Norrington rather than Ernest Dickerson, it stars Wesley Snipes, who had given up on trying to make a Black Panther film.

July 2000: The first *X-Men* film, which had been in development in one form or another since 1984, is enough of a success that twelve sequels and spin-offs appear over the next nineteen years.

April 2002: In *The Ultimates* #2, the Ultimate universe's version of Nick Fury appears, looking very much like Samuel L. Jackson. Two issues later, Fury notes that if anyone should play him in a movie, it should be Jackson: "That's not even open to debate."

Nick Fury discusses the question of who should play him in a movie in *The Ultimates* #4, 2002, written by Mark Millar and drawn by Bryan Hitch and Andrew Currie.

May 2002: *Spider-Man*, directed by Sam Raimi and partly based on James Cameron's script, opens; it's a gigantic hit.

December 2004: *Variety* announces a *Sub-Mariner* movie to be produced and directed by Chris Columbus, with a script by David Self. (No such movie is ever made.)

June 2005: In *Marvel Knights 4* #19, the Invisible Woman is furious that the film producer to whom the Fantastic Four optioned their history several years earlier, despite her attempts to "hold out for a better offer—from, say, a major motion picture studio like Fox," is "rushing some sure-to-go-straight-to-DVD *travesty* into production." In the real world, 20th Century Fox's *Fantastic Four* film (with its rights sublicensed from Constantin Film) is released that summer.

March 2008: *Marvel Adventures Iron Man* #9 is, arguably, the first comic to borrow imagery from the Marvel Cinematic Universe. Written and drawn in 2007, it's part of the "Marvel Adventures" line of self-contained, out-of-continuity, not-particularly-violent stories aimed at younger readers. The character Obadiah Stane is drawn to look a lot like Jeff Bridges in the *Iron Man* movie, except in a wheelchair and looking elderly: the first publicity photo of Bridges in *Iron Man* had been published in March 2007, and writer Fred Van Lente and artist Graham Nolan may have been making a guess based on his beard.

May 2008: The postcredits scene of *Iron Man* introduces the on-screen version of Nick Fury, played by Samuel L. Jackson, and is the first sign that the movies Marvel is planning might fit together into something bigger.

14

WHAT KINGS DO

ome of the major characters of the Marvel story—Spider-Man, the Hulk, the Fantastic Four—emerged more or less fully formed in their initial appearances, with the themes and quirks that make them special already in place. Black Panther didn't. The premise of the character, as we now understand him (especially in the light of his hit 2018 movie), seems straightforward: he's T'Challa, the king of the indomitable African techno-utopia Wakanda, and a brilliant strategist with superhuman abilities and a connection to a panther god. A lot of that premise was there already when Jack Kirby and Stan Lee introduced him in 1966, and he was presented as being a very big deal from the beginning. But almost all of the apparatus surrounding the Black Panther—the supporting cast around the king and the history of his nation that are now deeply integrated with that central concept—came about through slow accretion, as dozens of creators refined one another's labor over more than fifty years.

In particular, one writer is responsible for a lot of what we now think of as "Black Panther": the 1998–2003 sequence written by Christopher Priest crystallized everything the character had been until that point and defined what he's become since then. The tone of Priest's run was wildly different from any other Black Panther stories before or since—it's basically a political comedy—but Priest's central insight was that T'Challa isn't *actually* a superhero in the ordinary sense.* More than anything else, he's a monarch. (Even his high-tech costume is effectively a badge of state.) He succeeds when he acts in the interest of Wakanda, and he fails when he acts for any other reason, *even when* acting morally is contrary to the benefit of his nation. When people expect him to be something he's not, like a superhero, that's fine with him, because that perception becomes another weapon he can use in his capacity *as* a monarch.

But—as the narrator of Priest's *Black Panther* habitually observes—I'm getting ahead of myself.

Fantastic Four #52 (July 1966)
STAN LEE, JACK KIRBY, JOE SINNOTT

Black Panther's image dominates the cover and the first page of the issue in which he made his debut, created by Stan Lee and Jack Kirby at the peak of their powers.† They were introducing the first Black superhero in American mainstream comics, and they wanted to make sure everyone knew it.

Kirby and Lee had spent a while figuring out who the character would be. There's an early Kirby concept drawing of a version of him called Coal

---

*If this argument is starting to look familiar, that's no accident: it's also true of Thor, the Fantastic Four, the X-Men, and some other prominent characters.
† This is the issue published immediately after the one with which we started our tour; see chapter 4.

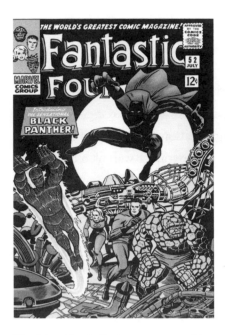

Black Panther's first appearance: the cover of *Fantastic Four* #52, 1966, drawn by Jack Kirby and Joe Sinnott.

Tiger,* who has a bright sunburst outfit, a big *T* on his belt, and no mask at all. Once he was renamed Black Panther, Kirby drew him in a black-and-gray costume with a half-face cowl—that's how he appears on an early draft of this issue's cover. By the time *Fantastic Four* #52 appeared, his costume was entirely black and covered his whole body. Did somebody realize that that would look cooler? Did somebody think that having a visibly brown-skinned character on a cover would be a problem in the South and decide not to risk taking a stand?† There are lots of theories and no evidence.

It's also worth noting that, while Black Panther was Marvel's first Black superhero, he wasn't their first African American superhero (that was the Falcon, who appeared three years later). He's introduced as being African royalty: not the king of Wakanda, but "hereditary *chieftain* of the Wakandas … and perhaps the *richest* man in all the world!" (The implication is that "the Wakandas" are a people or a tribe rather than a physical nation.)

Then there's his name. From a twenty-first-century vantage point, "Black Panther" seems like an obvious nod to the Black American revolu-

---

*Occasionally, someone suggests that "coal tiger" was then a commonplace phrase to describe postcolonial African nations or their leaders, especially Patrice Lumumba of the Democratic Republic of the Congo. I've been unable to find any reference to the phrase in that context that doesn't also mention Black Panther, though, so I'm dubious about it. (Also, there are no tigers indigenous to Africa.) In any case, Marvel much later introduced a couple of minor characters called Coal Tiger.

†For what it's worth, the Black character Gabriel Jones had appeared prominently on the Kirby-drawn covers of several issues of *Sgt. Fury and His Howling Commandos* at that point.

tionary politics of the mid-1960s. But the timing of this issue makes that more complicated. Huey Newton and Bobby Seale founded the Black Panther Party for Self-Defense in October 1966, about six months after *Fantastic Four* #52 went on sale; they took the group's name from the panther in the logo of Stokely Carmichael's Alabama voter registration project, the Lowndes County Freedom Organization. There's some chance that the names of the political group and the character weren't a coincidence, but they probably were.*

In 1966, there was louder demand for Black representation in American pop culture than there had ever been before, and also louder resistance to it. Only one of the Top 20 singles on Billboard's Hot 100 the week the Black Panther first appeared was by an African American act (the Isley Brothers, whose "This Old Heart of Mine" was number 15); *I Spy*, the first network TV drama with a Black star, finished its initial season later that month. And Mississippi's poll tax, the last one in America, was struck down by an appeals court ruling on April 8, 1966, four days before *Fantastic Four* #52 went on sale.

The story itself is problematic in fascinating ways, a mixture of racist tropes and ingenious inversions of them. It opens with the Fantastic Four flying in an ultra-high-tech airship, a gift from "an African chieftain, called . . . the Black Panther!" Reed Richards wonders aloud where the chieftain might have gotten it from; the answer is that his "little kingdom" is a high-tech wonder. Readers' first view of "the Wakandas" is in some ways an agglomeration of "deepest darkest Africa" and "Africa is a country" clichés, with spear-carriers and ceremonial dances and awkward Westernisms. The land Black Panther rules is also, from the very beginning, presented as the most technologically advanced society in the world: fabulously wealthy, luxuriously equipped, and justifiably proud of the traditional aspects of its culture, including its monarchy.

---

*Lee, interviewed by *Changes* magazine in 1970: "I made up the name Black Panther before I was conscious that there is a militant group called the Black Panthers."

Fantastic Four #53 (August 1966)
STAN LEE, JACK KIRBY, JOE SINNOTT

With the setup out of the way, the Black Panther explains his origin, which is very simple: he's king because his father was king, and his powers come from "a secret—handed down from chieftain to chieftain." (Divine right, basically.) He also discusses a bit of Wakandan history, which is so full of clichés that the Thing keeps pointing them out: "Look, kiddo—why don'tcha save yerself the trouble? I know the rest by heart! Everything wuz hunky dory until the greedy ivory hunters made the scene!"

In lieu of ivory hunters, the interloper in the Panther's story is Klaw (seen in Marvel's movies as Ulysses Klaue), whose pith helmet and all-white crew immediately mark him as a colonialist. Klaw's goal is the Wakandan "sacred mound" of vibranium—the world's only source of a fictional stand-in for uranium, an actual African natural resource, and the thing that's made the Panther and his people rich.

That's a lot of backstory for a comic book that also involves a battle with a gigantic red gorilla (and another with Klaw himself), but there are some very significant parts of the apparatus around the Black Panther that are still missing here—like his name. His late father is identified as "T'Chaka, the warrior king" in this issue, but he himself wasn't given the name T'Challa on panel until Lee and Kirby's *Captain America* #100, a year and a half later.

Avengers #52 (May 1968)
ROY THOMAS, JOHN BUSCEMA, VINCE COLLETTA

Having made a few more appearances alongside the Fantastic Four and Captain America, T'Challa comes to New York to join the Avengers here. (Why would an African monarch want to join an American superhero team? That question wouldn't be addressed until decades later, but he remained in *Avengers'* cast through 1971 and intermittently thereafter.)

He arrives at their headquarters to find three Avengers on the floor, apparently dead. Moments later, a white S.H.I.E.L.D. agent and policemen turn up and pull their guns on him, assuming he's responsible. John Buscema draws him with the half-face cowl of Kirby's early designs, so he's visibly Black whenever he appears, including the cover, although this issue refers to him only as "the Panther" rather than "Black Panther"—in fact, nobody's race is openly mentioned in the text of the story. By *Avengers* #56, he's "Black Panther" again, and once again has a full-face mask.

Avengers #73 (February 1970)
ROY THOMAS, FRANK GIACOIA, SAM GRAINGER

Two years later, *Avengers* was less hesitant to acknowledge race and racism, if still incredibly awkward about it. After a white supremacist organization, the Sons of the Serpent, attacks Black TV talk-show host Montague Hale, T'Challa goes after them and stops their agents' assault on a previously apolitical Black singer named Monica Lynne. The experience radicalizes Lynne: "What I want to know is, where were the police until the danger was over? Didn't you want to dirty your hands . . . to rescue a Black girl?" she asks a cop. Later, the Black Panther reveals to Lynne that he's a "soul brother," to her great surprise. ("Why haven't you let anyone know this before?" "I thought it was enough to be just a man! But now, I know it's time to stand up and be counted!") In the following issue, the Sons of the Serpent turn out to be led by Hale and a white talk-show host, who had been pretending to be racists to gain power for themselves.*

---

*When the Sons of the Serpent had first appeared in 1966's *Avengers* #32–33, their leader had been revealed as one General Chen, a dictator from a "hostile Oriental nation" who wanted to divide America. "White supremacist organization is secretly run by POC" is a questionable ironic twist even the first time; the second time, it's really just not a good look at all.

Fantastic Four #119 (February 1972)
ROY THOMAS, JOHN BUSCEMA, JOE SINNOTT

T'Challa notes in this issue that he's now called the "Black Leopard," explaining that "Black Panther" has *"political* connotations. I neither condemn *nor* condone those who have taken up the name—but T'Challa is a law unto *himself."* (Roy Thomas, who wrote this issue, has claimed that Stan Lee instructed him to make the change; in any case, it was reversed within a few months.)

The story involves T'Challa being imprisoned in "Rudyarda," a thinly fictionalized version of apartheid-era South Africa. At its end, the Thing blows off some steam by smashing a gate with segregated doorways.

Jungle Action #6 (September 1973)
DON McGREGOR, RICH BUCKLER, KLAUS JANSON, GLYNIS WEIN

Despite his occasional clashes with everyone from Doctor Doom to the Adversary, Black Panther really has only two durable nemeses: Klaw, the inextinguishable specter of colonialism, and Erik Killmonger, the maybe-justified-but-maybe-not figurehead of political rebellion, who desires T'Challa's power for himself. The second of those joins his story here, in the first episode of the bimonthly Black Panther serial Don McGregor wrote from 1973 to 1976.*

McGregor's Black Panther stories were enormously ambitious and thoughtful, although their poetic verbosity sometimes makes them a bit of a chore to read. For the duration of the feature's first storyline, "Panther's Rage," it was set in Wakanda, and its cast was almost entirely

---

*The wincingly named *Jungle Action* had previously been one of Marvel's reprints-nobody-asked-for titles: reruns of "white jungle queen" comics from the 1950s like *Jann of the Jungle.*

Black.* It brought back Monica Lynne, who was now T'Challa's girlfriend; it fleshed out Wakanda's geography and culture,† although it downplayed the high-tech vision of Kirby and Lee's Wakanda.

This issue ends with Killmonger having a showdown with T'Challa at the top of a waterfall, a scene reprised in the 2018 *Black Panther* movie. Killmonger is otherwise almost unrecognizable as the film's character: all we learn of him at first is that he's very big, sadistically cruel, has a pet leopard called Preyy, and has been leading a militia that wants to overthrow T'Challa's government. Subsequently, it's revealed that he, too, is a victim of colonialism: in his youth, he was captured by Klaw's forces, enslaved, and forced to mine vibranium.

Jungle Action #10 (July 1974)
DON McGREGOR, BILLY GRAHAM, KLAUS JANSON, GLYNIS WEIN

This is one of those moments where it's worth thinking about who's telling the stories in these comics, and how much "telling these stories" means (or doesn't mean) the same thing as "writing." There's one version of Black Panther's history where the character spends his first thirty-three years in the hands of white writers, being entirely the product of white Americans' ideas about Africa, and very often the vehicle for their stories about American Blackness.‡ (Those ideas, in practice, were usually sympathetic, and sometimes pretty right-on by the standards of the

---

*Alex Simmons, quoted in *The New York Times*: "There was a point where some of the editors said, 'Where are the white people?' And Don, this little short Scottish white dude from Rhode Island said, 'We're in Africa, we're in his kingdom!'"

†The first map of Wakanda as a physical nation appeared in this issue—although another map, two issues later, revised it. (The first indicated that it was on the Atlantic coastline of Africa, the second suggested that the Indian Ocean was somehow to its west. These days, it's usually drawn as being somewhere around Ethiopia and Kenya in eastern Africa.)

‡I am *also* white and American; my pronouncements on this stuff should be taken with an appropriate grain of salt.

times, but they were also iffy by definition.) In that recounting, Priest writing the *Black Panther* series in 1998 is the watershed.*

There's another way to look at the character's history, though, where this 1974 issue is a turning point for Black Panther, the first time one of his stories had a Black cocreator. Billy Graham became the regular penciler on the feature with this issue; he had previously penciled and/or inked the first seventeen issues of Marvel's *other* early-1970s series with a Black protagonist, *Luke Cage, Hero for Hire*, and coplotted most of them.

Graham opens the story with a visual flourish: it's a scene of the Black Panther wrestling a crocodile at the edge of a river, and both the battle and the story's title are reflected in the water. As usual, he makes space for McGregor's prolix captions. The first one begins: "The setting sun drips blood onto the River of Grace and Wisdom, each drop splattering in brilliant reflection from the mirror surface of the water, escorting night-tide over the jungle growth that flourishes about the river's banks."†

That visual symmetry—reflections are a recurring motif here—plays into a broader theme of "Panther's Rage." Over the course of thirteen issues, the Black Panther feature illuminates the contrast between T'Challa's domain, the surface of Wakanda, and what would, much later, become his domain: its literal and metaphorical underground spaces, occupied by both the dead and Killmonger's insurgent "death regiments." The centerpiece of this issue is a confrontation between T'Challa and a monstrous commander of the dead, King Cadaver, in a literal hall of mirrors; Graham begins that scene with a magnificently unnerving two-

---

*Or possibly 1993's *Deathlok* #22–25, the first time a Black writer (Dwayne McDuffie) got to tackle Wakanda at length.

†1975's *Avengers* #137, written by Steve Englehart, includes a little parody of McGregor's purple prose. "Thor," Black Panther declares, "the fine fool's gold of stark velvet *morning* seems to light the mottled tapestry of *desire* and *disaster* that comprises the legend of *life* for my people and *myself* in this hidden, half-slumbering nation-state we proudly proclaim *Wakanda*—but the amber eyes of *reason* widen as mauve shadows of *regret* creep all across the outside *worldscape*, and scream the bleeding need for *Panther's presence* at this time." Thor mentally translates: "'Nay.'"

page spread on which the edges of reflective panes also serve as panel borders.

Black Panther encounters King Cadaver in a mirrored room in 1974's *Jungle Action* #10, by writer Don McGregor and artists Billy Graham and Klaus Janson.

Jungle Action #24 (November 1976)
DON McGREGOR, RICH BUCKLER, KEITH POLLARD, AL WENZEL

The second Black Panther serial in *Jungle Action* brought T'Challa to America for a confrontation with the Ku Klux Klan. The series was canceled as of this issue, with its plot entirely unresolved;* Billy Graham had left several months earlier, going on to a career as a playwright and actor.

---

*Don McGregor didn't return to Black Panther until 1989, when he and artist Gene Colan collaborated on a loose, rambling serial in the anthology title *Marvel Comics Presents*. "Panther's Quest" concerned T'Challa's search for his stepmother, Ramonda, who had been kidnapped by South African white supremacists. McGregor also wrote a parody of "Panther's Quest" in Marvel's self-lampooning series *What The—?!* #9: when the Black 'n' Blue Panther's head is nearly crushed by a massive caption describing how much pain he's in, he grouses, "Do they pay this writer by the word?"

A note on the letters page apologizes: "We wish that we had time to bring the Panther vs. the Klan saga to a more satisfying close.... Don't think that the story of a T'Challa [*sic*] is at an end, however! In just sixty days BLACK PANTHER #1 will be making its appearance, brought to you by the man who co-created the King of the Wakandas—Jack Kirby!"

Black Panther #1 (January 1977)
JACK KIRBY, MIKE ROYER, DAVE HUNT

When Jack Kirby returned to Marvel in the mid-1970s, he could effectively write his own ticket. He took over *Captain America*, launched *The Eternals* and *2001: A Space Odyssey*,* and then began a fourth ongoing series—the first time his cocreation Black Panther had had a title named for him. It was a *very* sharp departure from the cerebral, intricate *Jungle Action* serial, none of whose characters besides T'Challa ever appeared in Kirby's stories.

Kirby was acting as his own editor (Archie Goodwin is credited as "consulting editor"), and anything that might have focused or directed his free-associative creativity is conspicuous by its absence. This first issue gets off to a weird, roaring start—T'Challa and a monocled collector named Mister Little burst into a house and discover "Alfred Queely—recluse, collector, and thief" murdered, holding a brass frog in his hand; then there's a fight with a strange armored swordsman, and Little notes that the frog is a time machine that once belonged to T'Challa's grandfather, then takes a jet-copter with T'Challa and blows up an aircraft pursuing them, and we find out that the frog was also owned by King Solomon and that it's responsible for Ali Baba's genie and the Loch Ness monster; then they're attacked and Little is apparently killed by minions of one Princess Zanda (princess of

---

*Both Arthur C. Clarke's novel and Stanley Kubrick's film had appeared in 1968, so 1976 was a little bit late to the post for a tie-in, but that wasn't about to stop Kirby. His *2001* series is now best remembered for having introduced the durable character Machine Man in its eighth issue.

what? shush), who has a gun that fires "nerve waves"; and then the frog summons an alien creature from the future that has the ludicrous pun "HATCH 22" written on its forehead; and—

Oh, right: Wakanda! Yes. Wakanda is mentioned only in the typeset caption at the top of the first page of *Black Panther* #1. The story is not set in Wakanda either—it's not clear where the story *is* set, but given that the cast flies to Africa in the third issue, it's probably not there. T'Challa gets a few Kirbyish fight scenes, but is otherwise irrelevant to the plot, which has nothing to do with monarchy or political power or anything else that's his domain as a character. There's no real reason this is a Black Panther story: it could just as well be a story about Captain America, or Mister Miracle, or Batman. (He doesn't actually make it back to Wakanda until issue #10, by which point we've already met a group called the Black Musketeers.)

Kirby stuck around for twelve bimonthly issues, then wandered away from *Black Panther* after leaving it on a cliffhanger; other writers and artists spent the last three issues of the series* attempting to tie up the remaining plot threads from both Kirby's story and, belatedly, "The Panther vs. the Klan."

Marvel Team-Up #100 (December 1980)
CHRIS CLAREMONT, JOHN BYRNE, BOB MCLEOD,
ROBBIE CAROSELLA, ET AL.

The then-current *X-Men* creative team of Chris Claremont and John Byrne collaborated on a short backup story for this anniversary issue. It's a team-up between Black Panther and the X-Men's Storm, including a brief flashback to the two of them meeting in Ethiopia in their youth. A throwaway line from that flashback—"They traveled together for a time"— took on a great deal of weight a quarter century later, as we will see.

---

*And, after *Black Panther* was canceled with #15, *Marvel Premiere* #51–53.

Black Panther #1 (November 1998)

CHRISTOPHER PRIEST, MARK TEXEIRA, BRIAN HABERLIN

Black Panther spent most of the 1980s and '90s as an occasional guest in other characters' comics, headlining only a pair of miniseries and some features in anthology titles. His 1998 series was the first time he was treated like a star attraction rather than a cult item. Christopher Priest and Mark Texeira's *Black Panther* #1 is one of the most spectacularly peculiar first issues Marvel has ever published, and a precisely pitched introduction to the bizarre but assured storytelling of the rest of Priest's five-year run as its writer. It does everything backwards, in much the same way that Ginger Rogers did everything Fred Astaire did backwards.*

The story opens on a full-page image that's as un-Black-Panther-ish as it could possibly be: a terrified, fragile-looking white man in his underwear, crouching on top of a toilet tank in a dilapidated housing project bathroom, aiming a handgun at an off-panel rat. This is our narrator, who presently identifies himself as "Everett K. Ross, Emperor of Useless White Boys." "The story thus far," he begins—a hell of a way to start a first issue.† Within a couple of pages, we find out that Ross works for the U.S. State Department (which has assigned him to accompany T'Challa in America) and is telling the story to his boss in Washington, D.C., although he's five flashbacks deep and halfway through the issue before we actually get to see the Black Panther costumed and in action.‡

Virtually the entire issue, in fact, is flashbacks and exposition and tomfoolery. There's a two-page image devoted to a scene of civil war within Wakanda, and another two-page image of T'Challa in suit and sunglasses, looking every bit like a 1998 hip-hop mogul and flanked by a

---

*And in high heels, as a 1982 *Frank and Ernest* comic strip by Bob Thaves put it.
†See also chapter 18.
‡Ross narrates most of Priest's *Black Panther*. As narrators go, he's not "unreliable" so much as "incapable of telling a story in a straightforward way."

pair of Amazonian women in minidresses.* A single-panel flashback to Ross listening to Kool and the Gang's "Jungle Boogie" in his convertible appears several times, as it will continue to do for the next few issues; Mephisto, Marvel's durable stand-in for the devil, shows up two pages before the end. *Black Panther* #1 makes *absolutely no sense at all* on a first reading, but it's not meant to be read just once. Its sense is meant to be unlocked by going over it a few times and returning to it after reading later issues.

Its writer is something of a wild card in the Marvel deck. Under his earlier name, Jim Owsley, Priest had started working for the company as a teenager in 1980. At the age of twenty-two, he became Marvel's first Black editor, and was overseeing the Spider-Man line a year later.[†] He also became the first Black writer of their superhero comics with 1983's *The Falcon* #1, and wrote a handful of Spider-Man comics (1987's *Spider-Man vs. Wolverine* one-shot is the highlight there), several years' worth of *Conan*, and the final fifteen issues of *Power Man and Iron Fist* before leaving Marvel for nearly a decade. He returned shortly before this series began, having changed his name to Christopher Priest a few years earlier.[‡]

For its first year or two, Priest's *Black Panther* is a manic, chronologically scrambled mass of narrative fragments that gradually click into place with one another, a serious story played as broad comedy, a puzzle box that keeps unlocking one side at a time while sealing up the next. Narratively, there was nothing else in mainstream comics like it in 1998—there still isn't, really.[§] Priest's conception of T'Challa, on the other hand, was

---

* They're the Dora Milaje, the king's personal guards, another concept that reappeared in the 2018 movie. (So did Ross, for no apparent reason other than to nod to Priest's work.)

†He clashed with *Amazing Spider-Man* writer Tom DeFalco, who later burlesqued him in *Thor* as "Aloysius R. Jamesly": a construction manager who insists his own vision for a building is more important than the architect's. Priest has described Jamesly as "a wicked rip at me, and largely deserved."

‡In credits, he's most often simply "Priest." He's never spoken publicly about the name change, but he is also an ordained minister.

§Chelsea Cain and Kate Niemczyk's 2016 *Mockingbird* series is as close as anyone's come to capturing its tone.

covertly a back-to-basics move, returning to the character as Stan Lee and Jack Kirby initially presented him in *Fantastic Four*. He's a ruler who puts his nation ahead of absolutely everything else; a technological and psychological genius who can code-switch fluidly but comes from a place that is culturally very different from America; a strategist who is so far ahead of the game that to be *permitted* to engage in conflict with him is to have already lost the fight. Priest's T'Challa always has a master plan that nobody can grasp until it plays out, and so does Priest in telling his stories.

Black Panther #8 (June 1999)
CHRISTOPHER PRIEST, JOE JUSKO, AMANDA CONNOR, JIMMY PALMIOTTI, VINCE EVANS, BRIAN HABERLIN

Black Panther was launched as part of a new, semiexperimental imprint, Marvel Knights, run by artists Joe Quesada and Jimmy Palmiotti.* The first wave of Marvel Knights books all had distinctive visual aesthetics and top-grade production values for their era; in the first few issues of *Black Panther*, Mark Texeira adds gray wash to his artwork for a painterly effect. The series is unmistakably Priest's show, though, not least because six different pencilers contributed to the series' first year.

Part of Priest's project as *Black Panther*'s writer was to address nearly every previous story in which T'Challa had appeared and to explain how all of those versions of him, with their disparate personalities and motivations, could be the same character. From that point of view, the period when he was operating in New York was particularly odd, as Everett Ross points out here: why would T'Challa have left the kingdom he ruled to

---

*Marvel Knights' other initial series were new takes on *Daredevil* and *The Punisher*, both formerly bestselling titles that had declined badly, as well as the perpetual also-ran franchise *Inhumans*. The imprint worked out well enough that Quesada became Marvel's editor in chief in 2000.

join the Avengers ("which I had always assumed was Greek for 'Gaudily Dressed Borderline Fascists,'" Ross quips)? The rest of the issue nods affectionately to Black Panther's history with the group, then answers the question: to spy on the Avengers from the inside, since they were potentially powerful enough to pose a threat to Wakanda. Even when he's been functionally indistinguishable from a superhero, he's been acting as his nation's king.

Black Panther #20 (July 2000)
PRIEST, SAL VELLUTO, BOB ALMOND, STEVE OLIFF

"Whatever you think he's doing, he's doing something else," Everett Ross says of T'Challa here, and that seems to double as Priest's statement of purpose for his *Black Panther*, as well as the source of most of its comedy. This issue is part of another story involving Killmonger, who once again engages in mortal combat with Black Panther at the same Wakandan waterfall where they fought the first time. But their physical battle is mostly symbolic: the real warfare is playing out in the marketplace. This time, Killmonger has tried to seize power by wrecking Wakanda's economy, T'Challa has responded by destabilizing the *global* economy, and the fight by the waterfall is not a melee but a formal challenge, with regular time-outs and scheduled breaks for the two of them to rest, argue, and chug sports drinks.

The cast, by this point, includes a young woman who calls herself Queen Divine Justice, a Chicagoan who's discovered that she's actually Wakandan royalty. Her first sight of Wakanda is the middle of a metropolis, where she's surrounded by stock tickers, a billboard for Killmonger's political party, and a gigantic ad for *Cats*. "So *this* is *Africa*," she says, with a look of wonder. "So primitive… so pastoral… it's just like I imagined it." Then she whistles for a taxi.

Black Panther #41 (April 2002)
PRIEST, SAL VELLUTO, BOB ALMOND, JENNIFER SCHELLINGER

Priest continued to work the disparate threads of T'Challa's history into his *Black Panther*. Storm reappeared in a story that hinted at an ongoing romantic spark between them. Klaw, from Lee and Kirby's *Fantastic Four*, returned, too; and so did Ramonda, from the Don McGregor and Gene Colan *Marvel Comics Presents* serial; and W'Kabi from *Jungle Action*; and Monica Lynne from *The Avengers*; and even Vibraxas, a young Wakandan who had debuted in a 1994 *Fantastic Four* storyline in which Black Panther had guest starred.

"Enemy of the State II," the serial that begins here, draws many of its byzantine plot's guest stars and concepts from Jack Kirby's 1977 *Black Panther* series, which Priest couldn't help but mock. It involves a second Black Panther, drawn by Sal Velluto and Bob Almond in a solid approximation of Kirby's mid-1970s style: a chortling, swashbuckling adventurer who claims to have ESP and often doesn't make a lot of sense. He—and, by implication, the Black Panther seen in the Kirby-written series—turns out to be a future version of T'Challa, suffering from a brain aneurysm and displaced in time by King Solomon's brass frogs. In the next issue, Kirby's character Princess Zanda reappears, still plotting global conquest even while she's working at a fast-food chicken restaurant's drive-through window. ("Vainglorious dullards! Speak into the chicken! *You must talk directly into the beak!*")

The shaggy-dog plot's punch line, though, returns to the cold-eyed seriousness of Priest's take on Black Panther's core motivations. He resolves a lengthy battle with Iron Man (both physical and corporate) by taking control of Tony Stark's armor and briefly stopping his heart. When Iron Man sputters his objections to those ruthless tactics, T'Challa puts him in his place: "We will never truly be friends until you stop thinking you are better than me—explaining this 'good' and 'evil' to a king."

Black Panther #50 (December 2002)

PRIEST, DAN FRAGA, LARRY STUCKER, JENNIFER SCHELLINGER

For *Black Panther*'s anniversary issue, Priest gave the series a sharp turn. Issue #50 opens with the Panther busting a series of small-time criminals and putting them into his service, telling them, "We will have an understanding between us. Speak of it to no man"—the same actions, and the same phrasing, that had appeared in #1. But T'Challa isn't actually in this issue, or the next: this Black Panther has a gun in each hand, and the man beneath the mask is soon revealed to be a biracial Jewish New York City cop, Kasper Cole.

Wakanda and its politics soon returned to *Black Panther*'s pages, but for the remaining year of its run,* Cole was this series' protagonist. Soon after it ended, Cole reappeared as the White Tiger, one of the stars of Priest and artist Joe Bennett's short-lived team series *The Crew*.

Black Panther #18 (September 2006)

REGINALD HUDLIN, SCOT EATON, KAARE ANDREWS, KLAUS JANSON, DEAN WHITE

The 2005–2008 *Black Panther* series, and the 2009–2010 relaunch that followed it, were mostly written by film producer/director/screenwriter Reginald Hudlin. The highest-profile moment of Hudlin's run was this issue: the wedding of the Black Panther and Storm, following up on the childhood relationship that had been established in Chris Claremont and John Byrne's story twenty-six years earlier and then touched upon in Priest's series.

Still, Ororo and T'Challa's mutual admiration leading to matrimony seemed to come out of nowhere, although Marvel hyped it up long in advance. (In the months before the wedding, there was even a *Storm* mini-

---

*Except for a two-issue fill-in with a different writer, set back in the T'Challa period.

series about Ororo and T'Challa's youthful romance, written by the best-selling Black novelist Eric Jerome Dickey.) The problem wasn't simply that Storm and the Black Panther never seemed to have much in common besides being superheroes with somewhat formal speech patterns and connections to Africa and divinity. It was that neither of them are actually superheroes, and not even for the same reasons—one is a champion of a cross-sectional group, the other a monarch of a physical nation.

The wedding itself coincided with the middle of the *Civil War* crossover that was then going on across the Marvel line, setting most of their major protagonists in conflict with one another, so it was presented as a "ceasefire": a big enough deal that most of the combatants show up to celebrate, along with real-world figures including Fidel Castro, Nelson Mandela, George W. Bush, and BET reporters Touré and Ananda. There's only the briefest of appearances by Hudlin's most enduring addition to the Black Panther story, T'Challa's sister, Shuri—in the comics, a grown woman who barely resembles the excitable, smartass teenage inventor played by Letitia Wright in the Marvel movies.

Black Panther Annual #1 (April 2008)
REGINALD HUDLIN, LARRY STROMAN, KEN LASHLEY, ROLAND PARIS, CARLOS CUEVAS, ET AL.

Set "several decades" in the future (King Solomon's frogs are once again involved), this one-off story is mostly giddy fan service. In this vision of what's to come, Wakanda rules over everything, and the son of T'Challa and Ororo is further cementing world peace by marrying Danielle Cage, the daughter of Luke Cage (now president of the United States) and Jessica Jones.* Also, Atlantis has been destroyed, Tony Stark has died in a failed attempt to attack Wakanda—that trick never works—and T'Challa

---

*Danielle was born in 2006's *The Pulse* #13; thanks to Marvel's sliding timeline, she's still a preschooler in new comics published in 2020. Another possible future version of her, as "the Captain America of 20XX," has appeared in several *Avengers* stories.

has retired and been replaced by Shuri, the current Black Panther and "the most powerful one in history."

Hudlin takes advantage of his story's *What If?*-ish setup to address a question raised by *Black Panther*'s Afro-utopianism: if Wakanda has been technologically ahead of the rest of the planet for centuries, was never colonized, and slaughtered any force that tried to conquer it, what did it do about the slave trade that afflicted the rest of Africa? (The regal, older Queen Ororo explains that Wakanda maintained an isolationist stance, because fighting the rest of the world over slavery "would require a ruthlessness that would threaten the moral fiber of the nation.")

Fantastic Four #608 (September 2012)

JONATHAN HICKMAN, GIUSEPPE CAMUNCOLI, KARL KESEL, PAUL MOUNTS

Shuri took over as Black Panther earlier than expected—she assumed the title and costume (and the Wakandan throne) when Reginald Hudlin and penciler Ken Lashley relaunched *Black Panther* in 2009. Between 2010 and 2016, there was no series simply called *Black Panther*. The miniseries *Doomwar* and *Klaws of the Panther* both featured Shuri; T'Challa, once again operating in New York City, became the protagonist of Daredevil's former series, which changed its title first to *Black Panther: The Man Without Fear* and then to *Black Panther: The Most Dangerous Man Alive*, expiring after a bit more than a year.

A T'Challa who isn't a king, though, is a T'Challa who is missing the thing that makes him what he is. Here, in an encounter with the panther god Bast, he becomes "King of the Dead"—the monarch of the "necropolis" beneath Wakanda, able to commune with all of the previous Black Panthers—at a moment when Wakanda's dead are about to become much more numerous.*

---

*This turn of events echoes his *Jungle Action* appearances: he's now effectively taken over the role of King Cadaver, whom he saw in the hall of mirrors in Billy Graham's first issue as artist.

Avengers vs. X-Men #9 (October 2012)
JASON AARON, ADAM KUBERT, JOHN DELL, LAURA MARTIN,
LARRY MOLINAR, ET AL.

The *Avengers vs. X-Men* crossover that ran through most of 2012 broke up the Panther-Storm couple (they respectively fought for the Avengers and the X-Men) with alarming swiftness. In a brief scene that opens the issue before this, the Sub-Mariner—also of team X-Men—floods Wakanda's capital city, triggering a ruinous war between Wakanda and Atlantis that would play out, mostly in the background, over the next three years' worth of comics. Here, in the aftermath of the flood, T'Challa tells Ororo that their marriage has been annulled by "the high priest of the Panther Clan" (i.e., himself). One page, boom, onward. In any case, he and Ororo turned out to be more interesting to read about as lovers ripped apart by ideology and the demands of state than as a happy couple.

New Avengers #21 (September 2014)
JONATHAN HICKMAN, VALERIO SCHITI, SALVADOR LARROCA,
FRANK MARTIN JR., PAUL MOUNTS

One of the central themes of the enormous, Jonathan Hickman–written *Avengers/New Avengers* serial of 2012–2015* is the conflict between monarchy and morality. Black Panther's role in it pushes that button hard. Without getting into the details here, there's a moment in this issue in which, to protect Wakanda, T'Challa would have to commit a genocidal atrocity. When he refuses to go through with it, the spirit of his father, T'Chaka, appears to him, and tells him, "You are dead to me.... You have no people. You are no Black Panther. You are no longer my son."

---

*See chapter 18.

The Ultimates #2 (February 2016)

AL EWING, KENNETH ROCAFORT, DAN BROWN

The 2016 *Ultimates* series concerned a superteam whose bailiwick was problems so large as to be essentially metaphysical. (Three of the group's five members were Black and a fourth Latina.) Black Panther, teleporting into deep space in this issue, sees a hallucinatory vision of T'Chaka telling him again, "You have no people! You are no Black Panther! You are no longer my son!"

Black Panther #1 (June 2016)

TA-NEHISI COATES, BRIAN STELFREEZE, LAURA MARTIN

The political essayist Ta-Nehisi Coates—the son of a (real-world) Black Panther—seemed, from one angle, like an odd choice to write a *Black Panther* series. His 2014 article "The Case for Reparations" had made waves, and in 2015 he'd won the National Book Award for *Between the World and Me*, as well as a MacArthur "genius grant." But unlike other famous-outside-comics writers who had written high-profile comics in the twenty-first century (like Eric Jerome Dickey with *Storm*, or Joss Whedon with *Astonishing X-Men*), he wasn't particularly known for his fiction at the time.*

Coates is also, however, a longtime comics nerd who has spent the better part of his life thinking about political power, and his five-year stretch as *Black Panther*'s writer was an immediate hit. Its opening image is, once again, a flashback to T'Challa on his knees as his father tells him, "You are no longer my son." T'Challa had returned to the Wakandan throne by this point, but the central question of Coates's story addresses a problem that had been conveniently overlooked for fifty years' worth of

---

*His first prose novel, *The Water Dancer*, was published in 2019.

Black Panther stories: Why would Wakanda, the most advanced nation in the world, have a hereditary monarchy as its seat of power in the first place?

"A Nation Under Our Feet," Coates's first, yearlong *Black Panther* storyline, is named after Steven Hahn's 2003 book about Black politics in the rural South after slavery.* In the context of Coates's story, it's also a reference to rulers holding their nations under their own feet. There are a lot of forces converging on T'Challa here, but the most challenging is a populist, antimonarchical uprising within Wakanda, whose slogan is "No One Man."†

Black Panther #6 (November 2016)
TA-NEHISI COATES, CHRIS SPROUSE, KARL STORY, LAURA MARTIN

Coates makes no secret of his affection for Priest's *Black Panther*, although the tone of his own version of the series is poles apart from it: stately, philosophical, subdued. He also has a very different conception of the Panther's relationship with other superpowered types, and here he pushes back against Priest's mischievous take on why he would have moved to New York to fight the likes of Ultron and the Masters of Evil. T'Challa calls in a group of allies to help him,‡ and notes in his narration that what originally brought him to America was a desire to expand his horizons: "I can now admit that I had it backwards. My friends, the Avengers, I did not join them to spy for my country. I spied for my country in order to join the Avengers."

---

*The story that followed it, "Avengers of the New World," wasn't particularly about the Avengers; it was named, rather, after Laurent Dubois's 2004 book about the Haitian Revolution.

†That's also an allusion to the hook of Kanye West's "Power": "No one man should have all that power."

‡They're the Crew—named after Priest's post–*Black Panther* project—who subsequently appeared in a miniseries of their own, *Black Panther and the Crew*.

Black Panther Annual #1 (April 2018)
PRIEST, DON McGREGOR, REGGIE HUDLIN, MIKE PERKINS, DANIEL ACUÑA, KEN LASHLEY, ET AL.

Shortly after the *Black Panther* movie came out, three of the character's past writers returned for this one-off victory lap. The short story written by Priest* brings Everett Ross back for a conversation he and T'Challa never got around to during his run (and throws in some scrambled chronology, for old times' sake); Don McGregor's story memorializes Monica Lynne (as well as his own artistic collaborators Billy Graham and Rich Buckler, to whose imagery its artist Daniel Acuña pays tribute); Reggie Hudlin returns to the utopian future Wakanda he'd imagined in the *Black Panther Annual* a decade earlier,† while acknowledging that Black Panther's story had already diverged from the path that might have led there.

Black Panther #1 (July 2018)
TA-NEHISI COATES, DANIEL ACUÑA

Hudlin's idea that Wakanda might someday rule over everything is appealing, but universal rule is only a utopia for the rulers. The most recent *Black Panther* series is again written by Coates and refracts that concept through the lens of the most familiar pop-culture narrative about colonialism: *Star Wars*'s rebels versus empire setup. Subtitled "The Intergalactic Empire of Wakanda," it's apparently set thousands of years in the future. Its oppressive, star-spanning imperial power is led by an emperor named N'Jadaka (the Wakandan name of Killmonger), and the

---

*After years away from comics, Priest had been writing DC Comics' series *Deathstroke* since 2016; one of its recurring antagonists was the Red Lion, president-for-life of a small African country. (Quiet coughing noise.)
†It's drawn by Ken Lashley, who had also drawn part of the 2008 *Annual*.

rule-flouting guerrilla warrior who's the hero of its slave rebellion is named T'Challa.

The relationship between those characters and the more familiar ones with the same names is only beginning to be revealed, more than a year into Coates's story, but he's working his way toward a sharp, subversive point. The powers of the Black Panther are the powers of the state; reversing the positions held by T'Challa and the insurgent who's been fighting him for decades on the page and on the screen makes it clear that the state's powers are not those of any kind of hero.

15

INTERLUDE: PRESIDENTS

The "sliding timeline" discussed back in chapter 2—the way Marvel has squished sixty years of publishing time into about fourteen years within the story—means that virtually every appearance by a U.S. president in its comics is now a "topical reference": something that didn't happen within the story quite the way it's shown. But presidents' appearances in Marvel's pages are a barometer of what the executive branch of the American government has signified in popular understanding across the past six decades: the universally acknowledged seat of power in the 1960s, an unreliable institution in need of repair in the '70s, the last hope for health care in the '90s, and more.

August 1963: John F. Kennedy (or, rather, his hair) appears in *Fantastic Four* #17, announcing his intention to push back against Doctor

Doom's threats: "We must move forward and proceed with great vigor! And now, gentlemen, if you'll excuse me, it's Caroline's bedtime!"*

September 1963: The wizard Merlin, revived from Arthurian times, attempts to find the president in the White House in *Journey into Mystery* #96, but concludes that the man he sees talking to Caroline is "too young." (Kennedy, then forty-six years old, was the youngest person ever elected to the presidency.)

June 1966: In *Tales to Astonish* #68, the Hulk's nemesis Glenn Talbot meets with Lyndon Johnson, who advises him, "Let's not jump to conclusions, major! Let us *reason* together!" A few months later, in *Tales of Suspense* #83, Johnson watches Iron Man fight the Titanium Man on TV, and muses, "If only the day would come when force is no longer necessary—when men would *reason* together, instead!"†

October 1970: In *Fantastic Four* #103, Richard Nixon tells the Fantastic Four, "Let me make one thing perfectly clear—our armed forces will be ready . . . in case you fail!" He repeats some variation on "perfectly clear" in 1971's *Captain America* #144 and in 1972's *Fantastic Four* #123 and *Incredible Hulk* #152.

January 1973: *Avengers* #107's final panel ends with the exhortation, "Use the power to vote—18." (That issue would have appeared on newsstands in October 1972, shortly before the first presidential election in which eighteen-year-olds could vote.)

January 1974: *Captain America* #169 revolves around an ad campaign by the fictitious Committee to Regain America's Principles. Its acronym

---

*"Great vigor" was a phrase Kennedy had used in an April 1961 news conference; his daughter, Caroline, was five years old at the time.
†Johnson was famously fond of quoting Isaiah 1:18: "Come now, let us reason together."

is a variation on CREEP: Richard Nixon's Committee for the Re-Election of the President, the organization at the center of the Watergate scandal.

May 1974: In *Marvel Two-in-One* #3, Daredevil sees his billy club "twisting slowly, slowly in the wind."*

July 1974: *Captain America* #175 concludes the "Secret Empire" storyline, in which the sinister cabal of that name has infiltrated the U.S. government. At the end, the Secret Empire's leader is unmasked just off panel (it's clear from the context that he's supposed to be Richard Nixon) and commits suicide in the Oval Office.†

The Secret Empire's leader reveals his identity in the Oval Office, in *Captain America* #175, 1974, by writer Steve Englehart and artists Sal Buscema and Vince Colletta.

---

*In March 1973, Nixon's domestic policy adviser John Ehrlichman had said (of L. Patrick Gray's nomination to run the FBI): "Let him twist slowly, slowly in the wind."
†Nixon resigned on August 9, several months after the issue appeared on newsstands.

The same month, "Roger (no surname or address given)" is credited with a very angry letter to the editors of *Creatures on the Loose* #30: "Where are you when it comes to Spiro Agnew, Gerald Ford, the gasoline crisis, Bebe Rebozo, the income tax deductions, the fact that the country seems to be folding up? . . . When we had prosperity, you did nothing but complain. Now you're as quiet as anything about the *real* enemy of this country: Richard Milhous Nixon! You disgust me!"*

May 1976: It turns out, in *Avengers* #147, that the president of Other-Earth (home of the Squadron Supreme) is Nelson Rockefeller—Gerald Ford's vice president in the real world—and that his mind is being controlled by the serpent demon Set.†

July 1976: The letter column of *Howard the Duck* #4 announces Howard's impending run for president with the All-Night Party. (The slogan on the campaign buttons sold by writer Steve Gerber: "Get Down, America!"‡) Over the following months, Howard survives assassination attempts from various industries he's antagonized, but a doctored photo ends up sinking his candidacy.

August 1976: Gerald Ford tells New Yorkers to take up arms against police and superheroes in *Daredevil* #136, thanks to a deepfake video created by the Jester.§ (In October 1975, the real Ford had announced that

---

*The unsigned response, in part: "We never have—and never will—take a position for or against an individual candidate or official. That is simply not our right. Moreover, on February 6th, 1974, as this letters section is being composed, we do not know whether or not President Nixon is guilty of anything!"
†On the same world, Nighthawk later becomes president, but is *also* possessed, this time by the Overmind. Other American presidents in various issues' alternate worlds have included Kitty Pryde, G. W. Bridge, Reed Richards, Captain America, Norman Osborn, the Red Skull, Luke Cage (see chapter 14), Kamala Khan (see chapter 20), and Doctor Doom.
‡It took me a solid thirty years to realize that the joke was that ducks have down.
§The term "deepfake" wasn't coined for another four decades or thereabouts, but it's the same idea.

he would veto federal assistance for New York City, then on the verge of bankruptcy; the *New York Daily News* famously ran the headline: FORD TO CITY: DROP DEAD.)

May 1977: In *Marvel Two-in-One* #27, Deathlok the Demolisher is brainwashed into attempting to assassinate Jimmy Carter at his inauguration.

November 1977: A mind-controlled Carter prepares to turn the White House over to Doctor Doom in *Champions* #16: "All of us heah are *prayin'* you'll succeed in *unitin'* this strife-torn world." He's about to quote Bob Dylan when Doom cuts him off with "SILENCE!"

September 1979: A speech by Carter concerning the energy crisis of the time—roughly a paraphrase of the "Moral Equivalent of War" address he'd delivered in April 1977, but apparently original to writer Chris Claremont—is the centerpiece of *Marvel Team-Up* #85. It's presented very sympathetically, although it's rendered in Carter's Georgia accent: "It mattuhs not whether world crude oil reserves are sufficient to meet this yeah's needs ... or those of the next decade."

October 1980: In *Captain America* #250, Cap considers running for president as an independent candidate with the "New Populist Party."*

February 1984: A street gang kidnaps Ronald Reagan and raises his consciousness by educating him about inequality in *The Falcon* #4. When he's released, Reagan goes on TV to announce, "I now have a deeper insight and a fresher commitment to the needs of the people—*all* the people."

---

*In that year's actual presidential election, independent candidate John Anderson won 6.6 percent of the vote.

September 1988: In *Captain America* #345, Ronald and Nancy Reagan are restored to human form after the villainous Viper turns them (and everyone else in Washington, D.C.) into snake people. The president declares that the problems came about because he'd delegated responsibilities to other people, and that anyway his own memory is very foggy.*

July 1989: The cover of *Amazing Spider-Man* #317 plays on a pair of George H. W. Bush quotes from the 1988 presidential campaign: "Has Venom become kinder and gentler? Read our lips, Spidey—NO WAY!"

August 1990: In *Fantastic Four* #343, the Human Torch realizes that he's on a parallel Earth when he discovers that Dan Quayle (then George H. W. Bush's vice president) is president.

1992: In *Marvel Collector's Edition* #1 (a comic given away to buyers of the candy Charleston Chew), Spider-Man tells the Eel, "I know Electro, I've beaten Electro to a pulp, and you, my confused friend, are no Electro"—a riff on Lloyd Bentsen's comeback to Quayle at the October 5, 1988, vice-presidential debate: "I knew Jack Kennedy. Jack Kennedy was a friend of mine. Senator, you're no Jack Kennedy."†

February 1992: In *West Coast Avengers* #79, George H. W. Bush and Dan Quayle react to the appearance of the demon Satannish: "How big is that thing, Dan?" "B-big enough to take people's minds off the economy, sir!" "My gosh! That *is* big!"

---

*Readers could not have missed the parallels to the Iran–Contra scandal, and to Reagan brushing off difficult questions on similar grounds.
†It remained a familiar enough quote that Kurse could paraphrase it in 1995's *Thor* #487: "I know Thor. Thor has been a friend to me. And you, deceiver—are no Thor!"

August 1993: In *Nomad* #16, Nomad has to pay for a painfully expensive prescription drug, and thinks, "It's up to Hilary [*sic*] now, I guess."*

February 1994: The supervillain Sidewinder, in *Captain America* #424, explains that he needs money for an operation for his daughter: "Until Hillary's national health care program goes into effect, I have no medical coverage or insurance. With my credentials, it's hard to get."

May 1994: Deadpool explains why he's acting heroically (for a change) in *Secret Defenders* #15: "What can I say? I go where the bucks are… and with Clinton's health plan 'round the bend, good medical benefits are a definite plus!"

March 1996: *Prime/Captain America* #1 involves an evil alternate-universe Bill Clinton, "who never got into Oxford and used his law degree to become a small-time government fixer."

May 2001: In *Amazing Spider-Man Annual 2001*, Aunt May notes that her friend Anna Watson, now living in Florida, "*thought* she was voting for that nice Al Gore and ended up voting for that *horrible* fellow instead. And I don't know if I'll *ever* understand *who* exactly this *Chad* person was?"†

September 2001: Hillary Clinton appears as president in *Fantastic Four Annual 2001*, thanks to a reality warp.

---

*Shortly after taking office in 1993, President Bill Clinton announced a task force on health care reform, headed by First Lady Hillary Rodham Clinton. The potential plan was the subject of enormous national debate before Congress failed to pass a final version in August 1994.

†The joke will be painfully evident to anyone who lived through *Bush v. Gore*, but the dispute over the 2000 presidential election involved "hanging chads"—bits of paper attached to Florida's punch-card ballots.

Barack Obama gives a thumbs-up on the cover of 2009's *Amazing Spider-Man* **#583, drawn by Phil Jimenez.**

May 2006: George W. Bush is only willing to communicate via a rubber duck in *X-Statix Presents: Dead Girl* #3. ("Mr. President can't hear you. My name's Ducky Wucky.")

March 2009: *Amazing Spider-Man* #583, featuring a backup story in which Spider-Man meets the newly elected Barack Obama—who had collected Spider-Man comics as a kid—goes into five printings (with Obama giving him a big thumbs-up on the cover) and sells more than five hundred thousand copies.

February 2010: In *Captain America: Reborn* #5, Steve Rogers returns as Captain America, possessed by his old Nazi nemesis the Red Skull, and attacks Bucky Barnes in front of the Lincoln Memorial while half-quoting Ronald Reagan's 1984 campaign slogan: "Time for a new morning in America." Shortly thereafter, once Rogers has shaken off the possession, Barack Obama gives him a presidential pardon in *Captain America: Who Will Wield the Shield?* #1.

August 2016: The *Vote Loki* miniseries concerns the trickster god's presidential campaign. (He loses, but the story's conclusion implies that his real goal was to swing the election by splitting the vote.) Loki's platform is simple: "I'm going to lie right to your face and you're gonna love it."

16

THE IRON PATRIOT ACTS

This leg of our tour is a bit different from its previous long segments, which have focused on particular characters or teams. But the dominant force within the broad Marvel narrative over the past fifteen years is *events*: the stories that are explicitly shared among multiple series and alter the environment in which all of those series take place.

Event comics annoy a lot of longtime readers, especially the more obsessive-compulsive readers among us, who fear that they'll have to buy dozens of other comics to understand what's happening in the particular series they like (mostly untrue, fortunately). They also sell better than almost any other new periodical comics, especially in collected form, and often boost the sales of ongoing series that tie in with them. There are now readers who *only* (or mostly) care about the more-continuous-than-not chain of event comics that began with 2005's *House of M* and runs through *Civil War* (2006), *World War Hulk* (2007), and onward.

No other kind of narrative art does quite what event comics can do:

examining pivotal moments in a huge, ongoing story from multiple perspectives at once, and allowing the audience to choose which of those perspectives they want to experience. Marvel's events often concern political crises of one kind or another, none more explicitly than the subject of this chapter.

The best work of fiction I've seen about life under the Donald Trump administration—the one that most accurately captures the slow-grinding despair and tension of that period in American culture—is "Dark Reign," which spans roughly three hundred issues that Marvel Comics published during the first year of the Barack Obama administration. Its cornerstone episode, *Dark Avengers* #1, came out January 21, 2009, the day after Obama's inauguration.

"Dark Reign" is the story of what happens after a genuinely malign individual ascends to political power and empowers his cronies to do what they will. The character in question is Norman Osborn, the sociopathic businessman who had first appeared as Spider-Man's nemesis the Green Goblin in the mid-1960s. For the entirety of 2009, he and his allies were everywhere, and nearly every Marvel series set in the present day on Earth became, to one extent or another, about survival in the time of Osborn.

More broadly, "Dark Reign" is about the way totalitarian regimes gain and keep power. They focus attention on a crisis, real or invented; they present a charismatic leader's harsh solutions as the only effective answer. As soon as they've attained power, they consolidate state forces under their control, undermine trust in the institutions that would ordinarily act as checks on them, and form covert alliances to defang or destroy resistance—all of which Osborn does.

Marvel didn't publish any comic book called, simply, *Dark Reign*, although there were a bunch that had "Dark Reign" in their titles.* The

---

*Some long-running series temporarily had a sinister little "Dark Reign" logo plopped above their titles, in a stylized typeface with the ragged outline of rotting wood.

story has no central narrative, just an overwhelming, fluctuating political atmosphere permeating comics published between December 2008 and December 2009, bookended by two more traditionally structured event comics: *Secret Invasion*, which ran through most of 2008, and *Siege*, which unfolded over the initial third of 2010. And its form—dozens of intersecting threads all moving from a shared starting point to a shared destination—is the sort of thing that can really *only* be pulled off in the context of corporate-owned mainstream comics.

As grim as the scenarios it depicts are, "Dark Reign" was hugely entertaining at the time of its publication, and it's remained so as the American political landscape has grown bleaker. It feels like a pointed satire of what the nation would become a decade later; its writers weren't clairvoyant, exactly, but they had a very good handle on the way far-right politics were already using media.

That's writers, plural: there wasn't a particular writer running the whole show, or a particular artist controlling its look. Still, three of the most interesting comics writers of that moment in mainstream comics had an especially strong impact on "Dark Reign," although one of them didn't actually write a word of it.

Thunderbolts #110 (March 2007)
WARREN ELLIS, MIKE DEODATO JR., RAIN BEREDO

The special presence was Warren Ellis, a caustic, intellectually omnivorous British writer with a particular gift for sprucing up long-running characters. (He generally tends to write a storyline or two, to lay out a new concept and demonstrate its execution, and then move on.) Ellis's voice and concepts echo throughout "Dark Reign," even in his absence.

In 2004, he and artist Adi Granov had relaunched *Iron Man* with a six-issue story called "Extremis" that effectively transformed Iron Man's alter ego Tony Stark, who was then still a representative of an aging generation of military technology, into a living mass of digital data occupying human flesh. Then Ellis moved on to *Thunderbolts*.

That series had been playing out variations on its clever conceit—a group of veteran villains pose as superheroes, doing the right things for the wrong reasons—since it began in 1997. A decade into its run, Ellis and artist Mike Deodato Jr. took over for a pair of bloody, viciously satirical storylines. Their Thunderbolts are an unstable group of thugs, manipulators, and amoral opportunists working for the American government under Norman Osborn's supervision, while backstabbing and scheming against one another.

Osborn, as Ellis writes him, is a terrifying figure, a rageful, murderous sociopath who has learned how to veil his madness. He presents his cruelty as seriousness and his vendettas as strategic alliances, and he's managed to convince everyone that he's a born leader, even as he's inches away from snapping.

He's also an expert at using right-wing media to shore up his power: this first Ellis and Deodato issue introduces "Fix News" ("Giving You Your Opinion"), which presents Osborn's rise as "a tale of true redemption." Midway through the story, we see an ad broadcast on the Fix channel for Thunderbolts action figures made by "Mittelwerk": an unsubtle conflation of toy maker Mattel with a World War II–era German weapons factory that ran on slave labor.

New Avengers #47 (January 2009)
BRIAN MICHAEL BENDIS, BILLY TAN, MATT BANNING, MICHAEL GAYDOS, JUSTIN PONSOR

This is the only Marvel comic in which Donald Trump has, to date, been shown on panel. (He appears very briefly, threatening legal action after Luke Cage has indignantly lifted his limousine out of traffic to let an ambulance through.) Trump's subsequent, uncharacteristic-for-presidents invisibility in Marvel's comics may or may not have anything to do with the fact that one of his major real-world donors and close associates, Ike Perlmutter, has been the CEO of Marvel Comics, and then of Marvel Entertainment, since 2005.

In any case, *New Avengers* #47 was written by the second of the three muses of "Dark Reign," the superprolific Brian Michael Bendis. Between 2000 and 2018, Bendis wrote more comics for Marvel than anyone else, sometimes juggling five or more simultaneous ongoing series; from 2004 to 2012, those always included *New Avengers*, and often at least one or two other *Avengers* series or miniseries that spun out of it.

Bendis was an unusual kind of writer for Marvel, much more deeply invested in characters' personalities and interactions, and how they express themselves in language and action, than in the specifics of plotting beyond landscape-altering incidents. The archetypal Bendis premise is "the balance of power has just radically shifted; now, how does everyone react?"

Bendis-era *New Avengers* was ostensibly about a team, but during line-wide events it often spotlighted a single character at a time. *New Avengers* #47–49 focused on how Luke Cage is affected by a power shift that took place at the conclusion of *Secret Invasion*, which was published the same day as this issue: Norman Osborn's abrupt rise to power.

Secret Invasion #8 (January 2009)
BRIAN MICHAEL BENDIS, LEINIL FRANCIS YU, MARK MORALES, LAURA MARTIN

The eight-issue *Secret Invasion* miniseries was the core of an event that had been foreshadowed for close to a year and ran through the second half of 2008, accompanied by a fusillade of tie-ins and spin-offs. Its premise was that Skrulls, the shape-changing aliens who had first appeared in Stan Lee and Jack Kirby's second issue of *Fantastic Four*, had covertly infiltrated the Earth (preparing to conquer it out of religious devotion), and had replaced superheroes and their allies with Skrull double agents. The setup suggested that the story would be resolved when the heroes beat the Skrulls, and then everybody could get back to their business.

The twist at the end of *Secret Invasion*, though, is that its "resolution" upends everything. Norman Osborn, backed by the Thunderbolts, charges into the final battle against the Skrulls and personally kills the invaders' leader—which is when he starts following the totalitarian playbook in earnest. Osborn immediately parlays his victory into first demonizing Tony Stark, who was at the time not just Iron Man but the director of S.H.I.E.L.D., and then assuming Stark's role as the person in charge of both American superheroes and national peacekeeping.* He also dismantles S.H.I.E.L.D., takes over its technological resources, and builds a new organization called H.A.M.M.E.R.†

The final image of *Secret Invasion* is not only not a denouement, it's a cliffhanger. Osborn, having moved into the Avengers' headquarters, meets in its basement with a group he's called together: Namor, Emma Frost, Doctor Doom, Loki, and the Hood, all of whom are, to one extent or another, very bad news. His initial speech to them trails off in midutterance...

Secret Invasion: Dark Reign #1 (February 2009)
BRIAN MICHAEL BENDIS, ALEX MALEEV, DEAN WHITE

... and resumes in this one-shot, published a week later. It's one of the "bottle episodes" that are among Bendis's specialties—a story set in the small rooms where political power-brokering happens, whose drama comes almost entirely from its dialogue.‡ The cabal Osborn has organized is

---

*All of this takes most of the story's characters by surprise, but it had been set up well in advance, too—partly in *Thunderbolts*, which was to be expected, and partly in *Deadpool*, which wasn't.

†Nobody ever figures out what H.A.M.M.E.R. might be an acronym for.

‡Its artist, Alex Maleev, had drawn most of Bendis's lengthy *Daredevil* run a few years earlier. He apparently uses photographic models for most of his characters, which is why Namor, whose facial features are usually drawn as not exactly human, looks really wrong for most of this issue.

made up of characters who have something to gain from an alliance. All but Loki oversee communities or nations (and Loki aspires to); all but the firmly criminal-minded Hood have variously been regarded as villains and as heroes. Osborn himself, as we see in the issue's coda, is still violently insane. And now they're running everything, even as they mostly regard one another with suspicion or hostility.

Uncanny X-Men Annual #2 (March 2009)
MATT FRACTION, MITCH BREITWEISER, DANIEL ACUÑA, ELIZABETH DISMANG BREITWEISER

Once Osborn and his cronies were in place, a substantial part of "Dark Reign" dealt with various kinds of political resistance. This story, which partly takes place during the same meeting as *Secret Invasion: Dark Reign*, sets up a thread in 2009's *X-Men* titles about resistance from inside the inner circle of a toxic power structure. Focusing on the history of the personal and political relationship between Emma Frost of the X-Men and Namor, the Sub-Mariner, it was written by the third of the major voices behind "Dark Reign," Matt Fraction.

Fraction is something of a disciple of Warren Ellis—he had been a prominent member of Ellis's online forum around the turn of the century. Like Bendis, Fraction specializes in constructing showcases for particular artists' gifts, and in deep dives into individual characters. In the service of setting up the roles both protagonists will play over the next year, the narrative here alternates between present-day sections (with rough-textured line art by Mitch Breitweiser, colored by Elizabeth Breitweiser with a deliberately limited palette—each scene is lit to include only gradations of one or two major hues) and flashbacks (with painterly, full-spectrum digital artwork by Daniel Acuña). Both Frost and Namor, it emerges, are certain that a covert partnership *within* Osborn's uneasy alliance could do them some good; they're also both willing to forfeit whatever principles they've got left to protect the people in their charge.

Thunderbolts #128 (March 2009)

ANDY DIGGLE, ROBERTO DE LA TORRE, FRANK MARTIN

One glitch in the premise of "Dark Reign" was the warm feelings Marvel's creators and readers generally had for the actual change that had just come to American government. Osborn running a black-ops team made some sense; Osborn as a national hero condoned by the Obama administration was hard to credit.

The two-part story that starts in this issue of *Thunderbolts* tries to smooth that over. Osborn, its first page informs us, has been given his new role "by the outgoing President." The new president is drawn as Obama, but isn't named within the story either. He brings Osborn aboard an Air Force One flight, along with the Hulk-affiliated psychiatrist Doc Samson, who confronts Osborn with evidence of his recent crimes. Osborn's defense is that, as the movie *Spider-Man: Into the Spider-Verse* put it later, anyone can wear the mask. To underscore his point, the plane is promptly attacked by a "Green Goblin." Osborn throws him out the hatch, then gets news media to propagate the idea that his quick thinking and heroism have rescued Obama from an assassination attempt by Samson and whoever was wearing that Goblin outfit. (The attack, of course, is Osborn's own plan, executed by the disguised Thunderbolts.)

Dark Avengers #1 (March 2009)

BRIAN MICHAEL BENDIS, MIKE DEODATO JR., RAIN BEREDO

For the four years leading up to "Dark Reign," the Bendis-written *New Avengers* had been Marvel's bestselling ongoing title and a focal point for stories whose effect rippled out to the rest of the line. But the overturning of established orders within the story extended to the presentation of the story itself; *Dark Avengers* elbowed *New Avengers* out of that top position for the "Dark Reign" year.

The opening insult of *Dark Avengers* is Osborn outfitting himself with a suit of Iron Man's armor that he's appropriated and repainted red, white, and blue, and declaring himself "the Iron Patriot"—a combination of Iron Man and Captain America. In case anybody has missed that this is a story about political propaganda, the first issue ends with him appearing on TV to introduce his team, declaring, "My name is Norman Osborn and I approve these Avengers!" Most of them are actually either dupes (Marvel Boy, the Sentry) or murderous psychopaths who can pass for the characters they're impersonating: "Hawkeye" is really Bullseye, "Spider-Man" is really Venom, "Wolverine" is really Wolverine's horrible son, Daken, and so on.

In its visual and narrative tone, *Dark Avengers* is an extension of Warren Ellis and Mike Deodato Jr.'s *Thunderbolts*. "While I was putting [*Secret Invasion*] together," Bendis later noted in an interview with the comics news site *Newsarama*, "Warren's *Thunderbolts* run made it very clear that if one would choose to do so, Norman was on track to head toward this kind of storyline, very organically, very in-character, and very much within the realm of what was going on. When Warren left *Thunderbolts*, I kind of raised my hand and said, 'Hey, you know that thing with the thing there? This is it.' And everyone said yes, including Warren, thank God in heaven, and I got to go write my Warren Ellis fan fiction." The resemblance between the two series also has a lot to do with the presence of Deodato, who's got a gift for evoking doomy, glowering moods: brutal industrial architecture, freezing-cold conference rooms, and dramatically canted angles.

New Avengers #50 (April 2009)
BRIAN MICHAEL BENDIS, BILLY TAN, MATT BANNING, JUSTIN PONSOR, ET AL.

Bendis's parallel series, *New Avengers*, spends the "Dark Reign" year on the defensive—the opposition faction to a regime that refuses to play by the rules. Its characters are constantly ambushed or compromised or in hiding, their resources (and the series' pages) spent on dealing with Osborn's associate the Hood and his army of conventional supervillains, while Osborn and company continue to cause havoc elsewhere.

This issue begins with the cast of *New Avengers* watching Osborn's televised announcement from *Dark Avengers* and reacting to it. The scene repeats identical panels of artwork several times in a row, both as a joking way of suggesting that nobody's moving and as a way to squeeze in dozens of word balloons' worth of Bendis's snappy, David Mamet–inflected dialogue.

Another of Bendis's signature gestures is incorporating pages drawn by guest artists into anniversary issues. Here, those make up a long, chaotic fight scene, each page narrated from a different character's point of view. The physical fight resolves nothing, though. The real challenge to Osborn comes at the end, when Ronin* goes on television to announce that "the Hood is working with or for Norman Osborn"—he doesn't even know which, or have any proof—and demand that they be stopped.

Dark Avengers #5 (August 2009)
BRIAN MICHAEL BENDIS, MIKE DEODATO JR., RAIN BEREDO

Considered as a superhero story, this issue of *Dark Avengers* is perfectly fine; considered as a satirical portrait of a sick administration, it's a gem. Its centerpiece is Osborn being interviewed on TV to respond to Ronin's accusations and to discuss his history as the murderous Green Goblin. Bendis's dialogue for him has the earnest timbre of a professional liar on a Sunday-morning talk show, as he explains away his supervillain career as a trauma that he's overcome ("I was suffering from a severe chemical

---

*Ronin is a costumed identity that's been used by a handful of different characters; here, as in *Avengers: Endgame*, he's Clint Barton, aka Hawkeye.

imbalance. One I was born with. Like millions of Americans"). Deodato gets those speeches across with superbly rendered body language: we see Osborn letting his eyes fall into shadow in sorrow, pausing for a prayerful moment, leaning back into his palms and half smiling.

A television interview with Norman Osborn in *Dark Avengers* #5, 2009, written by Brian Michael Bendis and drawn by Mike Deodato.

The rest of the issue is mostly devoted to what's going on back home with his "Avengers": they're squabbling with one another, jostling for dominance with insults and threats and a catastrophically dumb sexual liaison. Ares, the god of war, has a domestic life that's falling apart. The Sentry, ostensibly the most formidable member of the group, is so terrified of his own dark side that he's becoming untethered from reality. All that's holding Osborn's group together is the momentum of his deceptions.

The Invincible Iron Man #8 (February 2009)
MATT FRACTION, SALVADOR LARROCA, FRANK D'ARMATA

From 2008 to 2012, *The Invincible Iron Man* was written by Matt Fraction and drawn by Salvador Larroca—one of the longest continuous writer/artist runs in Marvel's history. It looked more like the then new Marvel Cinematic Universe than any other comic book at the time: Larroca drew most of his characters from photographic models, tended to stage scenes with the sort of wide horizontal shots one might see on a movie screen (sometimes with a touch of "lens flare" or blurring added by Frank D'Armata's coloring), and even borrowed a visual device from the first *Iron Man* movie, showing Tony Stark's face within the dark interior of the Iron Man mask, with the holographic projections he's "seeing" superimposed on it. The digital effects and textures of Larroca and D'Armata's artwork here already mark it strongly as a product of the consumer software of 2009. In this case, though, that's a good thing: old issues of *Iron Man*, in particular, are more interesting the more they reflect the technology of their moment.

The Fraction and Larroca *Invincible Iron Man* was built on the groundwork of Warren Ellis and Adi Granov's "Extremis" sequence from a few years earlier. Ellis had suggested there that the military-industrial complex—the web of institutions that Iron Man has always represented—had become much more about data and surveillance than about conventional armaments. Fraction runs with that idea for "World's Most Wanted," the *Iron Man* storyline that spans the year of "Dark Reign."

Cameras and video monitors are everywhere in this series, and technology and information are tools of control on every level*—and Iron Man is made of technology and information. He spends the year of "World's

---

*"World's Most Wanted" also brings back Iron Man's old nemesis the Controller, who makes little gizmos that literally enslave the people to whom they're attached.

Most Wanted" deliberately and progressively ruining himself as Osborn builds himself up; he erases his own memories and identity to keep them from becoming Osborn's assets. "Dark Reign" inverted the normal social and political order of the Marvel story, and *Invincible Iron Man* followed that prompt. Tony Stark, who had been an exemplar of genius and wealth for decades' worth of stories, becomes a desperate, isolated fugitive, making increasingly stupid mistakes as he heroically destroys his own mind. Even so, he remains as arrogant and manipulative as Osborn, if less cruel; whatever else Fraction's version of Stark is, he's always a recovering alcoholic whose sobriety has become another weapon of his obsessive need for control.*

All-New Savage She-Hulk #1 (June 2009)
FRED VAN LENTE, PETER VALE, ROBERT ATKINS, NELSON PEREIRA, TERRY PALLOT, MARTE GRACIA

Not every story that squeezed in appearances by Norman Osborn in 2009 was improved by it, but this one was. In principle, this miniseries is a wholly unnecessary piece of product, drawn in a generic American-mainstream-comics-of-2009 style, and has nothing to do with "Dark Reign": it's about the cloned daughter of the Hulk from a parallel world where women and men are warring tribes, on a mission to retrieve a Mc-Guffin from Earth-616. In practice, her fish-out-of-water adventure is enormous fun, partly because of its sly comedy—it turns out that the *calmer* this Hulk gets, the stronger she gets†—and partly because it's complicated by the patriarchal turf wars of the "Dark Reign" setting. Yet

---

*In one memorable sequence, Stark goes to visit his old AA sponsor, Henry Hellrung, the minor superhero Anthem, aware that he's subjecting his friend to a government raid and interrogation. He leaves a huge cashier's check with Hellrung, assuming that that will make everything better.
†The story's climax involves her whaling the bejesus out of the Dark Avengers as she meditates: "I flow with the universe. I bend like the supple reed. I envelop my enemies."

another kind of political resistance to totalitarianism, resistance from bureaucratic structures, is the deciding factor in *All-New Savage She-Hulk*'s conflict: the civil servants whose job is dealing with visitors from alternate realities have no patience for Osborn's crap.

The Amazing Spider-Man #595 (July 2009)
JOE KELLY, PHIL JIMENEZ, ANDY LANNING, CHRIS CHUCKRY

Before Ellis and Deodato's *Thunderbolts*, Osborn had always been primarily a Spider-Man character, but *The Amazing Spider-Man* was one of Marvel's few ongoing superhero series where he wasn't omnipresent in 2009. He was *present*, though, especially in the five-issue "American Son" sequence that begins here, which plays into some of the major themes of the broader Spider-Man story: fathers and sons, power and responsibility, journalism and open secrets. Beneath the unusually gruesome violence of its surface narrative, it's about Norman attempting to force his estranged son, Harry, to follow in his path (with another suit of patriotically decorated armor), and Harry betraying his principles to protect his own unborn son. And it addresses the role of the press in a time of malign government: Peter Parker and his coworkers at the news site *Front Line* know how horrible Osborn is, but they can't do anything about him without incontrovertible proof, and some of them risk their lives in the hope that such proof might exist.

Captain America: Reborn #1 (September 2009)
ED BRUBAKER, BRYAN HITCH, BUTCH GUICE, PAUL MOUNTS

The obvious move for a Marvel story whose subtext involves political corruption poisoning the cultural atmosphere of the U.S. would be to feature Captain America, who has usually been written as the aspirational version of national identity—a representative of what the country should be at its best. Steve Rogers was off the board as "Dark Reign" began, though, and spent most of it conspicuous by his absence.

At the time, Ed Brubaker had been writing *Captain America* since the beginning of 2005, working with a rotating group of artists including Butch Guice and Steve Epting.* Brubaker and his collaborators had made it less a conventional superhero series than an espionage thriller with an ensemble cast, and politics were never far from its surface. In early 2007, immediately after the *Civil War* crossover, Rogers was apparently killed off—the sort of thing that's usually reversed within a couple of months. Instead, Brubaker's *Captain America* did without its title character for years, finally getting his old sidekick Bucky Barnes (aka the Winter Soldier) to fill in for him.

The *Reborn* miniseries that replaced the regular *Captain America* title for the second half of 2009 concerned Rogers's inevitable comeback. Two things block the return of (the personification of) what the nation should be. One is the rot of America's leadership: Osborn's H.A.M.M.E.R. has commandeered the gizmo that's needed to bring Cap back, and Rogers's allies have to fight to retrieve it. The other is the bulk and weight of history: Steve Rogers is forced to reexperience his past, *Slaughterhouse-Five*-style, before he can return to save the present.

Dark Avengers/Uncanny X-Men: Utopia #1 (August 2009)
MATT FRACTION, MARC SILVESTRI, JOE WEEMS, FRANK D'ARMATA, ET AL.

Civic unrest can become a weapon in the arsenal of toxic government, and Norman Osborn takes advantage of it here—the payoff of the plot concerning Namor and Emma Frost's alliance that had begun in the *Uncanny*

---

*Brubaker wrote various Captain America–related titles, including *Winter Soldier*, *Steve Rogers: Super-Soldier*, and *Secret Avengers*, through early 2013—more than one hundred issues in all.

X-Men Annual earlier in the year. (Their resistance from within Osborn's cabal doesn't get them very far.)

At the time of this sequence, the mutant community of the *X-Men* titles, led by Scott (Cyclops) Summers, had largely settled near San Francisco. "Utopia," a crossover between several of those series and *Dark Avengers*, begins with a march across the Golden Gate Bridge by an antimutant organization called Humanity Now! They're roughly the Marvel Universe equivalent of the Proud Boys, right down to the uncanny resemblance between their shirt-and-tie look and the outfits worn by the leaders of white-supremacist rallies years after this issue was published.

The march leads to citywide riots, which are an opening for Osborn to fly in with his Avengers to fight the mutants and their allies, then to seize more power. By the time it's over, he's debuted his own, hand-picked "X-Men" team,* and dismissed the actual X-Men in a televised address as "the mutant menace, as led by the militant hate-monger Scott Summers."

Dark Wolverine #81 (February 2010)
DANIEL WAY, MARJORIE LIU, GIUSEPPE CAMUNCOLI, ONOFRIO CATACCHIO, MARTE GRACIA

"Dark Reign" extended *Thunderbolts'* villains-as-protagonists trick across Marvel's line. Several of Norman Osborn's Dark Avengers and secret associates were featured in individual miniseries, and a couple of them took over already extant series: Moonstone-as-Ms-Marvel bumped the regular (Carol Danvers) version of the character out of her own title, and *Wolverine* was retitled *Dark Wolverine*, with the familiar Wolverine's son, Daken, as its protagonist.

Moonstone and Daken both use sexuality and seduction as part of

---

Dark X-Men, starring that group, continued as a series of its own for the few remaining months of "Dark Reign."

their arsenals, and this issue focuses on the relationship between them. It begins with a solid gag—Moonstone flying off to meet Daken, wearing her stolen superhero outfit but blithely zooming past criminal incidents and cries for help. Then artist Giuseppe Camuncoli shows us how different Daken is from his father by borrowing and inverting the visual devices of the Frank Miller–drawn 1982 *Wolverine* miniseries, which used wide horizontal panels for its violent scenes. Here, the Miller-ish panel layouts depict the peaceful, meditative lie of an anecdote Daken tells about his youth in Japan; when the terrible truth is revealed, that form gives way to a page design as irregular as blood spatters. And the detail that this is *Dark Wolverine* #81 rather than, say, *Daken* #7, is a pointed joke of its own: seeing murderous pretenders move into the series of the characters they're replacing is like a more fun version of seeing a tobacco lobbyist appointed surgeon general.

The Invincible Iron Man #16 (October 2009)
MATT FRACTION, SALVADOR LARROCA, FRANK D'ARMATA

If you're trying to survive a political crisis, the allies you've got aren't necessarily the ethical exemplars you'd want, and as the "World's Most Wanted" sequence continues, that title takes on a second meaning. It's not just about Tony Stark as a fugitive, it's about him as an object of erotic desire and the way that's become one of his tools of control almost as much as it's one of Moonstone's or Daken's. Tony has a long history of using and discarding women—in the course of "World's Most Wanted," he sleeps with two different associates, knowing that they'll have to deal with the emotional consequences while he will literally have forgotten about it.

The women in Tony Stark's life carry most of the action of his series during the "Dark Reign" year, fighting onward for his sake through their own horrific traumas. His most dangerous enemy at this stage of the story isn't even Osborn but his half-mad ex-lover, Madame Masque, whose rage and desire are inseparable.* And as his mind is fading, his longtime assistant Pepper Potts—now with her own suit of armor,† and calling herself Rescue—gets to be the real hero while he runs away.

Dark Reign: The List—Punisher #1 (December 2009)
RICK REMENDER, JOHN ROMITA JR., KLAUS JANSON, DEAN WHITE

In the final stages of "Dark Reign," Norman Osborn is sufficiently emboldened by his successes that he draws up a checklist of eight specific goals, all but one of them petty pieces of personal revenge.‡ That premise played out as a series of *Dark Reign: The List* one-shots; the headline on Marvel's in-house ads for them was "The Iron Patriot Acts."§

One of the items on Osborn's list is "Kill Frank Castle," i.e., the Punisher, the nastiest of Marvel's long-term successes: a gun-crazy vigilante who goes around slaughtering mafiosi, drug dealers, thousands of security guards, and basically anybody else who crosses him, while rarely getting so much as a paper cut himself. He's a wish-fulfillment figure for bloodthirsty creeps; he's had his stylized skull logo co-opted by American police;¶ he's somehow inspired several movies and a TV series. In the early 1990s, he starred in so many series that there was a new *Punisher* comic practically every week, all of which treated him as uncomplicatedly admirable.**

The 2009–2010 *Punisher* series written by Rick Remender refreshingly presents Castle as a walking catastrophe who brings torture and

---

*"I hope you die. I hope we both die," she tells him, quoting the Mountain Goats' song "No Children."

†Her big moment in the film *Avengers: Endgame* involves a similar suit.

‡The remaining item on Osborn's list is "Control the World," by which he means not the Earth but a research facility first seen in *New X-Men*.

§The reference to the 2001 USA PATRIOT Act can't have been unintentional.

¶In 2019's *Punisher* #14, he specifically tells off police who use his symbol: "If I find out you are trying to do what I do, I'll come for you next."

**The *Punisher Armory* specials published between 1990 and 1994 literally consisted of Frank Castle describing his guns for ten issues.

death to everyone who dares to trust or care for him, and who is completely out of his depth when there are superpowered types around. It begins with Castle attempting to assassinate Norman Osborn, which gets him nothing but a year of escalating Grand Guignol horror. The climax of the first half of Remender's *Punisher* run (the half that intersects with "Dark Reign") is this one-shot, in which Osborn sends Daken after Castle. It's built up to be the fight of the Punisher's life, but when they finally face off, there's no contest. Daken butchers Castle and tosses his dismembered remains into a sewer. List item: checked off.*

Dark Reign: The List—The Amazing Spider-Man #1 (January 2010)

DAN SLOTT, ADAM KUBERT, MARK MORALES, DEAN WHITE

As "Dark Reign" approaches its end, it makes an argument about what kinds of resistance *do* work against a vicious and oppressive government— or rather, the separate stories that comprise "Dark Reign" collectively make that argument, whether accidentally or intentionally. Individual violent action, like the Punisher's, proves useless and suicidal. Sabotage, the tactic the heroes of 2009's *Agents of Atlas* series take, doesn't get very far. The isolationism practiced by the mutant community in various X-Men titles after the *Utopia* crossover isn't helpful either.

Journalism, though: that *does* do some good, elsewhere and especially here. The final item on Osborn's checklist is "Kill Spider-Man." As a costumed superhero, Peter Parker barely manages to survive his fight with the Iron Patriot in this story, but as a journalist, he manages to strike a real blow against the empire: he breaks into Osborn's corporate office, copies some damning images, and disseminates them by way of the press.

---

*I did say "first half." That's not the end of Castle's story, because of course it's not: he's stitched back together and reanimated thanks to a mystic gewgaw, then spends awhile protecting a society of monsters that lives underground. For the final few issues of its second half, that *Punisher* series was retitled *Franken-Castle*.

That's not what brings Osborn and his cabal down, but it chisels away at their defenses to the point where a few more hits do the trick.*

Siege: Embedded #1 (March 2010)
BRIAN REED, CHRIS SAMNEE, MATTHEW WILSON

"Dark Reign," since it didn't have a narrative core, didn't have a conclusion of its own. In January 2010, it was supplanted† by *Siege*, a relatively brief crossover designed to wrap up several years' worth of loose threads, including the Osborn plot. *Siege* was a much more conventional event than "Dark Reign," with a limited temporal and geographic scope, a central title, and a stack of tie-ins. Every issue of *Siege* appeared alongside an issue of the subsidiary miniseries *Siege: Embedded*, in which a pair of reporters set out to "kick Norman Osborn's ass. With journalism." They don't, exactly—and they spend a lot of pages fending off a right-wing pundit—but they do manage to reinforce Osborn's fall by documenting it.

Siege #2 (April 2010)
BRIAN MICHAEL BENDIS, OLIVIER COIPEL, MARK MORALES, LAURA MARTIN

The four issues of *Siege* itself are almost entirely devoted to a gigantic fight scene involving most of the principals of Bendis's titles from the preceding year, plus the original Captain America, Iron Man, and Thor, all restored to their power and back in the game.

The entire conflict, in miniature, is the final page of this issue. It's another variation on the repeated-image trick Bendis often uses: four nearly identical panels of Osborn in his red-white-and-blue Iron Patriot armor,

---

*Likewise, the yearlong "World's Most Wanted" storyline in *Invincible Iron Man* concludes with the surveillance that Osborn has been using as a weapon all year rebounding against him when it doubles as a tool of journalism: he knows he can't kill the helpless Iron Man when everyone's watching the fight on TV news.

†A handful of "Dark Reign"–branded issues continued to trickle out after *Siege* had begun.

seen from above as he looks toward the sky. In the first, Captain America's shield is just visible as a tiny reflection in Osborn's helmet. By the fourth, the reflection fills most of his mask, and the back of the shield itself has come into view at one corner of the panel—what we're seeing is the split second before it hits the Iron Patriot in the face. The caption says "TO BE CONTINUED . . ."—but at that moment, the rest of the story is obvious. Once the nation's conscience is back, *Siege* implies, everything will be fine.

The remaining two issues of *Siege* are just connecting the dots. Coipel and Morales draw everyone as if they're hovering in midair, with no ground and no gravity. Osborn isn't a threat anymore, just a babbling creep with green paint on his face; one slap sends him reeling, the next knocks him out. There are explosions and dramatic deaths, none of which stick for long. Barack Obama—now only shown in shadow, and not named—orders H.A.M.M.E.R. to disband, then assigns Osborn's political and bureaucratic powers to good old, trustworthy American Steve Rogers, who, during the page break before the concluding celebration, fixes most of the bad stuff

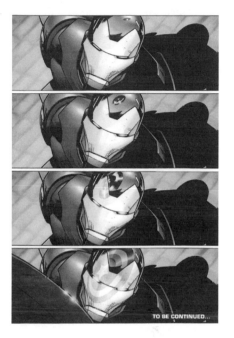

Captain America's shield, reflected in Norman Osborn's Iron Patriot armor: the final page of 2010's *Siege* #2, written by Brian Michael Bendis and drawn by Olivier Coipel and Mark Morales.

that's happened in the four years since Civil War began.* If we shadows have offended, think but this and all is mended, and so on.

---

*Iron Man, Captain America, and Thor, now alive and well and restored to their old identities again, even get to go on a little adventure together where they learn the Value of Friendship or something like that: the miniseries *Avengers Prime*, which takes place during the same page break.

Siege was immediately followed by a nonevent: "The Heroic Age," a shining banner that appeared on the covers of a handful of series. But there was nothing in particular connecting those comics to one another, and aside from *Amazing Spider-Man Presents: American Son*, a miniseries about the wreckage Osborn had left of his family, the Marvel line had much less to say about life after a political crisis than about life during it.

Osborn #1 (January 2011)
KELLY SUE DECONNICK, EMMA RIOS, WARREN ELLIS, JAMIE MCKELVIE, ET AL.

Six months after the conclusion of *Siege*, there was finally a belated coda to "Dark Reign": a miniseries in which the disgraced Osborn is transferred to a secret oubliette for supervillains, a sort of underwater Gitmo.* Osborn continues to insist that he's a political prisoner, "but that's all right . . . great men before me have ascended from prison cells to presidencies."

---

*Warren Ellis, the absent godfather of "Dark Reign," returned to write a backup story about one of the miniseries' supporting characters in its first issue.

17

INTERLUDE: MARCH 1965

The massive, intricate choreography of all the individual plots and character arcs within "Dark Reign"—the way each series' narrative strain, on its own, locks into place with dozens of others—has become a signature technique of Marvel's comics and movies. Like most of the contemporary elements of the Marvel story, it has its roots in the 1960s. In particular, there was a single month in the middle of that decade when the company's casual cross-promotion of its various titles shifted, almost as casually, into a new kind of storytelling.

In March 1965, Marvel's comics were still being distributed by Independent News, the company owned by their competitor National Periodical Publications.* Marvel had long since stopped adhering strictly to Independent's initial eight-titles-a-month restriction, but they didn't go too far over it. That month, they published eleven comic books, all of

---

*See chapter 5.

which showed up on newsstands, as usual, on either the first or second Thursday of the month. *Journey into Mystery* #116, *Patsy and Hedy* #100, *Rawhide Kid* #46, *Tales to Astonish* #68, and *X-Men* #11 came out March 4; *Amazing Spider-Man* #25, *Avengers* #16, *Fantastic Four* #39, *Sgt. Fury* #18, *Strange Tales* #133, and *Tales of Suspense* #66 came out March 11.*

The Marvels of that month appeared in a moment when American culture was shifting quickly. In the week between those two release dates, fourteen hundred Marines became the first American combat troops deployed to South Vietnam. Two groups of civil rights protesters attempted to march from Selma to Montgomery, Alabama; the first was attacked by the state's highway patrol, and the second was stopped by a court order. Bob Dylan's first Top 40 single, "Subterranean Homesick Blues," was released, and so was the Beach Boys' bittersweet, transitional *Today!* album. And the Roman Catholic Mass was partly conducted in vernacular languages for the first time.

Marvel was still far from the bestselling American comic book publisher at that point; the newsstands were ruled by the likes of *Superman, Tarzan, Archie,* and the Catholic Guild's *Treasure Chest,* which were very careful to preserve stasis. Nearly every issue of other publishers' series could be swapped out for any other, and no consequence endured beyond a single episode.† (Most of them also didn't credit their writers or artists.)

That month's Marvel comics *moved,* and moved in concert with one another. In *Amazing Spider-Man,* Mary Jane Watson appeared for the first time (with her face obscured), after being an entirely off-panel presence for months. In the World War II series *Sgt. Fury and His Howling Commandos,* regular cast member Pamela Hawley was killed off—an

---

*Some had May cover dates, some June, regardless of whether they were monthly or bi-monthly. Publication dates are from the very useful site mikesamazingworld.com.
†One kind of significant exception: in DC Comics' *Adventure Comics* #332, also published that March, the Legion of Super-Heroes' Lightning Lad lost his arm to "the Super-Moby Dick of Space."

acknowledgment of the cost of war at a moment when the U.S. was transitioning into another conflict. Even *Patsy and Hedy*, previously an *Archie*-style teen comedy, had recently become an ongoing serial (subtitled "Career Girls"): in #100, the girls, now graduated from high school, move out of their parents' homes.

Marvel's titles promoted one another, too, which was both canny marketing and farsighted storytelling. "The Mighty Marvel Checklist" in the letter columns of that month's superhero comics included brief plugs for the seven other superhero titles published that month, as well as *Sgt. Fury*.* Readers who followed more than one of them sometimes got to see little connections between them. That March's comics, though, did something new enough that it was startling: the events seen in five different series not only had lasting consequences, but had immediate consequences for *one another*.

In *X-Men* #11, the Scarlet Witch and Quicksilver quit Magneto's Brotherhood of Evil Mutants and return to their home in "central Europe." The next week, in *Avengers* #16, Iron Man, Giant-Man, and the Wasp all decide to leave the team (and Thor disappears: the Wasp notes that he "muttered something about a Trial of the Gods, and ran off"). They're about to disband when Iron Man's former enemy Hawkeye shows up, attacks them, and somehow convinces them to let him join. Quicksilver and the Scarlet Witch see a news report about that and write to ask if they, too, might join the Avengers, which they do at the end of the issue—meaning that the team now consists of Captain America and three characters who had previously been felons and terrorists.

The "Trial of the Gods" turns out to be what's keeping Thor and Loki busy in *Journey into Mystery* #116, while the Enchantress and the Executioner—who had slipped away from a battle at the beginning of *Avengers* #16—kidnap Jane Foster.

---

*The checklist didn't mention either *Patsy and Hedy* or *Rawhide Kid*, the teen-girl comic or the Western, although the latter *did* plug the superhero comics.

A page from the Thor story in 1965's *Journey into Mystery* #116, connecting it to goings-on in *Avengers*, *Daredevil*, and *Fantastic Four*. Script by Stan Lee, art by Jack Kirby and Vince Colletta.

But an unnamed kid sees the two villains and unsuccessfully tries first to contact the Avengers (who are evidently in a meeting, wrapping up their pre-lineup-change business), and then the Fantastic Four, whose headquarters are empty because the Frightful Four had left them for dead at sea in the previous month's issue. (In that month's *Fantastic Four* #39, they spend days traveling back on the ship that's rescued them.) The kid also sees Daredevil swinging past his window and tries to hail him, but Daredevil is preoccupied with trying to find the Sub-Mariner, which is to say that that *Journey into Mystery* scene takes place during the previous month's *Daredevil* #7.*

None of those stories require a reader to have seen any of the others for them to make sense; expository dialogue and footnotes provide whatever context is necessary. But readers who *had* seen more than one piece of the puzzle could feel them click together.†

---

*That issue of *Daredevil* would still have been on newsstands at the time: *Daredevil, Patsy Walker, Two-Gun Kid, Kid Colt Outlaw, Millie the Model,* and *Modeling with Millie,* all bimonthly, weren't published that March.

†A handful of much later stories return to that moment. The 1997 *Marvel Heroes & Legends* special, drawn by a group of veteran artists including both Steve Ditko and Dick Ayers, revisits the Avengers' lineup change. The same year's *Thunderbolts* #9 also centers on a flashback to the introduction of the new Avengers. *Avengers: Earth's Mightiest Heroes* #6–8, from 2005, fleshes out the events of *Avengers* #16, explaining how, for instance, the

What made that trick possible was that almost everything Marvel published, at that point, was by a small cluster of creators. Jack Kirby penciled, and probably coplotted or entirely plotted, that month's *X-Men*, *Avengers*, *Journey into Mystery*, and *Fantastic Four* (as well as the Captain America feature in *Tales of Suspense*, the Hulk feature in *Tales to Astonish*, and a few pages of *Sgt. Fury*). Wally Wood, then *Daredevil's* artist, helped Kirby out with the Daredevil figures in *Fantastic Four* #39. Stan Lee wrote the dialogue for everything Marvel published that month except *Rawhide Kid*, whose main feature was written and drawn by his brother, Larry Lieber.*

The other shift that's evident in that March's Marvels is a movement toward visual spectacle: there are a few images that serve less to advance a plot than to show off particular artists' gifts. In *Fantastic Four*, a full-page panel of "Reed's world-famous lab" is one of Jack Kirby's photo collages—not his first or his best (it's hard to mistake the curled-up bike chain near its top for an abstraction), but a forceful look-what-I-can-do gesture. And Steve Ditko's artwork for the Doctor Strange feature in *Strange Tales* #133 begins with one of my fa-

The opening page of the Doctor Strange story from *Strange Tales* #133, 1965.

---

group warmed so quickly to Hawkeye when he'd introduced himself by breaking into their building and assaulting their butler. (It was the butler's idea.) And 2017's *Avengers* #1.1 elaborates on the connections between the new team's debut and the Frightful Four's presence in *Fantastic Four* and *Journey into Mystery*.

*Rawhide Kid #46 also includes a short one-off story written and penciled by the brilliant, famously difficult Alex Toth (and inked into oblivion by Vince Colletta), one of only two stories Toth drew for Marvel in the 1960s.

vorite images in the entire Marvel corpus, the silhouette of Strange tumbling backward through an impossible space of geometrical abstraction. He's surrounded by circular nodes joined together with straight lines (Strange's body is behind most of them, but the shape of his cape curves in front of a few); behind him, there are not-quite-symmetrical starbursts and a huge, perfectly circular shape full of irregularly placed dots. It's beautiful and terrifying.*

It wouldn't be quite right to say that that March's comics were the most important turning point for the Marvel story, which had been turning all along. Still, there was *something* emerging from them, an implicit understanding that these individual series were systemically connected to one another, and that their characters could grow and change, or die, or redeem themselves.

---

*Part of the glory of that page is its coloring. Marvel's colorists weren't credited until the early 1970s, but Stan Goldberg did most of their coloring at that point in early 1965. Only eight colors appear on the page, as originally printed, and two of those (a hot red and a pale blue) are reserved for display text and a caption box; Strange's form is left white. But even when Marvel saved photostats of their '60s comics' line art to reprint them later, they don't appear to have saved color guides. The first few times that particular story was reprinted, it was recolored to substantially different effect. In the first reprint, 1969's *Marvel's Greatest Comics* #24, Strange's body is yellow, the yellow starbursts purple, the purple triangle behind him pale green, and the blue and green faces of the impossible shape he's passing through are uniformly dark blue. The newsprint on which Marvel printed comics was a slightly higher grade by that point, so the colors are less blotchy, but the fragile dots behind Strange's head seem to have been retouched to be much bolder.

A reprint in 1976's *Strange Tales* #184 returned to something like the original color scheme, but with much paler shades for everything. The 1984 *Doctor Strange Classics* series reprinted a dozen early episodes, reworked with painted color in place of the original flat tones; the episode from *Strange Tales* #133 was colored by Christie Scheele, who rearranged the colors of the big geometrical forms and added some glow effects to the circle behind Strange. And no color other than the black of Ditko's lines has been preserved in the version of that issue of *Strange Tales* that currently appears on Marvel Unlimited: now the background is hot reds, the starbursts have a digital glow at their center, and the circle is lilac with spots in three complementary shades. Does that violate anyone's artistic intentions? Maybe, maybe not; if Ditko had strong opinions about how his linework was colored, he never made them public.

18

THE GREAT DESTROYER

The comics Marvel published in March 1965 solidified the mechanics of their fictional universe: a setting where any story could affect what happened in any other. Fifty years later, writer Jonathan Hickman made that practice the centerpiece of an extraordinary sequence, knitting the historical peaks and dominant themes of the big Marvel story together, and blew up that universe along the way.

The mammoth story that Hickman serialized between the end of 2012 and the beginning of 2016, across ninety-three issues of four different series, is effectively the climax of everything Marvel had published up to that point and a gateway to everything afterward. Hickman's epic didn't look, at first, like a single enormous narrative, but he turned out to have planned its symphonic structure from the beginning and to have planted its seeds years before that. It's outlandishly ambitious and occasionally stunning. It doesn't just call back to comics by other creators spanning half a century, but makes some of them seem to foreshadow it, conceptually or even visually.

A lot of Marvel's best stories clearly reflect their moment in the culture that produced them. This one doesn't, for the most part, other than the way superhero stories have permeated popular consciousness, and maybe the general sense that everyone's destinies are controlled by a few, powerful people who are fallible even when they're not actually vicious. Most of its subtext and metaphors concern the big Marvel story itself: the creative processes that have shaped it, its overwhelming size and complexity, its relationship with its audience, those possibilities of change and finality that its form demands and those it rejects.

Hickman's story returns to a lot of the enduring questions raised in Marvel's comics from the Kirby, Ditko, and Lee period onward: the role of gods and the role of kings, where power really lives, what might be beyond the world we know. It provides resolutions, or at least way stations, for character arcs that had extended for years or decades: the rise of Miles Morales, Doctor Doom's questionable villainy and aspirations to divinity, the clash between the worldviews of Iron Man and Captain America, Franklin Richards's role as a never-aging anointed one (and as a stand-in for readers who become creators). It even addresses some of the enduring extradiegetic problems of the big narrative—readers' nostalgia for peak moments and strong feelings about "event comics," the conflicting urges for stories to both reach an end and never end, the necessity of having missed something important that happened in some comic book you haven't read. And it opened up Marvel's narrative to allow some of the changes that have come after it, particularly bigger roles for characters beyond the aging white men who dominated it for its first half century.

Like Brian Michael Bendis and Ed Brubaker earlier and Becky Cloonan later, Hickman had written and drawn independently published comics before he started writing mainstream comics. At Marvel, he cowrote the first few issues of 2009's *Secret Warriors* with Bendis before taking it over himself. His *Dark Reign: Fantastic Four* miniseries the same year led into a fine three-year stretch writing *Fantastic Four*, eventually joined by its companion series *FF** In 2010 and 2011, he also wrote a clever, history-spanning take on *S.H.I.E.L.D.*, drawn with delicate precision by Dustin Weaver, as well as a stretch of *Ultimate Comics Ultimates* and *Ultimate Comics Hawkeye* in which he first tried out Bendis's trick of telling a story from two different perspectives in separate series.

Avengers #1 (February 2013)
JONATHAN HICKMAN, JEROME OPEÑA, DEAN WHITE

In late 2012, Marvel launched or relaunched a cluster of comics, promoted collectively as "Marvel Now!" Hickman took over both *Avengers* and *New Avengers*, which Bendis had been writing for more than eight years at that point; the relaunched series were respectively drawn at first by Jerome Opeña and Steve Epting.

At the outset, Hickman's *Avengers* presents itself as being a big, fun adventure comic, and his *New Avengers* as a whole other thing, something shadowy and unsettling. Both series begin each issue with a "Previously in Avengers" page—usually a set of panels from earlier issues, explaining whatever's going on. In *Avengers* #1, though, the "Previously" page is four panels of visual abstractions, with captions that suggest the scope of what Hickman is up to.

> There was nothing.
> Followed by everything.
> Swirling, burning specks of creation that circled life-giving
> > suns.
> And then... we raced to the light.

It's an audacious gesture to start a series—especially one that was being promoted as Marvel's new flagship title—with a reminder that its

---

*See chapter 4.

readers have already missed something unless they've been around since the Big Bang. It's also an orchestral flourish, and the structure of Hickman's 2012–2016 story owes something to musical composition: themes, visual progressions, and verbal motifs recur constantly across it, often transposed or inverted or reharmonized.

The opening non-recap is followed by a brief overture: a series of cryptic flash-forwards to moments that would be seen in *Avengers* over the next few years. As the story's perspective downshifts from grand metaphysics to actual characters, Iron Man rouses Captain America from an unsettling dream—we see just one image of it, four hostile faces staring downward—and tells him that he's had a vision of a great machine, an Avengers group of unparalleled power and complexity. (Hickman, whose comics often include diagrams of various kinds, constructed one to represent the team's structure, with little character icons progressively added to its empty spaces as new members joined.)

It's worth noting that *Avengers* has never had a fixed set of protagonists. Its lineup change in March 1965, in fact, was the point at which the series' cast no longer included any of the characters who had appeared in its first issue. If *Fantastic Four* is about an extended family and *X-Men* is about a group with a shared identity, *Avengers* has always been about a professional organization, and a volatile one.*

/ / / / /

By its nature, *Avengers* is usually the home for stories that are broader in scope than most of the individual narratives devoted to the group's

---

*When *Avengers: Age of Ultron* came out in 2015, *The Wall Street Journal* analyzed which characters had appeared most often in the seven hundred–odd *Avengers* comics published up to that point. Captain America had been part of the group more often than not, with a few extended breaks; Iron Man, Thor, and the Vision were the only other members who had appeared in more than three hundred issues. (The Hulk had appeared a mere thirty-seven times—fewer than the likes of Starfox, Crystal, Sersi, and Goliath, none of whom have ever headlined comic books of their own.)

members—a framework that Marvel's movies picked up from their comics. *Iron Man* stories are about struggles for technological and industrial supremacy; *Captain America* stories are about struggles for American national identity; *Avengers* stories are about struggles for everything.

To put it differently, it doesn't usually matter much who's in the Avengers at any given time, only who they're fighting and why. The group's job is to make a show of force, often under the auspices of the American government; it's where power nominally lies within the Marvel story. The core group gathered by Iron Man and Captain America in Hickman's first issue is the lineup that would be familiar to readers who knew the Avengers primarily from the movie that had come out earlier that year: those two characters, plus Thor, the Hulk, Hawkeye, and Black Widow.*

The high-order threat they face first is a sidelong allegory for how corporate-owned comics work. The Builders, an alien race who are trying to control and reshape all of existence, have created three species who make and transform worlds. The Gardeners create life and accelerate evolution ("I'm an artist," declares one of them, Ex Nihilo). The Abyssi, who always accompany them, judge and shape their work (they're effectively writers; note that Hickman, a writer and artist who is writing but not drawing this story, indicates that artists carry most of the weight). The Alephs carry the Gardeners' and Abyssi's eggs and wipe away their failed creations (they're editors, in other words†).

There's some space opera around all that, in the course of which *Avengers* introduces a few new versions of old characters. One of them is Captain Universe, "the hero who could be you," a cosmic force that briefly possesses one person at a time and has turned up intermittently since

---

*That particular group of characters had never even all been Avengers in the comics at the same time until *Avengers Assemble* #1, published earlier in 2012.

†I picked up most of this interpretation of the Builders from a thoughtful post to Reddit's /r/comicbooks/ forum by someone with the username seer358. Thank you, whoever you are.

1979.* This version of Captain Universe is a broken woman, personifying a broken cosmos that is, by extension, a broken piece of fiction. She repeats the "there was nothing, followed by everything" speech a few times, but insists that something is wrong on the broadest imaginable scale.

Still, the overall tone of the story is jubilant. Another recurring phrase in Hickman's long story, initially used to describe what's being created in this issue, is "an Avengers world, the first of many." The world the Builders and Gardeners are shaping *is* Marvel Comics, the globally told and retold tale, the ever-expanding branded machine.

New Avengers #1 (March 2013)

JONATHAN HICKMAN, STEVE EPTING, RICK MAGYAR, FRANK D'ARMATA

The opening scene of Hickman's first *New Avengers* is the first statement of *that* series' central motif. In place of the grand abstractions of *Avengers*, we see Reed Richards of the Fantastic Four delivering the beginning of a grim speech that will reappear, with variations, over the course of the next few years:

> Everything dies.
> You. Me. Everyone on this planet. Our sun. Our galaxy.
>> And, eventually, the universe itself. This is simply
>> how things are.
> It's inevitable... and I accept it.†

---

*In 1994, there was an *X-Men/Captain Universe* comic that you could order by mail, in which the hero would in fact be you: it was available in editions with Captain Universe drawn as a man or as a woman, and your name would be lettered into the dialogue by computer, in the manner of personalized children's books.

†Hickman has a magpie's eye for interesting fragments of old comics, some of which his own comics echo, deliberately or accidentally. The "everything dies" speech evokes a piece of dialogue from Wolverine that opens 1996's *Uncanny X-Men* #337: "Things change. People change. You. Me. Every one of us... every day of our lives. The day ya stop changin'—is the day ya die."

That is an entirely different but equally perverse way to open a big-scale superhero series, and the rest of the issue is also at another pole from *Avengers* #1. *New Avengers* #1 isn't even really about a team: it's effectively a Black Panther solo story. In place of *Avengers*' grand Technicolor sweep, it's bitter, grim, tightly focused on loss and human cost, with colorist Frank D'Armata's palette largely constrained to sickly greens and sepias.

The group that's hearing that opening speech turns out to be the Illuminati, a coalition of the geniuses and kings who had been given dominion over the early years of the Marvel story: Reed Richards, Tony Stark, Stephen Strange, and the like. They'd first appeared under that name in a *New Avengers* sequence in 2006, which had proposed that they had been meeting in secret for decades' worth of comics, bending the course of events toward what they saw as the general good. At the point where Hickman's story begins, the Illuminati are two scientists (Richards and Stark), a sorcerer (Strange), and three monarchs of imperiled nations (Black Panther and the Sub-Mariner, as well as Black Bolt of the Inhumans). They all have obligations to protect their respective domains at any cost, and now they're in ethical quicksand.

Both *Avengers* and *New Avengers*, in the early months of Hickman's story, are largely devoted to men making plans and arguing. Anyone who was outside the halls of power, real or fictional, in Marvel's first decade is out of the loop, and that is exactly what leads to the disaster that's coming. "Save me from righteous men," the Black Panther prays to the goddess Bast in this issue's closing narration. His own righteousness becomes part of the problem too.

New Avengers #3 (April 2013)

JONATHAN HICKMAN, STEVE EPTING, RICK MAGYAR, FRANK D'ARMATA

As Hickman's first six-issue *Avengers* storyline was concluding, *New Avengers*' readers got to see a moment that recast the other series' meaning. *New*

Avengers #3 is as densely packed a comic as Marvel had published in decades (a *lot* happens in twenty-one pages). Its tension emerges from its characters' particular, conflicting ways of acting on their ideals.

What Reed Richards was explaining in the "Everything dies" speech—the plot device that drives the first four acts of Hickman's story—is revealed to have been "incursions," a loaded moral-reasoning puzzle along the lines of Philippa Foot's "trolley problem," with a simple if unsatisfactory set of rules. Every so often, two parallel universes collide, with their respective Earths as the point of collision. There is, conveniently, an eight-hour warning period. At the end of those eight hours, if at least one of the Earths has been destroyed, the universes somehow merge and everything's fine. If both Earths are still there, though, both universes cease to exist—and those other Earths tend to have their own superpowered protectors too.

And of *course* Reed thinks he can find a solution through weird science and human connection, and of *course* Namor responds to a disastrous success by flying off the handle at his allies, and of *course* military industrialist Iron Man solemnly lands on the idea of building doomsday devices, and of *course* the Black Panther places his nation over his personal morality. That's what they all *do*. Hickman builds the story around what an uncomfortable pleasure (but no less a pleasure for that) it is to see heroes doing terrible things that are nonetheless entirely consistent with who they have always been.

And of *course*, of *course*, of *course* the square-chinned idealist Captain America gives a stirring speech about resisting the very idea of genocidal realpolitik—so the Illuminati magically erase his memory of the whole thing. As his consciousness fades, he sees their faces staring down at him, the image we saw of his dream at the beginning of Hickman and Opeña's *Avengers*, as Tony Stark woke him up to tell him about his great idea for a bigger team.

Just that easily, Hickman shoves *New Avengers'* superheroes down a slope to hell, paved with their good intentions. The beautiful Avengers machine, we realize, is a lie: a distraction that Iron Man has sketched out to keep Captain America busy so he won't realize what's going on.* An "Avengers world" means a blighted and ruined world; "everything dies," rather than "there was nothing, followed by everything," is the real beginning of the story.†

Avengers Annual #7 (August 1977)
JIM STARLIN, JOSEF RUBINSTEIN, PETRA GOLDBERG

The first inkling that a Marvel story could be that nihilistic was a years-long sequence by writer/artist Jim Starlin that, like Hickman's, hopscotched between series, reaching its climax in this issue. Starlin has been illuminating his personal cosmology for his entire career, both in the context of his Marvel comics and elsewhere. In some ways, it's close to the sorts of delusions and hallucinations that only a few people are able to channel into art. (His stories have occasionally addressed the bonds between creation and madness.) It's nearly miraculous that Starlin was able to paint his idiosyncratic vision into Marvel's shared canvas and sell it as pop entertainment. It's genuinely miraculous that it became a centerpiece of Marvel's movies, the equivalent of William Blake's Urizen or Henry Darger's Glandelinians reappearing on cereal boxes and Halloween costumes.

Avengers Annual #7 involves a handful of Starlin creations that have become much more familiar through the movies: Gamora ("the deadliest

---

*The full Avengers team that would fill out the diagram is never completed, although a spin-off series, *Avengers World*, devoted its first fourteen issues to the kind of conventional team-adventure story Hickman was bypassing.

†Soon afterward, a character called the Black Swan—a harbinger of the incursions, whose role in *New Avengers* is mostly to insist that there is no hope—presents her own creation myth, an inversion of the one in *Avengers* #1: "There was everything. Followed by nothing. A swirling, gaping maw that swallowed life-giving suns. And then . . . we cowered in the night."

woman in the galaxy"), the six powerful stones known in the comics as the Infinity Gems, and most of all the death-obsessed philosopher-despot Thanos, about whom Starlin has been writing and drawing comics since inventing him in the early 1970s. Thanos (as well as Drax the Destroyer, yet another Starlin creation) had first appeared four years earlier in *Iron Man* #55. Starlin subsequently featured him prominently in *Captain Marvel* in 1973 and 1974, then in a 1975–1976 *Strange Tales* and *Warlock* sequence in which those series' protagonist Adam Warlock commits "cosmic suicide," killing his future self before he can become the villainous Magus. This issue's centerpiece is that confrontation, seen from the other side: Adam Warlock, his life in ruins, welcoming his death at the hands of his past self.

The Infinity Gauntlet #1 (July 1991)
JIM STARLIN, GEORGE PÉREZ, JOSEF RUBINSTEIN, TOM CHRISTOPHER, MAX SCHEELE, IAN LAUGHLIN

After *Avengers Annual* #7 and its immediate sequel, *Marvel Two-in-One Annual* #2, both Starlin and Thanos largely vanished from Marvel's new comics for more than a decade.* They came back, explosively, in 1990; a yearlong *Silver Surfer* sequence written by Starlin brought Thanos back into play, and led into this six-issue miniseries. Its premise—that Thanos has assembled the six stones of power into an omnipotence-granting glove—was directly borrowed for the 2018 *Avengers: Infinity War* movie. So was the climax of its first issue, in which Thanos kills half the universe with a snap of his fingers.

The Infinity Gauntlet was successful enough that it was followed by a

---

*Starlin did return for a handful of projects, notably the first book Marvel labeled as a "graphic novel," 1982's *The Death of Captain Marvel*; he also wrote and drew his creator-owned, not-part-of-anyone-else's-fictional-universe series, "Metamorphosis Odyssey"/*Dreadstar* for Marvel's Epic imprint between 1980 and 1986.

pair of sequels: 1992's *The Infinity War* (which doesn't much resemble the movie of that name) and 1993's *The Infinity Crusade*. Starlin has continued to use variations on its title for some of his subsequent stories about Thanos, from *Infinity Abyss* (2002) to *The Infinity Ending* (2019).

Infinity #6 (January 2014)

JONATHAN HICKMAN, JIM CHEUNG, DUSTIN WEAVER, ET AL.

The title of 2013's *Infinity* miniseries suggests that it, too, is a sequel to *The Infinity Gauntlet*—or, at least, a bustling crossover event prominently featuring Thanos. Written by Hickman and drawn by a small legion of artists, it draws the casts of both *Avengers* and *New Avengers** into a plot-dense but not very coherent storyline involving Thanos, an interstellar war on many fronts, the introduction of the Black Order that would appear in the *Avengers: Infinity War* film a few years later, and a desperate stratagem that results in the creation of a new generation of superpowered Inhumans.[†]

Invoking Jim Starlin's work as extensively as Hickman and his collaborators do here is, in part, a call to associative nostalgia: "Hey, we're doing big-scale cosmic stuff—pay attention if you remember enjoying those old stories!" But it's also a way to emphasize the spiraling horror that's at the center of Hickman's story, as it often was in Starlin's, the specter of murder appearing as a moral obligation for monarchs. The final image of *Infinity* is a visual homage to Starlin, an image nearly identical to the one with which he had concluded the first wave of his contributions to the Marvel story in 1977: Thanos frozen in stasis, his arms outstretched, reaching without grasping.

---

*Another Hickman diagram appeared in each issue: a flowchart explaining the chronological sequence of *Infinity* and its tie-in issues of *Avengers* and *New Avengers*.
†One of them is the new Ms. Marvel; see chapter 20.

New Avengers #13 (February 2014)
JONATHAN HICKMAN, SIMONE BIANCHI, ADRIANO DALL'ALPI

A version of Reed Richards, slightly different from the one we know, delivers the "Everything dies" speech, another world's champions come out of the sky, the terrible battle of the incursion begins, and then we see that all of this is being observed by *New Avengers'* regular cast, through a device created by the familiar Reed Richards.

New Avengers #14 (April 2014)
JONATHAN HICKMAN, SIMONE BIANCHI, ADRIANO DALL'ALPI

A version of Reed Richards, slightly different from the one we know, delivers the "Everything dies" speech, another world's champions come out of the sky, the terrible battle of the incursion begins, and then we see that all of this is being observed by—and so forth. The actual events of the previous issue and this one are different in most respects; their formal presentation is the same, and so is their outcome: the slaughter of an entire world.

Avengers #28 (June 2014)
JONATHAN HICKMAN, SALVADOR LARROCA, FRANK MARTIN JR., ANDRES MOSSA

While *New Avengers* is dealing with the incursion business, *Avengers* brings in doubles of the characters who starred in the first few Avengers stories, which is to say comics published fifty years earlier.* (They turn out to be those characters' sociopathic shadow selves; uncritical nostalgia

---

*That plot is a double of its own: the premise of one of the most successful "Marvel Now!" series, *All-New X-Men*, was that the original teenage members of the X-Men, from comics published fifty years earlier, had suddenly been transported through time to the present day.

for a silver age will betray you as surely as ignoring the past, Hickman implies.) That leads into this exceptionally clever issue. On its cover, various Avengers are caught up in a massive Hulk–Iron Man battle, and it looks like it's going to be another smashfest in the mode of 2007's *World War Hulk*: the return of the repressed vs. the military-industrial complex!

That's not actually how the story goes. We see the property damage the fight leaves behind, but the only "battle" depicted in the issue itself is a brutal conversation in a boardroom. By the time it's over, Hickman has implied that the physical fight isn't shown because it's not a real conflict: the smoke of battle is a smokescreen, a public pretext for more dealmaking by the men who rule in secret.

New Avengers #17 (May 2014)
JONATHAN HICKMAN, RAGS MORALES, FRANK MARTIN JR.

Instead of the "Previously in *New Avengers*" page that opens every other issue, this one begins with "Previously in *The Great Society*," and shows a scene we've seen before with characters we haven't: somebody called Sun God is giving his team an inverted version of the "Everything dies" speech ("Everything lives").

But wait—the Great Society? Sun God? Who? Did we miss something? No and yes: it's a crafty bit of metafiction. The Great Society had never appeared anywhere before that "recap." Their name comes from a cluster of domestic spending programs launched during President Lyndon B. Johnson's administration (slightly after the Avengers debuted, but in the right ballpark). They're stand-ins for the Avengers only at several removes, though; more obviously, they're a variation on the Squadron Supreme—who are, in turn, Marvel's longtime stand-ins for their competitor DC Comics' superhero team, the Justice League. Sun God, then, is Hyperion, who is effectively Superman (another version of Hyperion is already appearing in Hickman's *Avengers*); Doctor Spectrum shares her name with her Squadron counterpart, who might as well be Green Lantern; and so on. The implication is that we have shifted into reading another world's comic book. The horrible champions from another world who will come out of the sky, desperate and intent on genocide, are the ones we've been following all along in *New Avengers*.

New Avengers #23 (October 2014)
JONATHAN HICKMAN, KEV WALKER, FRANK MARTIN JR.

The pacing of the following half dozen issues is cruelly deliberate, poles away from the hypercompression of *New Avengers* #3. Their artwork (mostly by Valerio Schiti and Kev Walker) is open and airy, focused on the Avengers' body language as they come to the end of believing themselves to be righteous. Hickman's *New Avengers*, up to this point, has put its characters in situations where thanks to some contrivance or other they haven't actually had to become monsters. Now they have. They scream and hit one another, but the histrionics of "superheroes" have become meaningless. Here, they prepare themselves for the end of their own world—which doesn't arrive as scheduled. One last horrific, mutated reprise of the "Everything dies" speech explains why not: Namor, Marvel's very first villainous hero or heroic villain, has enlisted Thanos and company to help him murder one Earth after another.

Avengers #35 (November 2014)
JONATHAN HICKMAN, JIM CHEUNG, PACO MEDINA,
NICK BRADSHAW, ET AL.

"EIGHT MONTHS LATER" reads the opening caption of the next *Avengers* comic book to be published. It's the first nervy conceit of "Time Runs Out," a twenty-part serial-within-a-serial that bounces between Hickman's two *Avengers* series. Eight months, in Marvel story time, is a lot—it'd normally be at least three years' worth of comics, and Hickman's story dives right into its radically altered landscape of characters and relationships without explaining most of the changes.* Just as at the beginning of Hickman and Opeña's *Avengers* #1, you've missed something. Too bad; keep going.†

Most of the early scenes of "Time Runs Out" are focused on small moments: conversations, light action, scene-setting. The broader picture reveals itself by degrees. Everything is collapsing into chaos. Doctor Doom is up to something incomprehensibly big and awful. Hopes are successively, systematically extinguished. The question a reader asks shifts from "How are they going to get out of this?" to "They're not going to get out of this, are they?"

That's an *extraordinary* thing to think as one is reading a serial superhero comic. We know, of course, that there are going to be *Avengers* and *Spider-Man* and *X-Men* comics two years from now, that economics demand a way out. But it also registers as really, legitimately inescapable; this is a fourth-act sort of story, and everything about its structure feels like it's moving toward a final denouement.‡ "In 8 months ... time runs out!" declares a banner on this issue's cover, and the countdown continues along with the story.

Avengers #44 (June 2015)

JONATHAN HICKMAN, STEFANO CASELLI, KEV WALKER, FRANK MARTIN JR.

The last two Earths, now about to collide, are those of the familiar 616 universe and the Ultimate universe, its revved-up double that was created to draw in readers who didn't want to have to deal with backstory and that now has fifteen years of backstory of its own. The final issue of *Avengers* concludes with Iron Man and Captain America, the brothers in

---

Avengers World ran a few issues cover-billed as "Before Time Runs Out," unnecessarily spelling out some of what Hickman implies happened during that eight-month gap.

†The "five years later" transition in 2019's *Avengers: Endgame* movie probably owes something to this gesture.

‡Hickman ties off some of his plot threads and lets others drop; the apocalypse means not everything's going to get resolved.

arms whose irreconcilable conflicts have been a dissonant motif of the Marvel story since 2006's *Civil War*, meaninglessly beating each other to death as the world is ending. Then the S.H.I.E.L.D. Helicarrier, the great technological symbol of the point where their ideologies intersected, falls from the sky onto them. The two heroes' battle ends in the stupid violence that has never solved anything in their half century together, a mash of metal and blood. The last caption is "Everything dies."

Captain America and the Mighty Avengers #9 (August 2015)

AL EWING, LUKE ROSS, RACHELLE ROSENBERG

All of Marvel's superhero series came to a close around that time, some of them with stories labeled "Last Days," focused on their characters' actions at the end. The most affecting of those was in *Captain America and the Mighty Avengers*, a low-key spin-off about a branch of the team that acted as a community organization. Its final issue shows the last hour of the incursion from street level, and ends with a scene subtitled "You: 2 Minutes to Live." It's drawn from a first-person perspective: a doctor who's treating the injuries "you" incurred while saving schoolchildren thanks you for doing what you could even in the face of annihilation. "We were all Avengers," he says. "Every one of—"

And then there are no more images, just the white space of unprinted paper. A little device is pasted at the bottom of the page, as in most of the other final issues: "There is only *Secret Wars*."

Marvel Super Heroes Secret Wars #1 (May 1984)

JIM SHOOTER, MIKE ZECK, JOHN BEATTY, CHRISTIE SCHEELE

The title of *Secret Wars*—the 2015 miniseries that concluded the story Hickman had begun in *Avengers*, *New Avengers*, and *Infinity*—had a lot of baggage attached to it. The 1984 miniseries *Marvel Super Hero Secret Wars* was both an overwhelming commercial success and, conventional wisdom has it, an embarrassment: superhero comics' peak intersection of rapacity and artlessness, and the beginning of the crossover madness that's attached itself to the genre ever since. Conventional wisdom is mostly right about that.

The original *Secret Wars* was a brazen, cynical piece of product, created to promote a line of plastic toys. According to its writer, Jim Shooter, "Mattel's focus group tests indicated that kids responded positively to the words 'wars' and 'secret.' Okay." At the beginning of 1984, most of Marvel's major characters were shown disappearing into a mysterious structure in New York's Central Park, then reappearing somehow transformed. (Spider-Man had a new black costume, for instance, and She-Hulk had replaced the Thing in the Fantastic Four.) The explanations, we were told, would all appear in the twelve-issue *Secret Wars*.

In Shooter's story, dozens of heroes and villains were yoinked away to a distant planet called Battleworld by a functionally omnipotent entity called the Beyonder, and spent a year's worth of comics alternately having really big fights and delivering interminable gobs of expository dialogue about the importance of everything they were doing.* In any case, it worked: every issue of *Secret Wars* topped the sales charts, outselling even *X-Men*.

And something about the frantic escalation of Shooter and Zeck's *Secret Wars* stuck with a lot of the people who read it as kids in the 1980s. While Hickman and artist Esad Ribic's *Secret Wars* was being serialized

---

*In *Marvel Super Heroes Secret Wars* #11, having usurped the Beyonder's power, Doctor Doom speechifies: "Now, I am all-powerful! I have nothing to prove to lesser creatures—and none are my equal! I am complete . . . serene in my omnipotence! The dark, seething desires which once drove and shaped Doom are no more! Nothing in this universe—nothing of which you can *conceive*, no matter how cosmic in scope—could possibly merit my attention! For as eternity is to you . . . I am to eternity! I have transcended all concerns of this plane of existence." And so on.

in 2015, I mentioned it to a former comics fan I'd just met. "There's a *new Secret Wars*?" she asked. "Does it have the Beyonder? And is there a Battleworld? And does Doctor Doom become God?" It only kind of has Beyonders, I said, but there's definitely a Battleworld and Doctor Doom absolutely becomes God. "Okay, I'm in," she said.

Secret Wars #1 (July 2015)
JONATHAN HICKMAN, ESAD RIBIC, IVE SVORCINA

Hickman calling the final act of his story *Secret Wars* and building it around elements of the original *Secret Wars'* apparatus was an "Oh yeah? Watch *this*" move—both a declaration that he was going big and a boast that there was nothing in Marvel's history so benighted that he couldn't reclaim it. The 2015 *Secret Wars* #1 is the ultimate fight-scene comic book, in multiple senses. Fifty-seven characters are named and pictured on its cast-list page, and they're not even all the ones who play significant roles. The final incursion from *Avengers/New Avengers* has arrived, and everything is blowing up. If the issue had a soundtrack, it would be the "1812 Overture" and "The Ride of the Valkyries," played simultaneously at ear-splitting volume and crossfaded into white noise.

All that holds it together is Reed Richards's plan: a "life raft," with a handful of geniuses who can "relaunch humanity." At the very end of the gigantic Marvel story, Reed does exactly the same thing he did at its beginning, building a rocket and bringing his family on board with him. The first time, he was trying to break free of the Earth, and this time he's trying to break free of the collapsing reality of his narrative.

He failed in *Fantastic Four* #1, and now he fails again. The worlds collide and end, the universes crackle out of existence, the ship falls to pieces. Reed surrenders to despair and to the void. The last faint exhalation of color fades from the story. The pages go gray, then white—interrupted by a wordless, pale, perfectly symmetrical image of Doctor Doom's mask—

then black. The final page of the issue is faint gray type against empty blankness:

THE MARVEL UNIVERSE 1961–2015

THE ULTIMATE UNIVERSE 2000–2015

Strange Tales #146 (July 1966)
STEVE DITKO, DENNIS O'NEIL

Go back for a moment, though, to *Secret Wars* #1's image of the worlds smashing together. In a story as big as Marvel's, *everything* can be a reference to the past, even the end of all things. Steve Ditko's final Doctor Strange story, in this issue, involves the malevolent magical entity Dormammu* battling Eternity, the personification of all of existence, which Ditko draws as the silhouette of a cloaked human form, filled in with stars, planets, and just a fragment of a face. That scene includes a worlds-colliding panel composed exactly the same way, down to the positioning of the spheres.

Another nearly identical image appeared in 1992's *Marc Spector: Moon Knight* #41, part of the *Infinity War* crossover, drawn by Gary Kwapisz and Tom Palmer ("standard worlds merging scenario... everybody dies," ran a bit of dialogue in that panel, written by Terry Kavanagh). Another was in 2005's *Exiles* #64, by Tony Bedard and Mizuki Sakakibara, alongside a discussion of the multiverse's instability: "remove even one reality, destabilize entire metastructure." And yet another version—in which two versions of Earth, rather than colliding, are doubling like a cell in mitosis—appeared in 1980's *What If?* #22, the prophetically titled "What if Dr. Doom Had Become a Hero?" by Don Glut, Fred Kida, and Dave Simons.

---

*Ditko's design for Dormammu's head is an empty-eyed, open-mouthed face, rendered with nothing more than a handful of vertical lines surrounded by the shape of a flame. It's both terrifying and impossible to reproduce in any other medium; the *Doctor Strange* movie tried and fell short.

What If? #32 (April 1982)
MARK GRUENWALD, GREG LAROCQUE, ET AL.

More than two hundred issues of *What If?* in its various incarnations have appeared on and off since 1977: a series about what might have happened if things had gone differently at various junctures in the Marvel story. Its usual narrator is Uatu, the alien Watcher, who lives on the moon and sees everything that is and everything that might have been. Often, *What If?* has been something like what the historian Herbert Butterfield called "Whig history"—an argument that the story has gone exactly as it should have gone, because otherwise everything would have turned out much worse. This issue, "What if the Avengers Had Become Pawns of Korvac?" is a riff on a not very special *Avengers* sequence from a few years earlier. Korvac, the near-omnipotent antagonist from that story, appears on the front cover as silhouetted white space. Inside, Gruenwald cranks up the scale of the conflict, bringing in every cosmic entity who had yet been seen in Marvel's comics. After Korvac annihilates everything else on Earth, he ends the story (and his universe), and "all becomes nothing": dots spackled around the contour of Eternity, the shape of reality as Ditko imagined it, now full of inkless blankness instead of inky stars.

What If? #43 (February 1984)
MARK GRUENWALD, JACK ABEL, BEN SEAN

After everything ends, there's a sequel. On the first page of this issue's follow-up to *What If?* #32, the Watcher demands "behold," and points toward empty white newsprint.* Three superheroes return, from outside their universe, to the void left by the earlier story, and discuss how they might sacrifice themselves to restore what used to be. The ghost of

---

*Mark Gruenwald was mostly a writer and editor, and occasionally tried his hand at drawing; he didn't really draw any backgrounds in this story because there were none to draw.

Eternity appears to them—a trembling blue shape with nothing inside it—and tells them it doesn't want to come back.

Secret Wars II #9 (March 1985)
JIM SHOOTER, AL MILGROM, STEVE LEIALOHA, M. HANDS*

The original *Secret Wars* was swiftly followed by *Secret Wars II*, a big, tacky, ugly thing whose story continued each month in a handful of other series. Its final issue is a long, nonsensical fight scene whose artwork is mostly sloppy and overstuffed. Even so, it's got two sets of images with enduring potency.

One comes near the end of the story. There's a little black-and-white panel with a few dozen heroes' heads illuminated in light so bright it reduces them to half forms with no color at all; then a blank white panel; then the same treatment (one high-contrast panel, one empty one) given to the Golden Gate Bridge, to the Eiffel Tower, to the Earth and moon. It's the end, in the visual language we had for the end in 1985: the terrible illumination of Hiroshima, extended to everything we know.

On the next page, that sequence repeats in reverse. Nothing, then the world; nothing, then Paris; nothing, then San Francisco; nothing, then hot-lit superheroes and a broken machine.

The other visually resonant scene here is a clash between the Beyonder and the Molecule Man (an old *Fantastic Four* villain who went on to play a major role in Hickman and Ribic's *Secret Wars*). Each of them leans toward the other with one leg bent and the other extended, their hands glowing; behind them, there's a swatch of a Jack Kirby–style outer-space landscape, a dripping no-space in the mode of Steve Ditko's *Doctor Strange*, a horde of alien creatures, a figure-eight with an upper half that shows a

---

*The M in "M. Hands" stood for "Many," i.e., "This was running so late that everyone pitched in with coloring." Many's sibling, Diverse, also occasionally got a credit.

caveman and a Roman centurion agape at a dinosaur and a lower half that depicts a procession of alarmed human heads.

Giant-Size Avengers #2 (November 1974)
STEVE ENGLEHART, DAVE COCKRUM, BILL MANTLO

That image, too, has an antecedent, a scene from this climactic episode of a sequence about time travelers and cosmic forces. Here, it's the time-displaced Kang fighting with his time-displaced other self Rama-Tut* at the center of the image, with reality rupturing around them. Again, the figures are superimposed on a field of loops and fragments; again, all around them, there are bits of Kirby's stylized cosmos, Ditko's hallucinatory spaces, and fantastic, history-spanning figures. Doom's there too.

Secret Wars #2 (July 2015)
JONATHAN HICKMAN, ESAD RIBIC, IVE SVORCINA

Eternity, infinity, impossibility: after the end of everything, the story continues. At last, we learn the purpose for which Victor Von Doom has been amassing all that power for half a century of comics: to once again become God—not just the sovereign of everything, but the savior of everything. He's assembled a new Battleworld, composed of bits that he was able to save of the Earths of various realities, and created a history for it. It is, almost literally, an *Avengers* world, the material of Marvel's comics mashed into a ball so big it has gravity. Its sun is the Human Torch. There is nothing else—no stars, no space. There is nothing to it *but* the stuff of comic books strong enough to linger in memory.

It's Doom's own utopia, both a world that's perfect by his lights and a no-place that is every (extant) place, and he rules over it all, with no

---

*See chapter 4.

distinction between his divine and secular capacities. If some part of Battleworld becomes a threat to his supremacy, he erases that part and begins again. (To repeat a few questions from chapter 1: What do gods do? They create; they judge; they destroy. What do monarchs do? They protect their nations, even when that makes them monstrous. Can one entity be both? *Good question.*)

For most of the duration of the 2015 *Secret Wars*, in place of Marvel's other ongoing series, there were a cluster of miniseries set on Battleworld.* Only a few were direct substitutes: *Guardians of the Galaxy*, for instance, became *Guardians of Knowhere* (since there was no galaxy to guard). Most of the rest were revivals of past event comics or other fondly remembered past storylines, recast as zones of Battleworld. There was a *Civil War* where the war never ended, a similarly eternal *Days of Future Past*, a *Spider-Verse* and *Spider-Island* that were environments rather than incidents, an *Old Man Logan* trying to escape his realm rather than to enact vengeance. A running joke in all of the Battleworld comics was that any place where the word "God" would normally be used in dialogue, "Doom" appeared instead.

Secret Wars #9 (March 2016)
JONATHAN HICKMAN, ESAD RIBIC, IVE SVORCINA

The rest of *Secret Wars* itself is effectively a throne-room drama, an enormous game of *What If?* that rearranges the cast of *Fantastic Four* into new roles. The wild-card position Doom has always played is now occupied by Reed Richards. In the climactic struggle between the two men,

---

*The model for that publishing program was "The Age of Apocalypse" (see chapter 10), and the initial idea was apparently that they'd all stop for *Secret Wars*. In practice, some of them needed more time to wrap up their business, and the metaphysical, metafictional series *Silver Surfer* and *Loki: Agent of Asgard* (see chapter 12) extended their narratives into the white space where the universe had once been, taking their protagonists onward past the end of everything.

Esad Ribic draws their faces (one infinitely mutable, the other scarred and frozen behind metal) superimposed on each other in small, alternating squares, an echo of the chessboard that appeared in Jack Kirby's very first image of Doom back in 1962's *Fantastic Four* #5, in Jim Steranko's drawing of Doom in 1968's *Strange Tales* #167, and in Mike Zeck's restaging of Steranko's image in 1977's *Master of Kung Fu* #59.*

Alex Ross's cover artwork for this final issue of *Secret Wars* is even more allusive. It shows the clash between Richards and Doom in a composition that recalls the battles that were superimposed on fragmentary images in both *Secret Wars II* #9 and *Giant-Size Avengers* #2. The torn slivers of images that surround them are Ross's painterly reproductions of moments from various pivotal Marvel stories: Bruce Banner being struck from behind by gamma radiation, the birth of Franklin Richards, Tony Stark drunkenly staring at his reflection, and so on. Spider-Man appears in his pose from the cover of 1976's *Superman vs. the Amazing Spider-Man*, with just the tip of Superman's boot visible at the edge of Ross's painting. (Can't have Marvel without DC.)

When the conflict is ended, the story leaps months forward in time again for its coda. The familiar "prime Earth" (i.e., 616) is now the only one, at least for the moment. It's been restored, or remade, with just a couple of changes, like the addition of Miles Morales to its population.†
Reed and Sue Richards and their extended family of choice remain outside reality, surrounded by raw earth and speckled light; they will return someday, but not just yet.

Franklin Richards, who's now reached the age at which kids discover comics, has effectively become God, but not in the manner of Doom, who wanted to preserve the past and mold it to flatter himself. Godhood just happened to Franklin. He's dreaming up "whole universes," which then

---

*See chapter 8.
†See chapter 6.

Three reality-spanning clashes that echo one another visually: (*counterclockwise from top left*) Rama-Tut and Kang in *Giant-Size Avengers* #2, 1974, by writer Steve Englehart and artist Dave Cockrum; the Beyonder and the Molecule Man in *Secret Wars II* #9, 1986, by writer Jim Shooter and artists Al Milgrom and Steve Leialoha; and Reed Richards and Doctor Doom on Alex Ross's cover for *Secret Wars* #9, 2016.

become real. "All of this has to be catalogued. Recorded. Explored," his sister, Valeria, says. (That's what comics are there to do.) It's a symbolic turning over of the Marvel story from revivalists of bygone glories, like Doom, to a new generation (of characters, or readers, or creators).

The final words of Hickman's epic are "Everything lives." Thematically, that makes sense, but it's a corny note to end on, a sunny major flourish to conclude a thunderous minor-key fugue.* It's the kind of redemptive resolution Marvel's story has always promised—a capstone on half a million pages. But it's also not *the* end, because nothing gets to end forever. Thanks to *Secret Wars*' publishing delays, by the time its final issue appeared, almost all of Marvel's long-running series had already been relaunched and moved past that epilogue. *All-New, All-Different Avengers* was already on its third issue, for instance.

And what about everything Hickman and his collaborators had shown us in the previous three years? Oh, that happened, or mostly happened. When characters subsequently mention it at all, they suggest that there was some kind of huge crisis, but they got through it okay. As readers, we have once again missed something important. Everyone has. That's just how things are when you read superhero comics.

---

*Hickman still had a few loose ends to tie up—a brief parody of his own excesses in the comedy one-shot *Secret Wars Too*, the long-delayed final pair of issues of *S.H.I.E.L.D.*—but he otherwise retreated from mainstream comics for more than three years, returning to Marvel in 2019 to take over *X-Men*; see chapter 10.

19

INTERLUDE: LINDA CARTER

arren Ellis once noted that the omnipresence of super-heroes within comic books was "like every bookstore in the planet having ninety percent of its shelves filled with nurse novels. Imagine that. You want a new novel, but you have to wade through three hundred new books about romances in the wards before you can get at any other genre.... Superhero comics are like bloody creeping fungus, and they smother everything else."

Ellis, who has written some superb superhero comics,* makes a reasonable-sounding argument, on its face; it's an argument that could have been made just as well about crime comics in 1948 or romance comics in 1950. On the other hand, if there existed, say, an intricately inter-connected, occasionally extraordinary 2,700-volume *roman-fleuve* con-cerning the nursing staff at a particular hospital over six decades—or

---

*See chapter 16 for more on him.

a half-million-page comics epic about the same subject—and it had become a touchstone of contemporary culture, I bet I'd be interested in that too.

Around the beginning of Marvel, there was a moment where things *could* have gone that way. In the fall of 1961, Martin Goodman's comics line started putting a little logo on its covers: "M C," which might have stood for Marvel Comics. The first series to bear that logo on its debut issue, two months before *Fantastic Four* #1, was *Linda Carter, Student Nurse*,* a collaboration between Stan Lee and artist Al Hartley.

Lee and Hartley had been working together for years at that point, mostly on teen-comedy series like *Patsy Walker*, and they'd experimented with some short-lived comics about young professional women, like *Meet Miss Bliss, Della Vision,* and *Sherry the Showgirl.* Nurse comics were also part of Marvel's history already: they'd published thirty-six issues of the fluffy comedy *Nellie the Nurse* between 1945 and 1952, then one more in 1957, the same year as the more dramatic one-off *The Romances of Nurse Helen Grant.* There was even a little nurse-comics boom in the early '60s— during its relatively brief existence, *Linda Carter* was joined on newsstands by other publishers' *Cynthia Doyle, Nurse in Love; Nurse Betsy Crane; Nurse Linda Lark; The Nurses; Registered Nurse; Three Nurses;* and *Sue and Sally Smith, Flying Nurses.*

Linda Carter, Student Nurse belonged to a section of Marvel's early line that doesn't get discussed much: comics about young women making a place in the world for themselves, through school and into careers. (The first issue begins with Linda stepping out of a taxi at the generically named "Metropolitan Hospital" to begin her first day of training; Lee's narration announces that hers will be "a life filled with humor, thrills, and glamorous romance!")

Millie the Model and *Tessie the Typist* and *Hedy of Hollywood* and

---

*"Isn't that—" Almost. You're thinking of Lynda Carter, who played Wonder Woman on TV from 1975 to 1979.

their ilk were a significant part of what the company had published in the 1940s and '50s. As with their more forward siblings, monster comics, their aesthetic got absorbed into the superhero stories, although they themselves took longer to disappear: *Patsy and Hedy* kept going until 1967, *Millie the Model* until 1973.

Linda Carter, on the other hand, only lasted nine issues, never found its feet as a series, and has unsurprisingly never been reprinted. Still, I think of it, rather than *Fantastic Four*, as being where the collective Marvel story really begins, for three reasons.

The first panel of *Linda Carter, Student Nurse* #1, 1961, by writer Stan Lee and artist Al Hartley.

The first is that it was part of Marvel's first shared-universe, multiple-series crossover, which was published immediately after *Fantastic Four* #1—and didn't involve any superheroes. Patsy Walker appeared in *Kathy* ("The Teen-Age Tornado") #14, in a story that revolved around Kathy and her friend Liz respectively having their fashion drawings published in that month's *Patsy and Hedy* #79 and *Patsy Walker* #98. The latter issue guest starred model Millie Collins, who in turn met Kathy in *Life with Millie* #14. Shortly thereafter, Linda Carter visited Patsy's school in *Patsy Walker* #99, and Millie got a gig modeling for Jack Kirby—who appeared as a character—in *Millie the Model* #107.*

The second reason is that Linda Carter became part of the fabric of the Marvel Universe, although she took a while to get there. After *Linda Carter, Student Nurse* ended in January 1963, she vanished for almost a decade before briefly reappearing in 1972's *Night Nurse*. That series concerned Linda and her roommates, Christine Palmer and Georgia Jenkins, all nurses working the night shift at the renamed Metropolitan General Hospital. No superheroes were involved in that one, either; it lasted four issues.

Thirty years later, she came back again, and stayed. 2004's *Daredevil* #58 introduces a secret medical clinic, run by a woman known only as "the night nurse," where injured superheroes can go to get treated, no questions asked. The night nurse and her clinic have continued to appear here and there in Marvel's comics ever since (she assists Captain America's allies in *Civil War* and has a brief romance with Doctor Strange in the 2006 miniseries *Doctor Strange: The Oath*). It was eventually revealed that she's Linda Carter, and that she found her real purpose in life after superheroes saved her.†

The third reason I like to think of *Linda Carter, Student Nurse* #1 as the real starting point of what I read for this book is that the big Marvel narrative becomes strangely beautiful if it's Linda's story. It's ridiculous to think of any one character as *the* protagonist of this half-million-page

---

*The new superhero comics' characters didn't encounter one another until more than a year later: in March 1963, the Fantastic Four appeared in *The Amazing Spider-Man* #1, and the Hulk appeared in *Fantastic Four* #12.

†Linda's former roommate, Christine Palmer, returned a few months after her. Still working at the re-renamed Metro-General Hospital, she was part of the supporting cast of the 2004–2005 *Nightcrawler* series; played by Rachel McAdams, she had a significant presence in the 2016 *Doctor Strange* movie. Claire Temple, a doctor introduced in 1972's *Luke Cage, Hero for Hire* #2, appeared in a capacity much like Linda's "night nurse" gig in some of Marvel's 2015–2018 TV shows, played by Rosario Dawson.

epic, of course, but—what if that were true? What would it mean if the Marvel story is really about *her*, as comparatively little time as she's spent on panel?

The Marvel story is understood, too often, as a story for boys; with Linda at its center, it also belongs to a specific tradition of stories for girls. It's a story in which science and knowledge are defining forces; as Linda's story, it's about a woman who begins the most important part of her education on its first page and continues to learn even when she steps away from our view.

Linda Carter lives in a world more dangerous and

Linda Carter returns as the Night Nurse in *Doctor Strange: The Oath* #1, 2006, written by Brian K. Vaughan and drawn by Marcos Martin and Álvaro López.

overwhelming than anything she could have imagined when she first arrived at Metropolitan Hospital. If Marvel's body of comics is her story, it's about how that world has changed around a woman who has a perspective like that of the story's readers—someone with no special powers or more-than-human gifts. Linda's life has given her just what the old con man Stan Lee promised when she first appeared: thrills, but also humor and glamorous romance. What she's learned from the marvels that saved her is how to be brave and kind—and also that it can be fun for her to give herself another name, and sometimes wear a little cape.

20

GOOD IS A THING YOU DO

Superheroes are everywhere—so ubiquitous in popular culture that it's easy to take for granted that everyone knows what, exactly, they are, and what stories about them do. People instinctively recognize a superhero story on sight, and almost always describe the conventions of the genre wrong, in part because Stan Lee and his collaborators changed those conventions more than half a century ago and public perception still hasn't caught up.

"Vigilante crime fighters with secret identities," for instance, sounds reasonable—but as far as Marvel's characters are concerned, the "secret identity" paradigm is mostly dead. It fits Spider-Man, pretty much, and eventually started applying to Daredevil again, after many years when it didn't.* But it's barely described any other major character in the Marvel story for a while, and it was never true of most of them in the first place.

---

*Daredevil was outed in the press in 2002's *Daredevil* #32, and it was public knowledge that he was Matt Murdock until that genie was stuffed back into the bottle in 2015.

"Crime fighters" is also not quite right. Again, it's occasionally true of Spider-Man and a few others, but it never fit the Fantastic Four, and it's been decades since we've seen Black Panther or Doctor Strange or the X-Men do anything that actual law enforcement might otherwise handle, other than the occasional quick scene in passing. "Capes and tights"? A lot of them still do wear form-fitting outfits; not so much capes anymore, and when any of them other than Superman, Batman, or Thor affect a cape, it's usually in a very deliberate "look, this person is wearing a cape" sort of way (as with Linda Carter). "Kid sidekicks"? For readers born after 1960 or so, that's basically just Batman.

It's closer to say that the conventions of superhero characters—which aren't inflexible—are that they have unusual abilities, aliases that aren't standard names,* and distinctive costumes. They're sympathetic; their audiences are generally meant to identify with superheroes' central drives, except when they're explicitly invited *not* to. Superheroes' antagonists are characters whose ideologies are opposed to the heroes' ideologies in some way—which means that they often represent something these stories' audiences fear. (Sometimes villains' ideologies are also sympathetic.) And that conflict usually plays out as physical action, or something else that's visually interesting.

The two most interesting Marvel superheroes to have emerged in the twenty-first century[†] both provide timely perspectives on what the superhero concept has come to mean. Squirrel Girl and the current Ms. Marvel[‡] are both young women, the audience that Marvel mostly forgot about or neglected for decades. They're both students; Ms. Marvel is the daughter of Pakistani immigrants, and although Squirrel Girl is white, her supporting cast is made up almost entirely of people of color. Their ideologies

---

*There are a couple of recently prominent exceptions to that, Jessica Jones and Luke Cage, but even they used to have superhero names: Jewel and Power Man, respectively. And Doctor Strange is literally a medical doctor whose last name is Strange.
†One of them technically first appeared in the twentieth century, but she didn't really become the character she is now until 2015.
‡There was a different Ms. Marvel from 1977 to 2012; we'll get to her shortly.

Kamala Khan arrives on the cover of *Ms. Marvel* #1, 2014, drawn by Sara Pichelli.

and drives reflect a contemporary audience's real concerns. In Marvel's early years, American youth were worried about crime, and Communism, and having their secrets revealed. Now they care about social injustice, and systemic oppression and corruption, and having their voices ignored and their identities erased.

Both Squirrel Girl and Ms. Marvel are even more invested than their readers in the idea of superheroes; they've grown up in a world that's had them for real, ever since they can remember. The *Ms. Marvel* and *Unbeatable Squirrel Girl* series that began in the mid-2010s each had a single writer (and just a couple of long-standing artists) for five years. Both characters began those series as superheroes of a kind close to the received understanding of what those are—fighting crime, carefully maintaining double lives and secret identities—and ended them in a slightly different place. Their stories, like Spider-Man's, are coming-of-age stories, but they're about the way people grow up *now*.

Ms. Marvel #1 (April 2014)

G. WILLOW WILSON, ADRIAN ALPHONA, IAN HERRING

Sara Pichelli's cover artwork for the first issue of *Ms. Marvel* looks, at first glance, like a close-up of a costumed superhero. Look again: she's not in costume at all, but every element of Pichelli's drawing foreshadows what this series is going to be. Kamala Khan, in the first image we see of her, is wearing a T-shirt with the *old* Ms. Marvel's stylized lightning-bolt logo, along with a paisley scarf—which isn't the scarf that will be part of her costume. We can't see her eyes, or the part of her face where her mask will be, but we can see that her skin is brown, contrasted with the bright pink of the comic's title. Her right hand is decorated in rings and bracelets (she's a teenage girl whose family's culture is important to her), and it's making a fist (she's also pretty badass). In her left, she's holding three schoolbooks (she's a student whose parents expect a lot of her academically, and her stories always address how her new role puts additional demands on her time). Their spines read "U.S. History" (this will be a series to which real-world history matters a lot), "Hadith to Live By" (she's Muslim and proud), and "Illustration & Design" (one of the things she wants is to make culture of her own).

Kamala Khan is yet another of Marvel's collective creations, her real-world origin too complicated to be attributed to a single originator. She emerged from conversations between editors Sana Amanat and Stephen Wacker about Amanat's experience growing up as a South Asian Muslim in New Jersey, as well as writer G. Willow Wilson's interest in creating a teenage Muslim superhero. ("Sana and I initially had very modest expectations for this book," Wilson wrote five years later. "Our goal was to get to ten issues.") Artist Adrian Alphona came up with the images of Kamala and her supporting cast, although her costume was designed by Jamie McKelvie.

The visual style that Alphona and colorist Ian Herring developed for the series announces: *This is kind of like those other superhero comics, but it's actually different.* The borders of Alphona's panels here are drawn freehand rather than ruled.* They wobble a little; they suggest that they were made by a particular person. Alphona's lines are ultra-thin and a little uneven, with no variation in weight and effectively no areas of solid

---

*Most of the other artists who have drawn Kamala-era *Ms. Marvel* haven't done that, although Nico Leon, who drew most of the 2015 series, did. It's otherwise a very rare technique in superhero comics, with the prominent exception of Gabriel Hernández Walta's artwork for *The Vision* (2016).

black. (The darkest solid color on *Ms. Marvel*'s pages is usually the brown of Kamala's hair.) His characters are always slightly distorted, like gentle caricatures; Kamala, when she uses her powers, becomes much more so.

Herring's colors (he colored every issue of the two *Ms. Marvel* series written by Wilson) are particular to *Ms. Marvel*, too: a palette of pastels and light sepia tones overlaid with gray washes to augment depth, and a marbled watercolor effect that appears in larger open areas of the line-work. The lettering, by Joe Caramagna, mixes uppercase and lowercase type for dialogue, unlike most other comics set in the Marvel Universe.* The overall effect is to make *Ms. Marvel* look much more personal and handmade than *Avengers* and *Spider-Man*, but not outside their ballpark altogether.

As its cover suggests, this first episode of Kamala Khan's story isn't about a superhero, but about somebody who longs to be one. The only conventional action scene in *Ms. Marvel* #1 is a brief glimpse of Kamala's Avengers fan fiction. We see her hanging out with her high school classmates and struggling to fit into their social orders, as goofily charming as she is; we see her squabbling with her strictly religious parents, sneaking out of her house to go to a party, falling unconscious in a mysterious mist, and experiencing a hallucinatory vision of heroes—espccially Carol Danvers, formerly known as Ms. Marvel, the heroine Kamala longs, most of all, to be like.

Ms. Marvel #1 (January 1977)
GERRY CONWAY, JOHN BUSCEMA, JOE SINNOTT, MARIE SEVERIN

"At last!" the cover of the first *Ms. Marvel* #1 declared, thirty-seven years earlier. "A bold new super-heroine in the senses-stunning tradition of

---

*Kamala's narration is all uppercase, implying that she understands herself as belonging to the world where everything's in caps.

Spider-Man!"* That's an odd way of putting it, but mid-1970s Marvel was *really* interested in reconstructing the Spider-Man formula and in appealing to nostalgia in general. Ms. Marvel's initial costume is modeled on (the earlier, male) Captain Marvel's, except that it exposes her midriff and legs. Her secret identity is Carol Danvers, a minor supporting character from *that* Captain Marvel's early stories.† Her supporting cast, at the beginning of the series, is the *Daily Bugle* staff, which she shares with Spider-Man. Even the title of the issue is a callback: "This Woman, This Warrior!" is stamped from the mold of *Fantastic Four* #51's "This Man... This Monster!"

Ms. Marvel wasn't the first superheroine with a Marvel series of her own; that had been the Cat, whose 1972–1973 series was axed after four issues. But there weren't many others at the time. Later in 1977, the first issues of both *Ms. Marvel* and *The Cat* were reprinted in a book called *The Superhero Women*—one of several paperback anthologies of Marvel's comics published by Fireside Books about that time. Since there weren't enough solo comics about superheroines to fill it out, the book also included appearances of superpowered women from *Amazing Spider-Man* and *Fantastic Four*, stories involving the chain-mail-bikini-wearing barbarian Red Sonja and the villainous Hela, and a 1971 Stan Lee and John Romita Sr. oddity called "The Fury of the Femizons" (Sample dialogue: "I have been ever loyal to the United Sisterhood Alliance—and to its creed... Sexuality! Solidarity! Superiority!").

---

*The cover also calls her "the most mysterious woman warrior since Madame Medusa"—a member of the Fantastic Four's supporting cast who had starred in exactly one solo comic book, *Marvel Super-Heroes* #15, in 1968.

†Ms. Marvel's name owes something to *Ms.* magazine, which had begun in 1971 and had featured Wonder Woman on an early cover. In the 1977 *Ms. Marvel* series, Carol Danvers, who had been the head of security at an Air Force base in her earlier *Captain Marvel* appearances, became the editor of a women's magazine.

Marvel Age Preview #2 (March 1992)
RENÉE WITTERSTAETTER ET AL.

In the ensuing decades, Marvel sometimes did a little bit better at telling stories about women characters—but not *much* better.* This sixty-eight-page special details all the projects Marvel was planning on publishing in 1992, divided into eighteen categories—"Big Guns," "Science Fiction," "Movie/TV Tie-Ins," and the like. In the middle of it, two pages are devoted to a section called "Female Readers," which lists three titles: *Barbie, Barbie Fashion*, and a sequel to Barbara Slate's 1989 one-shot *Yuppies from Hell*. (The last of those never came out.) Of the remaining 102 titles described in the special, two are named after women characters: *Silver Sable* and *She-Hulk*.

It's worth noting that before superhero comics made their early-1960s comeback, the company that would become Marvel published a surprisingly high number of comics starring women. In April 1957, for instance, there were seven of them, out of forty-eight issues total: *A Date with Millie, Jann of the Jungle, Lorna the Jungle Girl, Millie the Model, Patsy and Hedy, Patsy and Her Pals*, and *Sherry the Showgirl*. (That's not counting romance anthologies,† whose protagonists were always women—just series whose titles named particular women characters.) In the superhero era, that changed. Since the mid-'70s, there have often been only one or two running at any given time, and occasionally none—between the end of *Codename: Spitfire* in 1987 and the beginning of *The Sensational She-Hulk* in 1988, for instance.

Now it's changing again. Of the eighty-five new Marvel issues cover-dated March 2020, thirteen were solo titles starring women. (Thirty-eight others were solo titles with male protagonists; the other thirty-four were not named after a specific character.) It's not parity, but it's not noth-

---

*Ditto for publishing stories written or drawn *by* women, which is a whole other problem.
†The company published five of those that month: *Love Romances, True Tales of Love, Lovers, My Love Story*, and *Stories of Romance*.

ing, either, and the turning point seems to have been the beginning of 2012's *Captain Marvel* series.

Captain Marvel #1 (September 2012)
KELLY SUE DECONNICK, DEXTER SOY

The first *Ms. Marvel* series ended in 1979, and Carol Danvers joined the mass of Marvel's rootless characters. She was depowered and repowered; she changed her superhero name to Binary for a while, then to Warbird, and then back to Ms. Marvel for a series that ran from 2006 to 2010. The original Captain Marvel had died in 1982, and that name had been handed off among a few other characters since then. Here, Carol claims it. The 2012 *Captain Marvel* series took as a given that she was finally living up to her potential, and that doing so made her a big deal. It wasn't quite a bestseller, but its fans were *very* enthusiastic—an organized group called themselves the "Carol Corps"—and mindshare matters more than single-issue sales anyway: this is the version of the character that led to the hugely successful 2019 *Captain Marvel* movie. Carol Danvers's identity shift also left the name "Ms. Marvel" open again, which was where Kamala Khan came in.

Ms. Marvel #5 (August 2014)
G. WILLOW WILSON, ADRIAN ALPHONA, IAN HERRING

The new Ms. Marvel's origin story is slow moving, as such things go, but thoughtful. Her powers—she can change the size and shape of her body in ways she can't always control—are a witty metaphor for what teenage girls go through in general. (The pitch-perfect word she uses to describe what she can do is "embiggen," a neologism from a 1996 episode of *The Simpsons*.) She idolizes Carol Danvers to the point that she disguises herself as blond and white at first, but quickly realizes that that's not really her.

It's not until this issue that she gets her costume and works out how to use her abilities. This is also where Wilson formulates Kamala's statement of purpose: "Good is not a thing you are. It's a thing you do."

That line crystallized Ms. Marvel: it pointed the way forward to everything she's become. It sounds very simple, as if it applies in a generic way to superheroes, but it doesn't. Kamala's goal is not to live up to her responsibility (like Spider-Man), or punish the guilty (like the Punisher), or protect her people (like the X-Men), or defend her kingdom (like Black Panther), or make up for the sins of her past (like Black Widow), or uphold American ideals (like Captain America). She wants, above everything else, to *do good* in the world, and the most interesting conflicts in her stories come when she struggles to understand what good she *can* do—what the right course of action would be, and what she might lose by taking that path.

Ms. Marvel #6 (September 2014)
G. WILLOW WILSON, JAKE WYATT, IAN HERRING

After all those decades of trying to reconstruct the elusive recipe that had made Spider-Man work, mostly by mimicking the wrong aspects of its premise, Marvel finally landed on it again with *Ms. Marvel*. Kamala Khan is, effectively, a twenty-first-century Peter Parker: a misunderstood teenager with an alliterative name, trying to find her way in the world. Like him, she's outside the center of the action (in Jersey City rather than Forest Hills); like him, she's trying to balance the academic demands and social labyrinths of high school with a personal calling that keeps her up all night, while she withholds the most important thing about herself from the people she cares about most. And like Spider-Man, Ms. Marvel makes almost any scene she's in funny. She's not a wisecracker like him, but her earnest, over-the-top enthusiasm about absolutely everything is a consistent source of comedy. (On meeting the X-Men's Wolverine in this issue: "I can't believe it. I'm gonna pass out. I totally put you first in my fantasy hero team-up bracket!")

Even so, Wilson tweaks the Spider-Man template a little, especially in ways that follow from Kamala's enthusiasm for doing good for its own sake. The first few issues of *Ms. Marvel* had set up Sheikh Abdullah, the imam of the Khan family's mosque, as a sort of J. Jonah Jameson figure, a blustering old man who would perpetually make life harder for her. Here, Kamala's forced to talk to Sheikh Abdullah about why she's been sneaking out of the house. She tells him that she's been helping people (while skimping on the details), and he surprises her, and us, by being entirely supportive: he advises her to "do what you are doing with as much honor and skill as you can." ("I thought you were going to warn me about Satan and boys." "I've been giving youth lectures at this mosque for ten years. If I still have to warn you about Satan and boys, I should lose my job.")

Marvel 75th Anniversary Celebration #1 (December 2014)

JAMES ROBINSON, CHRIS SAMNEE, JORDIE BELLAIRE, BRUCE TIMM, STAN LEE, ET AL.

The short story that begins this anthology imagines various characters' whereabouts at the moment *Fantastic Four* #1 began, around fourteen years' worth of Marvel time earlier. Dr. Donald Blake is planning a vacation to Norway, Peter Parker is showing his uncle Ben some photos he's been taking, and so on. Its final scene is Kamala Khan as a very little girl, playing with a Captain America ball as her mother calls her in for dinner.

This issue also includes the final story Stan Lee wrote for Marvel—a comics adaptation of his *first* story, "Captain America Foils the Traitor's Revenge," a short prose piece from 1941's *Captain America Comics* #3. And it's got a one-page gag cartoon about Marvel's favorite laughingstock of a character, Squirrel Girl, imagining how silly it would be if she had her own comic book.

The Unbeatable Squirrel Girl #1 (March 2015)
RYAN NORTH, ERICA HENDERSON, RICO RENZI

Squirrel Girl had first appeared in 1991, in a one-off Iron Man story (published in the inventory-dumping anthology *Marvel Super-Heroes*) by writer Will Murray and artist Steve Ditko: a teenage girl with a bushy tail who somehow defeats Doctor Doom by commanding squirrels to do her bidding. You could say that she was Ditko's last significant Marvel co-creation, except that it was a long time until anyone thought of her in those terms. For nearly twenty-five years, she was a *can you believe we published this?* character, turning up as the ultimate Z-lister among the buffoons of *Great Lakes Avengers* and as bizarre comedy relief in *New Avengers*, where she was Luke Cage and Jessica Jones's nanny, who kept winning impossible battles off panel.

Then writer Ryan North and artist Erica Henderson came up with a fresh take on her for this 2015 series, and suddenly she was a character that people laughed with, not at. *The Unbeatable Squirrel Girl* raises the question of what kind of contemporary character would thrive at the old superhero paradigm of fighting superpowered fiends and monsters, and its answer is "someone who is incredibly good at creative nonviolent conflict resolution."

That's its central joke, which only gets funnier with repetition. Squirrel Girl really is unbeatable, and not because she can bench-press more than anybody else or anything like that (although she *is* awfully strong and durable). It's because she's kind and insightful and curious and finds ways for everybody to come out of conflicts with their underlying interests addressed. She "enjoys fighting crime," as she puts it at the beginning of the first issue (singing her own personal theme song, to the tune of the 1960s animated *Spider-Man* series' theme), but her idea of fighting crime has less to do with beating up criminals than with convincing them to turn their skills to more socially productive uses.

Like *Ms. Marvel*, *Squirrel Girl* declares with its visual style that it's "a superhero comic, but not like *other* superhero comics." Henderson's line art is broadly cartoony, with thick, expressive brushstrokes and distinct body language for every character. (Squirrel Girl's chin comes to a point, making her head look a little like an acorn.) Colorist Rico Renzi sticks almost entirely to flat tones, aside from the occasional bit of scenery; letterer Clayton Cowles uses a *Ms. Marvel*-style upper- and lowercase typeface, and many pages include a line of commentary from North in tiny gold type at the bottom, as an extra gag.*

True to the archaic "dressing up and fighting crime" model, Squirrel Girl has a sidekick (a squirrel named Tippy-Toe) and, when she stuffs her tail into civilian clothes, a secret identity, which she's not terribly good at protecting: undergraduate computer science student Doreen Green. As the series begins, Doreen meets her roommate, Nancy Whitehead, who defends the forbidden presence of her pet kitten in their dorm on the basis that "obeying an unjust law is itself unjust."

That's a tossed-off joke, but it's also a precept that Doreen internalizes over the course of the series. A lot of this first issue's seemingly throwaway gags go on to become part of the fabric of her story, like the "Deadpool's Guide to Super Villains" trading cards she carries (which conveniently serve as exposition for readers who are unfamiliar with certain characters). She encounters long-standing Spider-Man villain Kraven the Hunter, and convinces him that what he should really be hunting is Gigantos (undersea "biological doomsday weapons" that first appeared in 1962's *Fantastic Four* #4); Kraven goes on to appear several times later on, as Squirrel Girl's staunch ally. And at the end of the issue, Tippy-Toe alerts her that the squirrels have discovered something huge and terrifying approaching the Earth: Galactus.

---

*North has used that same trick in various other comics he's written—it's a clever print equivalent of mouse-over text, and a nod to his background in webcomics.

Fantastic Four #48 (March 1966)
STAN LEE, JACK KIRBY, JOE SINNOTT

If this book was a tour of a real place, *Fantastic Four* #48–50 would be the spot with T-shirt hawkers lined up across the street from it—it's so doggedly regarded as a definitive story from Stan Lee and Jack Kirby's peak that it's hard to see it clearly through the walls of its reputation. Galactus, an enormous alien in purple armor, arrives on Earth with the intention of devouring its energy and destroying it. He's accompanied by his herald, the Silver Surfer, a metallic-skinned man on a flying surfboard. The Fantastic Four try to stop them, but the deciding factor ends up being the Thing's girlfriend, Alicia, convincing the Surfer to rebel against his master.

The Galactus Trilogy is corny and overwrought, and its pacing is bizarre—the Galactus plot doesn't even begin until midway through #48, and ends midway through #50. It *should* be camp, in Susan Sontag's sense of "failed seriousness." But it doesn't fail. Kirby and Lee are so intensely committed to the gravity of their story that it actually delivers the feeling of plummeting toward the void and being miraculously spared.

Ever since then, Galactus has mostly been a presence of overwhelming, impossible catastrophe in Marvel's comics, a world-exterminating force, older than the universe itself, against which there can be no resistance. His presence signifies that a story in which he appears is meant to be taking place on the level of what one character in *Fantastic Four* #49 calls "the great cosmic game of life and death." Which is to say: he is *all the way* out of Squirrel Girl's league.

The Unbeatable Squirrel Girl #4 (June 2015)
RYAN NORTH, ERICA HENDERSON, RICO RENZI

Too bad. Doreen Green is the only one who knows Galactus is coming, so she's just going to have to deal with him. At the end of *The Unbeatable*

Squirrel Girl #3, she flies to the moon (in one of Iron Man's suits of armor) and confronts him; the first page of #4 is Doreen taking a selfie as she sits atop the fallen Galactus on the lunar surface, saying, "Well, gosh, *that* wasn't so hard after all!" The bottom of the page is captioned "The End!" Turn the page, and there's the letter column. Done.

Turn the page again after the letter column, and there's another caption: "Okay, Fine, I Guess It's Not the End." Squirrel Girl, it turns out, has saved the day by befriending Galactus and finding him an uninhabited planet full of nuts that he can devour instead. ("Then we came back to the moon to lie down because we all over-ate, and here we are!") That also seems like the kind of one-off gag that would never be referred to again—but even as *The Unbeatable Squirrel Girl* refuses to take anything too seriously, it plays scrupulously by the rules of the Marvel universe's continuity.* Everything we see happen becomes part of its history.

Ms. Marvel #19 (December 2015)
G. WILLOW WILSON, ADRIAN ALPHONA, IAN HERRING

When Marvel's entire line of comics ended and started again as a result of *Secret Wars*, *The Unbeatable Squirrel Girl* just treated it as a semester break: apocalypse was too heavy for its sort of comedy. *Ms. Marvel*, though, took advantage of that moment to show how Kamala Khan would react to the imminent end of everything. Its last four issues before the break, #16–19, all take place during the chaotic eight hours before the universes collide. Kamala finally meets Carol Danvers, the mentor she's been longing for, who helps her rescue her kidnapped brother but breaks the news to her that the world is probably ending.

Not wanting to die without telling the truth about herself, she reveals

---

*When she meets Spider-Man on her college's campus, it's specifically during a particular *Amazing Spider-Man* sequence; near the end of North's run as *Squirrel Girl*'s writer, there's a tie-in to the big crossover event, *War of the Realms*, which resolves a plot thread from that story.

to her mother that she's Ms. Marvel. Once again, Wilson gets to show how Kamala's insistence on doing good, above all else, can upend superhero clichés: her mother embraces her and tells her that she'd figured it out a while ago, and that "if the worst thing you do is sneak out to help suffering people—then I thank God for having raised a righteous child."

The Unbeatable Squirrel Girl #8 (July 2016)
RYAN NORTH, ERICA HENDERSON, ANDY HIRSCH, RICO RENZI

A supervillain, to Squirrel Girl, is somebody who needs to reconsider their actions and use their gifts for better purposes; a monster is something that's lashing out because its needs aren't being met and that deserves some compassion. The three-issue sequence that begins here opens with an incident that initially seems unrelated to the rest of the story: Squirrel Girl is with the rest of the New Avengers,* battling a monstrously huge bug that's attacking New York. Then she figures out what's actually going on—it's a tree lobster, a (real-world) species of insect that was recently saved from extinction and is now being bred in captivity. "Did you get loose and accidentally get exposed to cosmic rays and become giant?" she asks the tree lobster. (It nods.) "Aw, sweetie. You're probably just hungry, huh?" (It nods again.)

Most of the rest of this episode is devoted to Doreen dealing with her unrequited crush† on her classmate and ally, Chipmunk Hunk, who had joined her supporting cast along with Koi Boi‡ (they both have exactly the powers you'd expect). In a disastrous attempt at distracting herself

---

*She belonged to that team during its 2015 series—an entirely different set of characters from the New Avengers discussed in chapter 18.

†One of the quiet virtues of *The Unbeatable Squirrel Girl* is that it really captures the social environment of college: being pushed together with strangers by chance, becoming fast friends with them, feeling attracted to some of them, and learning to live with that attraction not being reciprocated.

‡Koi Boi is a trans man, which is not signaled until a scene in *Unbeatable Squirrel Girl* #9 where the heroes are changing into their costumes and he's wearing a binder.

with online dating, she goes out with a "super hero truther." Just as he's trying to convince her that "advanced animatronics are being used in so-called 'super hero' false flag operations," the Mole Man, the subterranean villain who goes all the way back to *Fantastic Four* #1, attacks with *his* giant monsters.

Again, compassion and empathy are Squirrel Girl's first line of defense. The Mole Man explains that her influence has led to Kraven attacking the monsters in his domain. Her response is to offer a heartfelt apology, in the language of social justice activists, self-improvement books, and no other superhero comic book *ever*: "Dude, I accept the truth of your lived experiences, and I'm not going to tell you that your feelings are wrong."

Squirrel Girl makes peace with the Mole Man in *The Unbeatable Squirrel Girl* #9, 2016, written by Ryan North and drawn by Erica Henderson and Tom Fowler.

He's so impressed that she hasn't simply attacked him that he immediately proposes marriage to her—and then, when she declines, starts sinking the surface world's landmarks and announces that he'll only stop if she agrees to go on a date with him. That's another trope* for which *Squirrel Girl* has no patience (the cover of #10 is the Mole Man tipping a fedora and saying "M'lady"). The solution to her problem comes in the form of still another monster who needs understanding: Tricephalous, a three-headed, fire-breathing creature who's also got a half-century-long history in comics, and who turns out to have loved the Mole Man all along. It's the early Marvel formula again: monsters + romance + superheroes + topicality = entertainment.

Ms. Marvel #8 (August 2016)
G. WILLOW WILSON, ADRIAN ALPHONA, TAKESHI MIYAZAWA, IAN HERRING, IRMA KNIIVILA

Civil War II was one of the messier moments of Marvel's 2010s. A grand-scale crossover event launched at the same time as the release of the 2016 *Captain America: Civil War* movie, it was ostensibly a follow-up to the massively successful *Civil War* crossover of ten years earlier. This time, instead of Captain America being at odds with Iron Man over a question that mirrored the national conversation, Iron Man and Captain Marvel were bickering over a question that's only meaningful in fiction: If somebody with precognition sees visions of future crimes, is it okay to arrest their perpetrators before they happen?[†]

In place of the first *Civil War*'s gradual build-up, *Civil War II*'s conflict was abruptly plunked down onto its cast. Captain Marvel's position (yes, lock them up, and punch anyone who says otherwise) is fairly inconsistent with her character as established, and not especially defensible. And the central *Civil War II* miniseries, written by Brian Michael Bendis, is slackly paced—it ended up running an issue longer than planned.

---

*See, for instance, 2012's *New Mutants* #37, in which Magma goes on a date with the devil Mephisto in exchange for his rescuing her team.

†That question had *already* been posed in fiction: Philip K. Dick's 1956 short story "The Minority Report," which had been made into a film in 2002 and a TV series in 2015.

The *Civil War II* tie-ins in Marvel's other series included some terrific stories, though. The sequence in *Ms. Marvel* that connected to it, issues #8–11, begins with a flashback to Kamala Khan's great-grandparents being displaced from Bombay to Karachi during the partition of India in 1947. (That kind of calamity, Wilson implies, is what happens in a *real* civil war.) The body of the story concerns Carol Danvers asking Kamala to oversee a "predictive justice" team in Jersey City, and the disastrous consequences of that project leading Kamala to fall out with her former idol and mentor. As she notes, making predictions about who's going to commit a crime looks a lot like profiling.*

All-New All-Different Avengers Annual #1 (October 2016)

G. WILLOW WILSON, MAHMUD ASRAR, TAMRA BONVILLAIN, MARK WAID, CHIP ZDARSKY, ET AL.

A running joke-that's-not-really-a-joke in *Ms. Marvel* is that Kamala's hobby is writing fan fiction about other superheroes. That's another thing that makes her a contemporary character: it's pretty common for the young women who are now the most dedicated readers of comics† to make up their own stories and share them with one another.

This annual, from the brief period when she was a member of the Avengers, elaborates on that. It's an anthology of short faux-fanfic stories, framed by a sequence of Kamala being alarmed to see "totally inaccurate fanfic" about herself and her teammates. One is a satire of wish-fulfillment amateur writing that takes a sharp turn into mocking the sexist jerks who infest fan culture ("You've shown me the error of my ways! No more social justice warrioring for *me*!" says the story's "Miss Marvel," as Kamala, reading it, all but bursts into flames); another imagines Ms. Marvel and

---

*To underscore that point, Kamala gets pulled aside for an extra security patdown at an airport as *Ms. Marvel* #12 begins.
†Just not necessarily *superhero* comics.

Squirrel Girl meeting for the first time, beating each other up in an arcade game, and then going out for macarons.

The Unbeatable Squirrel Girl #26 (January 2018)
RYAN NORTH, MADELINE MCGRANE, ERICA HENDERSON, CHIP ZDARSKY, TOM FOWLER, ET AL.

Participatory fandom is also an ongoing thread in *Squirrel Girl*—Nancy
Whitehead draws her own "Cat Thor" stories, and the series' letter columns featured readers' cosplay and drawings. This issue is an anthology
of ten short comics "by" Squirrel Girl and her superhero friends. (Like
that *All-New All-Different Avengers Annual*, it's freed from even the stylistic grammar of in-canon stories.) It was actually drawn by a group of
cartoonists whose work is mostly as far outside Marvel's usual kind of
visual representation as Erica Henderson's. One of them is *Garfield* creator Jim Davis, who draws a parody of his own newspaper strip, with
gluttonous cat Garfield and his hapless owner Jon replaced by Galactus
and the Silver Surfer.

The Unbeatable Squirrel Girl #31 (June 2018)
RYAN NORTH, ERICA HENDERSON, RICO RENZI

Henderson left *Squirrel Girl* in mid-2018, although she continued to
draw its covers and the odd interior page. Her final issue before Derek
Charm took over as the series' main artist (working in a very similar
mode) is a jewel, and the final word on another antiquated superhero tradition: the idea of heroes going "on patrol," like beat cops, looking for
trouble to fix.

Doreen and Nancy, for plot reasons, find themselves experiencing time
so quickly that the rest of the world is effectively standing still. They have

no real way to communicate with anyone but each other; they know they'll live out the rest of their lives in the span of a couple of days. And so they devote themselves to "patrolling" New York for that brief time, keeping everyone safe and solving whatever problems they can.

This isn't the first time North and Henderson have shown us a version of Squirrel Girl as an old woman, still happy to be doing what she does;* a life of kindness, they suggest, is a sustainable life.

Exiles #1 (June 2018)
SALADIN AHMED, JAVIER RODRÍGUEZ, ÁLVARO LÓPEZ, JORDIE BELLAIRE

The same month, the first issue of *Exiles*—a new incarnation of a long-running title about versions of characters from many alternate universes—introduced a possible future Kamala Khan. She's scarred, gray-haired, and heavily armed, one of the last defenders of Jersey City in a catastrophic timeline. The name "Ms. Marvel" makes her angry to hear. She's just called "Khan."

All-New Wolverine #33 (June 2018)
TOM TAYLOR, RAMON ROSANAS, NOLAN WOODARD

The "Old Woman Laura" sequence that concluded the *All-New Wolverine* series was a vision of Laura Kinney, the second Wolverine, in a possible future (a parallel to the "Old Man Logan" storyline from ten years earlier that did the same for the first Wolverine). In its first episode, also published the same month, there's a brief scene in which we see what Kamala Khan is up to in *that* future: she's the president of the United States.

---

*The first is the story that appeared in issues #2–5 of the second series.

Ms. Marvel #31 (August 2018)
G. WILLOW WILSON, NICO LEON, SALADIN AHMED, GUSTAVO DUARTE, IAN HERRING, ET AL.

The fiftieth issue of *Ms. Marvel* (counting the relaunch) is a celebratory jam, with Wilson and Nico Leon, who was then the series' regular artist, joined by three other writers* and three other artists. It's about a party, too: a sleepover, with three of Kamala Khan's closest friends, and a sign that she's reached a small social milestone with her peers. (Despite its embiggening and villain-punching action, all of the series' memorable moments are about Kamala's relationships with her family and social circle.) After various interruptions, including a team-up with Miles Morales (Spider-Man), she reveals her double identity to her friends. They've known for a long time, too, of course.

The Unbeatable Squirrel Girl #50 (January 2020)
RYAN NORTH, DEREK CHARM, ERICA HENDERSON, RICO RENZI

"This book is an experiment," Ryan North wrote in the first issue of *The Unbeatable Squirrel Girl*: "can a book like this find an audience? Will people TRULY read a comic about someone who dresses up like a rodent-like animal and fights crime in a major metropolitan area, even if that animal ISN'T a bat?" It did, in fact, find its audience, though more as paperback collections than as periodical comics, and survived remarkably long by contemporary standards: fifty-eight issues (including eight of the pre–*Secret Wars* series) and a standalone graphic novel, *The Unbeatable Squirrel Girl Beats Up the Marvel Universe*.

When series conclude these days, their creators usually have at least enough advance notice to wrap up outstanding plots. That wasn't always

---

*One of them, Saladin Ahmed, wrote Kamala Khan's next series, *The Magnificent Ms. Marvel*, after Wilson concluded her five-year run a bit later.

the case; final issues used to end with an apologetic little notice that their story would be continued somewhere, or worse. One of the final comics Jack Kirby drew before leaving Marvel, 1970's *Silver Surfer* #18, ends with a cliffhanger and a next-issue blurb, but the next issue never appeared.*

Squirrel Girl, though, had a very soft landing, announced long in advance. Its final storyline, in issues #47–50, is a thematic wrap-up, bringing back most of Doreen Green's antagonists at once—notably Doctor Doom, her antagonist from her first appearance, who had repeatedly turned up in *Unbeatable Squirrel Girl*, in person or by proxy. He's arguably her ultimate nemesis, but for a very different reason than he's the Fantastic Four's. Doom sees Reed Richards as a dangerous rival, and Squirrel Girl as a persistent nuisance. She believes that everyone can be helped to become better than they are; Doom believes that he's already perfect and that it would be beneath him to accept help from anyone.

Thanks to her enemies' machinations, Doreen Green is outed as Squirrel Girl and her home is destroyed. But as she faces impossible odds in a showdown in Central Park, everyone she's helped and befriended over five years' worth of her comics, from her superpowered classmates to Kraven the Hunter to the Mole Man, turns up to help *her*. (Lots of squirrels, too, of course.) Finally, as all seems lost, her "close personal friend" Galactus shows up to fix everything: "This *deus* is here to *ex machina*, so let's get to it," he says.

Galactus does, in fact, magically resolve everything that needs to be resolved, thanks to his Power Cosmic.† Surprisingly, that doesn't include making anyone forget Squirrel Girl's secret identity: "I want to share my

---

*That cliffhanger wasn't resolved until twenty-nine years later, in *Webspinners: Tales of Spider-Man* #4–6.
†The Power Cosmic—whose name is an *extremely* Stan Lee inversion—is also used by the Silver Surfer, who explains it in a Dan Slott–written conversation in 2014's *Silver Surfer* #3: "How are you talking in space?!" "I possess the Power Cosmic." "How am I breathing in space?" "The Power Cosmic." "And I'm not freezing because . . . ?" "Power Cosmic." "That's very . . . convenient." "*That's* the Power Cosmic."

whole self with the world," she explains. "I don't want to have to hide who I am anymore." The double life is a superhero tradition that's outlived its purpose. Her final step on her journey to coming of age as a heroine is shedding that too.

Squirrel Girl and Galactus have one more conversation on the moon. He tells her that they'll both have changed by the next time they meet, and that, thanks to the Power Cosmic, he knows that "everything in this universe, everything we've shared from the very beginning of our stories—will always exist, ready to be revisited by those with the power to see it."

The first time I read *The Unbeatable Squirrel Girl* #50, I was reading it aloud with my son—we'd been reading the series together since it started—and when I reached that line, I had to choke back tears.

21

PASSING IT ALONG

I've been filling up long white boxes with comics since I was about ten years old. If you've been to a comic collector's house, you've seen them: the uniform cardboard rectangles, just at the limit, when they're full, of what a sedentary adult can hoist. I've never thought of myself as a serious collector—I don't think I've ever paid more than ten bucks for a single back issue, and I don't care about condition at all. I buy comics to read, I've always said (with a deliberate shrug), and I hold on to them to read them again.

If I'm not a collector, though, I'm an accumulator for sure. Some people keep boxes full of photos they've taken; boxes of comics do the same thing for me. I used to have distinct memories of where and when I bought every issue I owned, where I first read it, what the air and light were like that day in that room. Now I've got too many for that to be true, but the particular physical copies of comics I read when I was a kid, or that affected me strongly later on, still set off those associative chains: staring at the overwhelming masses of text in *Avengers Annual* #10 on the guest-room bed of my grandparents' house, sipping an oversize soda as I read *Web of Spider-Man* #32 on a break from my phone-polling summer job, calming my nerves with a little stack of Brian Michael Bendis and Alex Maleev's *Daredevil* while my wife and newborn son slept.

My wife and I figured that, given our predilections for visual art and music and writing, we'd probably have an artsy sort of kid—a drummer for our band, our joke went when she was pregnant and he was kicking. But you don't get to pick the kid you get, and the extraordinary one we got is *really* into science and math. Almost from the time Sterling could talk, he made it clear that concrete, interestingly complex systems were what set his gears turning: the periodic table of the elements, the orbits of the planets, Minecraft. As a young child, he was perfectly fine with watching Pixar and Disney movies and so on, but given the option, he preferred nature documentaries.

Sterling's always been a pretty introverted, quiet kid. For many years, I struggled with how to be a good father to him, and thought a lot about how we could bond better. I worried, neurotically, that the kid I loved just sort of tolerated my presence. I often wondered if there were any enthusiasms that we might share someday, since our interests are so different. I live for music; he can mostly take it or leave it, aside from certain video-game soundtracks. He loves games, but I don't have the reflexes for most of the ones he enjoys.

Comics, we eventually discovered, were something that we absolutely could share. But only certain kinds of comics: Jamie Smart's *Bunny vs. Monkey* and Roger Langridge's *Snarked!* and Don Rosa's *Uncle Scrooge* and Bill Watterson's *Calvin and Hobbes* and . . . well, most other kinds of comics aimed at kids, but not the Marvel and DC stuff I'd been devouring since I was about his age. "*Superhero* comics?" I'd tell my friends, imitating what I imagined to be his thought processes. "That's what my *dad* likes."

Then, around the time Sterling turned ten, a local organization invited me to teach a four-week class on the history of American superhero comics. I assembled some slideshows for it, and he asked if he could see what I'd put together. Of course, I said. So I walked him through the outline of it, and I could sense the tumblers lining up in his brain. He didn't care about the costumes or the action or the characters especially, but he could see that it was a complicated system. And if there's one thing he likes, it's complicated systems. A few days later, he came to me and said, "Hey, Dad? I'd like to try to read all the Marvel superhero comics, in order. Not publication order, but continuity order. I want to read them all in the order the events happened to the characters."

Okay, I said, we can certainly try that. But if we start a story and it's not so interesting to you, let me know and we'll just skip to the next one, okay? We spent a few hours puzzling over the order in which we'd get to various series, then dove in, reading the earliest ones together. He liked it when I read out loud to him, and I liked doing that, too, so that's mostly how we operated at first.

We hit a pothole almost immediately. One of the first things in our reading order was "Weapon X," Barry Windsor-Smith's visually spectacular but violent and wrenching origin story for Wolverine. I got a chapter or two in and suddenly remembered how gruesome and sad it is. Uh, can we skip over this one, kiddo? No, he insisted, I want to see this!

To my relief, the early Fantastic Four and Hulk stories totally connected with him. (They were stories made to thrill ten-year-olds, and fifty years after they were created, they still worked just fine for that purpose.) He had lots of questions about them all, and *I could answer them*—the first time that had really happened between us. We were having fun together, more than ever before. I was pretty sure it wouldn't last more than a couple of weeks, but I was determined to savor that time.

On a family vacation, we brought along the first *Fantastic Four Omnibus*, which he reveled in, bursting out laughing at Stan Lee's corny jokes. (He thought it was hysterical how often characters said "Bah!" So we started a blog called *Marvel Bah!*, documenting every time somebody said it. There's a "Bah!" on the cover of *Avengers* #1, he was tickled to discover.)

Loki unleashes a "Bah!" on the cover of 1963's *Avengers* #1, drawn by Jack Kirby and Dick Ayers.

He got through 1962, then 1963, and wanted more. I kept the reading order updated for him, figuring out how to integrate *Untold Tales of Spider-Man* and *X-Men: First Class* and all the other continuity inserts; he especially enjoyed the bits where he could jump back and forth between multiple series published decades apart, all flowing into one another as if that's how it had been intended from the start.

And as I dug through my long white cardboard bins for yellowed copies of *Marvel Super-Heroes* and *Tales to Astonish*, I realized: *This* is why I kept these. This is my payoff for scouring discount piles for back issues and hauling them from house to house, for never selling them off or throwing them out. Reading this stuff is fun for me, and going back to the old comics keeps my past alive in my mind, but what I like best is sharing them—and getting to share them with my kid is *exactly the thing I always wanted.*

I still understood that his interest was liable to wane at any time: getting over brief phases is what kids do, and arguably what I had failed to do. But he kept reading and reading—when he got to 1966, and the first real crossover between series (a fight between Iron Man and the Sub-Mariner that begins in *Tales of Suspense* and concludes in *Tales to Astonish*), his mind was blown. After a few months, when he'd reached 1968, he came to me and said, "You know, Dad, I think I've read enough of sixties Marvel now. I've gotten up to where Captain Marvel shows up." (Oh, well, I thought, this was great while it lasted. But he wasn't done.) "I've decided

I'm much more interested in the modern crossover era." (In so many words.) "Can we jump forward to *Civil War*?"

We absolutely can, I said, and we dove back into reading-order making, which continued to be a bizarrely fun part of the process in its own right. I wondered how "the modern crossover era" would go over with him: the fictional world that had been shaped for the benefit of ten-year-olds had evolved into something different, or tried to. A lot of those later stories, I suspected, might go over his head, or be too intense for him.

I shouldn't have worried. He was *totally* into it—the plot threads tightly strung between two or ten or thirty series at once were exactly what he was looking for. So Marvel crossovers became our shared ritual, the thing we did on afternoons and weekends: sitting on the couch, reading through *Civil War* and *Secret Invasion* and *Avengers vs. X-Men* together. (Around then, I started thinking: What if I just went ahead and read everything myself? What might come of that?)

He developed likes and dislikes; as soon as our *Civil War* reading got to the tie-in issues of Brian Michael Bendis's *New Avengers*, he noted that "this writer is *really* good." (Bendis is especially good out loud, which I suspect was part of the appeal.) For a few years, he didn't particularly like *X-Men*, aside from Bendis's 2012–2015 *All-New X-Men* run, which he went back to reread. His delight in *Deadpool*, on the other hand, convinced me that maybe there was more there than I'd thought.

Other than *Deadpool*, he didn't like the particularly violent or gory stuff at all—he avoids the Punisher whenever possible (fine by me), and the Grand Guignol incarnation of *Moon Knight* from the mid-2000s got an instant "Let's skip this" from him. He adored the big plot twists, though, so I was careful to avoid spoiling them. (Every time someone was revealed as a Skrull in *Secret Invasion*, he whooped with glee.)

Reading with me also gave him a chance to show off his steel-trap memory: he pointed out visual allusions to stories we'd read months earlier, recalled everyone's names and origins, and generally fact-checked everything we read. At one point, I was trying to remember where the Red Ghost had first appeared, and he immediately said, *"Fantastic Four #13."* How'd you remember that? I asked him. "Because #1 is the Mole Man, #2 is the Skrulls, #3 is the Miracle Man, #4 is the Sub-Mariner, #5 is Doctor Doom, #6 is Sub-Mariner *and* Doctor Doom, #7 is Kurrgo, #8 is the Puppet Master..." You've read those stories *once*, I said. "Yeah!"*

We worked our way forward until we'd run out of crossovers, and by then he'd gotten somewhat less draconian about wanting to read absolutely everything in order. He's still very particular, though. As far as mainstream comics go, he is Team Marvel all the way. (One complicated system of this kind is exactly enough for him.) I tried him on some *Batman*, which left him cold; a few times, I suggested he might enjoy having a look at my beloved *Judge Dredd*, an idea he spurned with his toe.

Anything that prominently features villains—Loki, in particular—is his idea of a good time. He can take or leave *Doctor Strange*, but when Loki briefly claimed the title of Sorcerer Supreme for himself, he was all over it. *The Superior Spider-Man* is his all-time favorite comic—he liked it so much that his mom, who's never been a big comics person, wanted to get in on whatever was delighting him, so we started an ongoing family ritual of reading an issue of *Spider-Man* together every night.

Comics from the 1970s, '80s, and '90s, on the other hand, don't interest him at all, aside from the first couple of years' worth of *Thunderbolts*, which I suspected correctly that he would be into. He once asked if I could pick "something kind of old" for him to read on a car trip—"like from maybe 2003?" (I handed him the first volume of *Runaways*, which, to my relief, went over like gangbusters too.) And comics as physical objects are much less interesting to him than they are to me (he's fine with them, but

---

Howard the Duck #16—a bizarre piece of illustrated prose concocted in 1977 by writer Steve Gerber in response to a blown deadline—includes a scene in which Howard asks his cocreator to name the villains in the first fifty issues of *Fantastic Four*. As Gerber is rattling them off, Howard interrupts him: "I just wanted ya to see for yourself how much trivia you were carryin' around in your head! It's gotta be crowdin' out the important stuff, or keepin' it safely suppressed."

usually prefers to read on a tablet). Good for him: he'll never have the urge to lug those heavy white boxes from place to place.

We started watching the Marvel Cinematic Universe movies, first at home and then, when we ran out of DVDs to borrow, in the theater on their opening weekends—the only movies besides *Star Wars* that he's actively enthusiastic about going out to see. We found games that were easy enough for me to play with him and jammed full enough of lore that we could both enjoy them. (Thumbs up to *Lego Marvel Superheroes 2*, which gave us lots of excuses to look up some of its deep-cut characters.)

And—it *worked*. We bonded over Thing-vs.-Hulk fights and *Secret Empire* and Otto Octavius. It's given us a shared body of knowledge that we can talk about or draw on for conversations about other things. Reading comics has brought us closer than we had ever been before. It's happy time we spend together.

I asked Sterling once if there was a particular character with whom he identified. He thought for a moment and said "Peter Parker. The version from the sixties." Oh, the bitter, frustrated science whiz who's trying to find his place in the world? "Mm-hmm!" he said with a sly grin. "How about you?" I told him that I hadn't been able to think of anyone. "Really?" he said. "I'm surprised you didn't say Brain Drain"—the gloomy existentialist brain with a robot body from *The Unbeatable Squirrel Girl*. Touché, kid.

I still have to remind myself regularly that I shouldn't count on it lasting. He's a teenager now. At some point, he will likely dismiss all of these comics as the childish things he's put away, like '60s Peter Parker walking away from the trash can with his costume in it. At some point after that, he might come back to them, or not.

I suspect he'll find *some* kind of complicated story to explore when he gets older. As different as he is from me, our minds work in similar enough ways that I can't imagine he'll stop enjoying that process. If he does find himself back in the mountain of Marvels, or if he never leaves it, I hope he finds its glorious imaginary world changing all the time, keeping pace with the real one in which he lives, and I hope he appreciates it for chang-ing. I hope, too, that what he cares about is the story itself—the charac-ters, the images, the imaginative leaps and eleventh-hour improvisations that hold it together—and its creators, rather than the business entity that stamped a logo everywhere on it. A story can never leave you; a corpora-tion can never love you back.

ACKNOWLEDGMENTS

Writing this book took a lot longer than I imagined it would, and it wouldn't have been possible without the enthusiasm and patience of a great many people. Thanks to my parents, first off, for encouraging my youthful passions (and for storing a whole lot of comics for me for many years).

Sarah Lazin, my eagle-eyed agent, worked wonders in finding a home for *All of the Marvels*. At Penguin Press, Ed Park started it on its journey, and Scott Moyers gave the manuscript a very hard (and much-needed) kick and saw it through to the end.

Three friends made particularly tremendous contributions to this book's final form. The extraordinary Katie Pryde's enthusiasm, insights, and encouragement kept me going even when I was lost in the Negative Zone. She's batted around ideas about comics with me for years, and I'm pretty sure she improved every single page here. Katie also hosted a string of events at her store, Books with Pictures, that let me test-drive some of this material. Stephanie Burt is the kind of reader every writer dreams of having, and doubly so when a manuscript is still taking shape; her ability to spot what's necessary and still missing is unparalleled. Jessica Bruder's pep talks kept me afloat, and her big-picture notes made my arguments much clearer. Also, she laughs at the same things I do, which I appreciate.

I couldn't ask for a better angel on my shoulder than Lori Matsumoto, who enthusiastically cheered me on at every step. I couldn't ask for a better devil on my shoulder than Daphne Carr, who lovingly roasted me when I tripped myself up and showed me the path to do better. Talking to Bryan Stratton and Robb Milne from the *Marvel by the Month* podcast helped me sharpen several sections; Joshua Glenn let me cast light on some odd moments of Marvel history at his site, HILOBROW. William F. Wu's insights into *Master of Kung Fu*, both decades ago and when we corresponded, did a lot to shape my ideas about that series. Tim Maloney gave me some excellent advice that made the final few months of this project a lot easier.

Jay Edidin and Miles Stokes, and their podcast *X-Plain the X-Men*, are models of pouring enthusiasm onto the ridiculous to make it hilarious. Rahawa Haile, Annie Nocenti, Franklin Bruno, Diana Schutz, Gavin Edwards, Naomi Clark, Andréa Gilroy, Chris O'Leary, and Evan Narcisse all miraculously showed up exactly when I needed to hear what they had to say. Jane Cavolina copyedited the manuscript with precision worthy of Hawkeye. Catharine Strong at Aevitas; Ben Clark at the Soho Agency; Ed Lake at Profile; and Mia Council, Alicia Cooper, Yuki Hirose, Gloria Arminio, Colleen McGarvey, Shina Patel, Meighan Cavanaugh, Claire Vaccaro, Alyson D'Amato, and Will Staehle at Penguin all made this book's path substantially smoother. And Multnomah County Library's Sterling Room for Writers provided a quiet, calm space to work.

Thanks to all of my patrons from the 616 Society message board—it's a joy to talk comics with all of you. Extra thanks to Andrew Boscardin, Tony Bleach, Daniel Restrepo, Sam Cowling, Scott Ashworth, Paul Gilbert, and Kian Ross, who all gave me valuable feedback and suggestions on various chapters. Thanks, too, to the Hermenauts, MCP'ers, Redditors, and chatters who were more of a support system for me than they could have imagined.

This book is, in its way, one big expression of gratitude to the writers and artists and editors who created the fantastic, colorful worlds in which I've spent so much happy time. You've made something I will always carry with me.

And I'm grateful, most of all, to Sterling Wolk and Lisa Gidley, who inspired me and encouraged me every day of this long, bizarre project. I'm so glad I get to share these stories with you.

APPENDIX

MARVEL COMICS: A PLOT SUMMARY

Look closely enough at the mountain of Marvels, and of course you'll see a story. Any one panel suggests what happens before and after it; any one page has motion and communication and characters; any one issue is obviously a piece of a history. Take a few consecutive issues together, and the action rises and falls, splits and converges. Pull away a bit more, to the point where you can observe different series at the same time, and the story starts to make less sense—the parts might connect to one another, or might not. A month's cross-section of the whole thing will probably be a mess of colors and violence, passionate speech and conflicting goals.

Pull back still further, though. From a distance, the mass of thousands of Marvels takes on a definite form again. That shape wasn't molded intentionally, for the most part. It was assembled one little sheaf of pages at a time, improvised by creators who mostly followed the improviser's rule of "yes, and"—but sometimes didn't, or contradicted one another by accident or deliberately, or saw their job as maintaining "the

illusion of change." To the extent that it *is* intentional, that's only because it was hammered into a design agreed upon by a small number of
those creators, working in concert. But all of it bears the unmistakable
marks of the moments in which each part of it was made for money,
read for pleasure, then laid atop the last little sheaf of pages. The story's
shape emerges from its cross talk and disarray like constellations from
the stars.

The contours of the story often resemble the contours of the cultural
environment and moment in which it was produced, in a broad and distorted way, in part because it's made up of the work of so many distinct,
individual voices trying to create something that would be entertaining
and meaningful to their audience (and to themselves) in that moment. It's
blinkered in a lot of ways, of course, not least because those voices have
predominantly belonged to white American men—as open and pluralistic
as most of Marvel's creators have usually tried to be*—and addressed readers who were often implicitly assumed to be the same. But it's what we've
got; there's nothing else like it.

The story's overall shape breaks down, remarkably neatly, into six phases
so far, even though the divisions between those phases weren't intentional
(with a single exception). They can't have been: the creators involved with
them were just trying to hit the next month's deadline. Nonetheless, as
with other cultural and historical shifts, there are moments at which, in
retrospect, it's apparent that *something different* started happening.

The plot of the Marvel story is not its skeleton but its spine. It has
branches, subbranches, systems that are all but independent of it. This
consideration of the biggest themes that emerge from it is subjective and
incomplete;† the patterns you see if you explore those territories will be

---

*The "Stan's Soapbox" editorials by Stan Lee, published in every issue for years and rever-
ently reprinted after his death, preached a bighearted if fuzzy sort of universalism: "Sooner
or later, if man is ever to be worthy of his destiny, we must fill our hearts with tolerance."
†In particular, I've omitted a *lot* of things that happen beyond Earth.

different.* This is a map drawn from memory, but it's better than no map at all.†

I. 1961–1968

The first phase of the story spans a period when American nationalism (and terror of the Communist bloc) was paired with startling technological innovation. Both of those trends are mirrored in Marvel's early years, in which we meet most of its major characters and discover the locations where the better part of what follows will take place.

The story doesn't have an entirely clean starting point. There's a prologue that had been going on since 1939, and even more prehistory was added later, extending to a million years ago, when the spirit of vengeance rode a woolly mammoth and space gods first arrived to judge the Earth. Still, the standard line is that the Marvel tale—both the main body of the narrative and the industrial product of the company that made and sold it—begins in the autumn of 1961.

The characters we see most, at first, are a cluster of girls in high school who are thinking about their future (Patsy Walker, her friend Hedy Wolfe, their acquaintance Kathy) and young professional women in their circle (model Millie Collins, student nurse Linda Carter). Their world is a peculiar one. The "marvels" that abounded in the late 1930s and '40s have mostly receded into the yellowing past, but there are reports of monsters practically every week—creatures from under the earth's surface with

---

*Marvel has also attempted to summarize its own plot a few times: 1985's *The Marvel Saga*, whose twenty-five issues mostly covered the period from 1961 to 1966; 2012's *History of the Marvel Universe*, covering 1961 to 2011 in forty-eight pages; and 2019's *History of the Marvel Universe*, six issues that take the form of Franklin Richards and Galactus reminiscing at the end of time.
†In the interest of readability, I'm doing two things in this timeline that I've tried to avoid in the main body of this book: I'm conflating in-story and real-world events and their respective timelines, and I'm repeating a few points that appear elsewhere without pointing toward the particular chapters in which I go into them in more detail.

doubled consonants in their names, or aliens from outer space, some of which can change their shape to look like ordinary people.

Suddenly, there's a major shift in the forces shaping the world—bigger even than Sputnik or the Berlin Wall. A scientist, Reed Richards, and three of his associates take a ride on an experimental rocket and pass through radiation that transforms their bodies. They call themselves the Fantastic Four, and their exploits make headlines.*

After they defeat some subterranean monsters and an army of shape-changing aliens called Skrulls, more weird science starts to turn up, created by weirder scientists: "unstable molecules," as Richards calls one of his inventions. Atomic radiation has transformed the power structure of the world, and its secrets are still the great destabilizer in the game of nations. A bomb test gone wrong turns scientist Bruce Banner into the part-time monster the Hulk, his transformations triggered initially by nightfall, but later and more enduringly by anger. Radioactivity also plays a decisive role in the origins of Spider-Man, of Daredevil, and of the mutant teenagers who become the X-Men—"children of the atom." All of those characters are underdogs, given power they never asked for at a terrible cost. Marvel presents *itself* as an underdog, too: hungry and earnest, open to innovation, not yet on top of the heap but pushing hard to get there.

More scientific geniuses get in on the new craze. Hank Pym, another brilliant scientist who is himself unstable, devises a way to make people grow and shrink and to communicate with ants, calls himself Ant-Man, and gives his socialite girlfriend, Janet Van Dyne, similar powers as the Wasp. Arms manufacturer and technologist Tony Stark, injured in a military hot zone, builds himself a suit of armor and calls himself Iron Man.

Another wave of transformation has nothing to do with even the fanciful empirical science we've seen. A "master of the mystic arts," Dr. Stephen

---

*Headlines are a big deal at this point. During this part of the story, we often see recent events summarized in the form of the front page of a newspaper, the place where the culture records what's important to it.

Strange, has set up operations in New York's Greenwich Village and is dealing with metaphysical menaces, like the personification of nightmares. A physician named Donald Blake discovers a magical walking stick in Norway that transforms him into the Norse god Thor; shortly thereafter, Thor's brother, Loki, the god of mischief, tricks his way out of the tree in which he's been imprisoned for centuries and starts causing trouble again.*

Some further trickery by Loki leads to Thor joining forces with Iron Man, Ant-Man, the Wasp, and the Hulk. They call themselves the Avengers, and promptly get security clearance to act as semiofficial representatives of the U.S. government. That incarnation of the group immediately mutates. After they encounter still another shape-changing alien, the Hulk leaves, and the others promptly find World War II–era superhero Steve Rogers, Captain America, frozen in an ice floe and miraculously still alive. Cap, as everyone calls him, got his power from something called the Super-Soldier Serum—a formula whose name we'll be seeing again—and is the only person on whom it ever worked before it was lost. (Or so we are led to believe.) Shortly before the end of the war, there had been a battle in which he had been frozen, and his sidekick, Bucky Barnes, had been killed. (Or so we are led to believe.)

Cap is one of the keys that unlock the prehistory of the Marvel story. The other is the Sub-Mariner, Namor, the ruler of Atlantis, who had appeared in comics back in the 1930s and '40s and now turns up in *Fantastic Four*, as an amnesiac living in a flophouse. Both of them bring a familiar theme from mythology to the new narrative, too: the king who sleeps under a mountain. Namor is literally a king who's been unconscious of his kingdom, and his moral compass is that of a king—neither good nor evil, but devoted to protecting his realm. The reawakened Captain America is a good monarch, a natural leader who is entirely benign; he's the still-youthful epitome of the Greatest Generation, but he is no

---

*As we soon learn, every body of mythology is literally true within the Marvel universe. The traditional stories told in our world about immortal gods, especially those who take human form, are simply how somebody on Earth-616 has documented interesting events.

longer whole. Bucky Barnes, who was supposedly even more innocent, is now gone.

Who do these heroes fight? As always, their enemies represent what American culture fears most—sinister entities lurking "behind the Iron Curtain" (there's a curious reluctance about naming Russia or China outright), or their agents (like the Black Widow, who is a Soviet spy in her earliest appearances, and her cat's-paw, Hawkeye). Spider-Man fights a lot of inventors and scientists; Doctor Strange fights mystical forces. Doctor Doom, who eventually fights everyone, is most of those things at once and more, because he will take any kind of power he can get. He's a monarch, too, and in the first panel of his first appearance, Doom is moving human-shaped figures on a chessboard, next to books labeled "Demons" and "Science and Sorcery."

The heroic teams also fight time travelers, the people who can alter the triumphalist narrative of American history more efficiently than anyone else. Over the course of a year or so, remarkably similar covers on both *Avengers* and *Fantastic Four* introduce time-traveling villains Immortus, Kang the Conqueror, and Rama-Tut, all of whom wear green-and-purple ensembles that echo Doctor Doom's.* (To be fair, a lot of villains were wearing green and purple at that point.)

A strain of Marvel's story that starts to emerge around 1965, though, is that almost nobody is entirely beyond redemption. In the middle of that year, the composition of the Avengers abruptly shifts: Captain America, the only holdover from the previous version of the group, is joined by three ex-villains. Eventually, nearly every antagonist from this period will return in a more sympathetic context.

A final piece of heroic infrastructure materializes in the mid-1960s, too: S.H.I.E.L.D., a quasi-military, quasi-law-enforcement, espionage-based organization with very broad powers and lots of impressive gear, vari-

---

*At one point, Doom and Rama-Tut float the possibility that they might turn out to be the same person; they don't, but Rama-Tut, Immortus, and Kang eventually do.

ously depicted as affiliated with the U.S. government or with the United Nations.* (What's good for America, as far as the story is concerned at this point, is what's good for everybody.) It's run by Nick Fury, a tough secret-agent type who's already been starring in *Sgt. Fury and His Howling Commandos*, a series about the squad he commanded during World War II.

Espionage and counterespionage are very big at the time in newspapers and fiction—from the 1960 U-2 incident and James Bond on down to *Get Smart*—and S.H.I.E.L.D.'s rise is accompanied by a new class of antagonist. Overlapping secret societies are jockeying for power all over Marvel's world: the anarcho-scientific organization A.I.M. (Advanced Idea Mechanics) in their hot yellow "beekeeper" suits, the crypto-Nazi cabal Hydra, the purple-robed Secret Empire.

Having covered the Eastern and Western Blocs, the scene-setting part of the story expands beyond them. We meet the Inhumans, an evolutionary offshoot of humanity who have cloistered themselves away in a domed city called Attilan.† We visit Wakanda, a technological utopia within Africa, and the Savage Land, a tropical region within Antarctica where dinosaurs still roam. Beyond the world we know (and closer to the visions seen by the psychedelic explorers of the mid-'60s), there's the Negative Zone, a space within space of utter otherness, and the Dark Dimension, an equally alien realm ruled by the nightmarish, flame-headed Dormammu.

---

*It's established, much later, that S.H.I.E.L.D. has existed in some form since it was founded in ancient Egypt by Imhotep, and that it's generally been a secret organization devoted to defending the world from threats without calling attention to its existence—a benevolent conspiracy. The error of the modern incarnation of S.H.I.E.L.D. may have been going public. In the course of the story, it's been disbanded at least three times. Its base of operations, the Helicarrier, is a wonder of military technology—an aircraft carrier that is *itself* airborne—but, beginning in the late 1970s, Helicarriers will fall out of the sky about as often as hailstorms. The writer Matt Fraction's list of what "literally everyone does, the first time they write for Marvel: 1) Try to crash a helicarrier, 2) And Nick Fury's there, 3) So's Spider-Man."

†Attilan is variously purported to be in the Alps, the Andes, or the Himalayas, until it eventually ends up on the moon, and is subsequently relocated to the Hudson River.

And then there's outer space, which has so far mostly been represented by hostile visiting aliens. In an issue published in early 1966 (shortly before the Soviet craft Luna 9 made the first soft landing on the moon), a god arrives from space to end the world: the planet-devouring Galactus, a force so huge he's incomprehensible. "We're like ants . . . just ants . . . ants!!" exclaims the Fantastic Four's panicked Human Torch, as he tries to grasp the scale of which he's just been made aware.

Even after that threat of annihilation is averted, the poor Earthlings who are still struggling to travel as far as their own moon can't ignore their planet's existence in a much bigger context. Another galactic empire, the Kree, is operating in competition with the Skrulls, and Earth becomes a beachhead in their cold war. (A Kree captain who's conveniently named Mar-Vell arrives on Earth and starts calling himself Captain Marvel.)

Small things can matter as much as large ones within this story, though: the issue in which the Fantastic Four defeat Galactus famously concludes with a long sequence in which the Human Torch, who's just saved the world, goes off to start his first year of college. Less wealthy characters don't have that option, and as the U.S. steps up its bombing campaign in Vietnam, Marvel's comics start to address that war's effects on its cast. Patsy Walker's boyfriend, Buzz Baxter, enlists in the Army immediately after his graduation from high school. A few months later, he comes back from Vietnam wounded and traumatized; he can barely speak to Patsy. Flash Thompson, Peter Parker's high school tormentor and Spider-Man's biggest fan, enlists as well. He'll do better for himself in the military, until he loses his legs in a firefight in the Persian Gulf many years later.

As the quotidian rhythms of Marvel's pre-superhero comics are absorbed into the bigger story, the ordinary women who were those comics' protagonists fade from view. The business of being human goes on in superhero stories, though. Professor Charles Xavier, the X-Men's leader, dies (temporarily); Reed and Sue Richards of the Fantastic Four have a baby, Franklin Richards, whose birth involves a great deal of difficulty, including a trip to the Negative Zone. Franklin serves as a symbol of the story's recognition of itself and its own emerging power, and his arrival signals a shift in the overarching narrative.

II. 1968–1980

On or about August 1968, human character changed, and so did Marvel's characters. The second phase of the grand Marvel story spans 1968 to 1980, a period of political turbulence, extrapolation from the fantastic creations of the first seven years, and creative stagnation punctuated by bolts of invention.

As the Communist and quasi-Communist threat in Marvel's pages recedes (and as America's reservations about the Vietnam war grow more serious), a new archvillain surfaces: Mephisto, a devil who's closer to Faust's Mephistopheles than to the biblical Satan. His only desire is to punish, tempt, and ruin the good. He's the natural foil to the knowledge seekers and scientists introduced in the first act, although it'll be a little while before he meets them.

Romance comics—with short stories whose characters are only ever seen once—return to Marvel for a few years, beginning in 1969. They are, more directly than ever before, about young women trying to negotiate the cultural shifts of the time.* Throughout this period, Marvel's creators are still overwhelmingly male (and white), but the culture of the time acknowledges a little more easily that their protagonists need not be. An initial ripple of titles starring particular women, *The Cat*, *Night Nurse*, and *Shanna the She-Devil*, is followed later in the decade by *Ms. Marvel*, *Spider-Woman*, and *She-Hulk*. And the origin of the first Black superhero with his own series mirrors that of Captain America: as the result of more

---

*A 1972 issue of *Our Love Story* "dedicated to the fearless, fabulous females of women's lib!" begins with a story called "The Movement... Or My Heart!"

Super-Soldier-Serum-related experimentation, the unjustly convicted prisoner Carl Lucas gets superstrength and unbreakable skin. He renames himself Luke Cage and hangs out his shingle as a "hero for hire."

The tone of the story abruptly turns grimmer and weirder in 1972, as a new wave of B-movie monsters pours onto the stage: Dracula and Frankenstein's monster and a werewolf and a living mummy from ancient Egypt, as well as the flaming-skulled supernatural motorcyclist Ghost Rider. Another attempt to re-create the Super-Soldier Serum turns scientist Ted Sallis into the Man-Thing, a mindless swamp creature that burns anyone who feels fear. All of those compromised and monstrous protagonists are now much more interesting, in practice, than the previous wave's superheroes, who are still restaging their old battles. The scariest new character, though, is the cunning alien Thanos. Like Doom, he's devoted himself to amassing as much power as he can; unlike Doom, he's doing it because he worships Death.*

As the Watergate scandal unfolds in our world and deals an enduring blow to Americans' trust in government, a wave of rebellion against patriarchal authority emerges in the Marvel story. John Jameson, the son of Spider-Man's foil, J. Jonah Jameson, becomes a kind of sci-fi werewolf. Shang-Chi, the son of a "devil doctor," shakes off his father's influence and seeks his own path in the world; so does the son of Satan himself, Daimon Hellstrom, a rebel like his old man. Even little Franklin Richards manifests reality-shaping mutant powers, forcing his father to temporarily shut down his mind.

With the collapse of established orders, though, what's left turns out to be chaos. Frank Castle, a military veteran whose family has been killed in mob crossfire, rejects the American legal system outright and devotes himself to killing those he feels have escaped justice, calling himself the Punisher. Adam Warlock, an Adam Kadmon–ish "perfect man," discovers

---

*That's with a capital D; Death appears to Thanos as a hooded woman who rejects his love.

that his own future self is the despotic figurehead of an intergalactic religion; Thanos, who has an eye on a powerful jewel in Warlock's possession, helps him to commit "cosmic suicide." And after he witnesses the president being unmasked as the head of a criminal empire and killing himself in the Oval Office, Steve Rogers briefly gives up being Captain America and wanders America under the name Nomad.

Several months after that story is published, the real-world Richard Nixon resigns; the new president, Gerald Ford, is a Nixon appointee whose brief term is marked by economic and diplomatic chaos. Within the Marvel story, during the Ford administration, new characters are dropped into unfamiliar environments and struggle to survive their power dynamics. Ex-soldier Jim Scully falls through the Bermuda Triangle and lands in a world of dinosaurs and aliens, where he becomes known as Skull the Slayer. High school student Richard Rider accidentally becomes a member of the Nova Corps, an alien police force fighting against Skrulls, but doesn't understand what he's supposed to be doing until it's nearly too late. A mostly mute alien comes to Earth and briefly has adventures as Omega the Unknown, until he's killed by trigger-happy police. The cynical, irritable Howard the Duck finds himself accidentally exiled from his duck-dominated parallel Earth to the Marvel world of "hairless apes."

The antiheroes of the early 1970s mostly fall quiet within a few years. But some of that period's developments—a new generation that's unlike the old, heroes who aren't only white men anymore, intimations that American culture might be a weapon aimed at its underclass—are filtered into the most notable Marvel characters of this stage's second half: a new team of X-Men, an international, mixed-race, mixed-gender group that assembles to fight one last impossible monster with an assonant name, a living island called Krakoa. One of the new X-Men, Wolverine, will go on to become one of the most prominent figures of the Marvel story; he turns out to be a product of still more attempts to create a super-soldier.

The temptation and threat of devil archetypes, teased at the beginning of this period, resurfaces in 1980, as a Satanic figure called Nicholas Scratch possesses Franklin Richards. And the emergence of Dark Phoenix, the monstrous shadow self of the X-Men's Jean Grey, followed by her death, concludes this part of the story and reverberates through the next.

III. 1981–1989

The devils heralded by Mephisto come into power in the third phase of the story, which begins around the time of the election of Ronald Reagan and continues until, roughly, the end of 1989 and the fall of the Berlin Wall. It's full of malign forces below the ground, and clandestine replacements and substitutions. Despite the political rhetoric of that era, the fears reflected in Marvel's comics have less to do with annihilation from the other side of the Iron Curtain than with systemic oppression at home, and with gods' and leaders' helplessness against the devils. The problem, the story suggests, is not an "evil empire," but the empire of evil.

This is also the period when the ascending American counterculture crosses paths with a declining mass culture—when the generation that overlaps with both mainstream comics' older readers and their younger creators realizes that the independent art being made in underground circles is often more potent than the art that has big money and big intellectual-property institutions behind it. Marvel can no longer really claim to be a scrappy underdog, so there's a lot of anxiety in its comics about an impending inversion of the order of things, but also a certain amount of excitement.

The dissonant opening fanfare of Marvel's 1980s is another *X-Men* story, "Days of Future Past," a horrific vision of a barbed-wire future in which most of the heroes are dead (but Franklin Richards is still around as an adult). *Daredevil*, meanwhile, rises up to become one of the most significant parts of that decade's Marvel story, depicting Manhattan as a modern-day antecedent of the "Days of Future Past" hellscape: looming towers in which business is done and squat bars in which the fallen brawl, with society's outcasts crawling through tunnels beneath the streets.

The next devil to arrive is Asmodeus, who torments Ghost Rider in early 1981. He's followed by Belasco, the ruler of Limbo, who twists Illyana Rasputin (the little sister of the X-Men's Colossus) into his demonic apprentice. The Norse fire demon Surtur returns to bring about Ragnarok, the apocalypse of the gods, heralded by a colossal hammer striking an anvil ("DOOM!") in every issue of *Thor* for a year. Still another devil figure makes his first appearance in *Uncanny X-Men*: the Adversary, a malign trickster god summoned by another kind of shape-changing alien, a Dire Wraith.

A second version of grown-up Franklin Richards, different from the one in "Days of Future Past," briefly appears in the modern day: he's accidentally aged his body to maturity, but his mind remains a child's. Any similarity to superhero comics progressively aiming at older readers and greater conceptual complexity, while continuing to balance on the premises of stories aimed at small children, may or may not be intentional.

Most of the major players disappear for a moment, then return changed, with their stories no longer just intersecting but swirled together. They were all kidnapped (the first miniseries to be called *Secret Wars* reveals) by a seemingly omnipotent figure called the Beyonder, who whisked them away to fight one another on a cobbled-together planet called Battleworld. The Beyonder is a god with no conception of good or evil, a child smashing action figures together to see which will break first. Doctor Doom, though, knows the difference and has chosen his side; he seizes the power of a god and saves everything, not for the last time. *Secret Wars* is swiftly followed by *Secret Wars II*, in which the Beyonder shows up on Earth and spends a while investigating what it means to be human and "incomplete"—to, like any reader, not know the entire story.

As another consequential baby is born—Scott (Cyclops) Summers's son, Christopher, later known as Nathan—everything flips upside down.

The crucial moments of the Marvel story start to take place underground (in the subterranean tunnels of the outcast mutants who call themselves the Morlocks), underwater (where a cocoon containing Jean Grey's living body appears), or in various underworlds (like the Asgardian Hel in which Thor is cursed by a death goddess). Villains are raised up and heroes brought low. Charles Xavier abandons his students, turning over the education of the New Mutants team he's brought together to his former archenemy, Magneto. Cyclops abandons his wife and newborn son to join his resurrected ex-girlfriend in X-Factor, a group that pretends to oppress mutants in order to protect them.

Over the course of 1986, things get dark. The Morlocks are massacred in their tunnels. Doctor Doom briefly becomes the emperor of the world. More substitutions and inversions follow: the familiar, politically progressive Captain America, Steve Rogers, is replaced by right-wing athlete John Walker; the green, monosyllabic Hulk, who's been smashing things for a quarter century, is replaced by a smart, irritable, gray Hulk. The Avengers are diminished by degrees, then disband.*

All the pent-up underground heat from this phase of the story boils over in 1989's "Inferno," a linewide crossover in which the parental abandonment and heroic abdication of the past few years results in Hell erupting into Manhattan. In that sequence's wake, the Fantastic Four are replaced by impostors, who go back underground for a bizarre replay of the original team's first story. It's implied that the real Fantastic Four may remain there forever after, the monarchs asleep and dreaming under the mountain.

As this phase of the story draws to a close, Loki plays a substitution game on a grand scale, convincing villains to attack one another's enemies, in another linewide crossover, "Acts of Vengeance." At last, *New Mutants* #87 introduces a "new" character called Cable: a huge guy with a glowing eye, a scar over the other eye, shoulder pads, pouches, and a mammoth gun. He promptly assumes control of the young militia that Charles

---

*(Very briefly.)

Xavier assembled, although he's entirely physical where Professor X was entirely cerebral. In a few years, we will learn that he is Nathan Summers, grown to adulthood in the terrible future. His reappearance marks a transition to the next phase of the story, foreshadowing its chaos and duplication and big, loud imagery.

IV. 1990–2004

The emotional investment Marvel's readers had made in the 1980s is swapped out for a double-your-money bubble in the '90s; the artistic promise of the previous decade's experimentation is eclipsed by financial promises Marvel can't keep, backed by increasingly incoherent exploits of wasp-waisted babes and muscle-bound men with pouches and bandoliers and cannons. (The crash of "DOOM" reappears as an inescapable drumbeat in the first storyline of Todd McFarlane's 1990 *Spider-Man* series.)

The antagonists of the story's fourth phase are internal: people the protagonists or the public have come to think of as friends and allies, and have invested with power. Everyone turns out to have a dark side or a shadow self, a double of some kind. *Spider-Man* begets *Venom* and *Carnage* and *Scarlet Spider*. *Iron Man* begets *War Machine*. *Thor* begets *Thunderstrike*. *Captain America* begets *Nomad* and *U.S.Agent*. *Fantastic Four* begets *Fantastic Force*, a group led by still another grown-up version of Franklin Richards, who now goes by the very '90s name Psi-Lord.

But before the universe's cast is doubled, it's halved. Thanos, who's been all but entirely absent from the story since 1977, returns with a new piece of cosmology: the jewel that Adam Warlock possessed is one of six Infinity Gems that each control some aspect of existence.* He assembles them all into an omnipotence-granting glove, with which he tries to impress Mistress Death by making half the population of the universe dis-

---

*Like the earlier Cosmic Cube and M'Kraan Crystal, they're magical jewels that can bring about anything the plot requires.

appear. *The Infinity Gauntlet* is followed by the even louder crossovers *The Infinity War*, in which a slew of characters' artificial doubles are running around, and *The Infinity Crusade*, which brings Mephisto and Thanos into conflict with a "goddess" who is one of Adam Warlock's shadow selves. Each of those stories is, nonetheless, resolved by everything being reset to its precatastrophic state.

After "The Age of Apocalypse" replaces the *X-Men* comics themselves with sinister doubles for a few months, another gargantuan, ill-defined menace comes into being: Onslaught, who is approximately the dark side of Charles Xavier combined with the dark side of Magneto. The Avengers and Fantastic Four appear to be killed fighting him, but are actually saved by young reality shaper Franklin Richards, who creates a doppelgänger of Earth itself, on which his parents and their friends can safely remain until he can bring them home.

The September 11, 2001, attacks on the World Trade Center* and the Pentagon are the biggest shock to the American psyche in decades. The Marvel story's immediate reaction, like that of every other arena of pop culture, is performing sentimental concern—there's an infamous issue of *Amazing Spider-Man* in which everyone is helping out at the World Trade Center site, and Doctor Doom sheds a tear.†

The security-versus-privacy debate that subsequently surfaces within the national conversation echoes in two sequences, both published in the spring of 2002, that ceremonially sacrifice the superhero genre's attachment to "secret identities": Tony Stark reveals his dual identity as Iron Man to the public,‡ and Matt Murdock is outed as Daredevil by a news-

---

*Attacks on the World Trade Center had been a staple terror-fantasy of Marvel's comics for twenty-five years: it had been dematerialized in 1976, set ablaze in 1980, shattered by Nazis in 1983, had a plane flown at it in 1991, bombed in 1994 and 1996, and so on.

†Thanks to the Marvel universe's sliding timeline—see chapter 2—that issue is now out of continuity, since everything from *Fantastic Four* #1 onward has now taken place well after 2001.

‡That moment is echoed, six years later, by the conclusion of the first *Iron Man* movie.

paper report. Those are followed by one of the most pointed pieces of American self-examination Marvel has yet published, *Truth: Red, White & Black*, in which it turns out that the creation of the Super-Soldier Serum that gave Captain America his powers involved unethical, fatal experiments on African American men, very much like the real-world Tuskegee syphilis experiment.

Throughout this phase, the story has been looking back on itself—sometimes nostalgically, sometimes critically—and by 2004, it's trying to shake off its repetitions. Thor destroys Asgard in an attempt to break the Ragnarok cycle. In *Avengers Disassembled*, published at the same time, Avengers Mansion is blown up, a handful of familiar characters die, and the Avengers are discredited and disband.

As the final crashes of the long '90s reverberate, Linda Carter, one of the young professional women whose lives have been overshadowed by the marvels of their age, reappears after thirty years or so off panel; she calls herself "the night nurse."

V. 2005–2015

The 2005 launch of *New Avengers* begins the fifth movement of the Marvel story, a chain of linked events that continues for a decade. The Big Bads of this era, a bit surprisingly, are utopians: people who have a vision of a perfect world, usually (but not always) under their leadership, and are willing to do whatever it takes to get there. That means that the struggles of Marvel's protagonists are mostly with one another, and with the consequences of their actions. The story again echoes what's happening in the culture of its time: clashing factional ideologies, struggles for collective identity, technology moving faster than anyone can follow, and the persistent sense that the world is being shaped by behind-the-scenes conspiracies.

Iron Man integrates his armor into his body with something called Extremis, described as both "a virus" and "a super-soldier solution," that essentially upgrades him to a living supercomputer. Meanwhile, the original super-soldier solution—Captain America, a living metaphor for American military force as a vector for American ideology—is feeling the backlash of history; his long-lost World War II–era partner, Bucky Barnes, has returned as the Winter Soldier, now a brainwashed assassin.

Just then, the world is briefly transformed into a utopia for superheroes—some superheroes, at any rate. In *House of M*, the Scarlet Witch has altered reality so that she and her friends get what (they believe) they want: now mutants are the dominant caste rather than a loathed underclass, and her family is royalty. (The consequences of that transformation go horribly wrong, as do the consequences of its reversal.)

The Illuminati, a secret coalition of the geniuses and kings who used to be the story's uncomplicated heroes, decide that the next superpower-related disaster could rebound on them. They betray their old friend the Hulk and conspire to strand him in outer space so he can never endanger Earth again. (That plan goes horribly wrong too.) They're right, though: a big cultural shift is one catastrophe away, which is how *Civil War*, a more expansive story than Marvel has ever published, begins.

The New Warriors, a minor superhero team, are being filmed for reality TV when they're involved in an incident that kills most of them and destroys a chunk of Stamford, Connecticut. In the ensuing uproar, the U.S. passes legislation requiring everyone with superpowers to register with the government or be sent to an extradimensional prison. The conflict between those who believe that's necessary, led by Reed Richards (who has taken it upon himself to "solve everything") and the military-industrial complex's champion Iron Man, and those to whom it's anathema, led by small-*l* libertarian Captain America, escalates into a conflict that spills over into almost the entire Marvel line*—a new, more violent security-versus-privacy debate. The proregistration forces are ultimately

---

*Linda Carter, the night nurse, is briefly seen working as a medic on Rogers's side.

victorious, and Captain America is taken into custody and seemingly assassinated; the political allegory in *Civil War* is not subtle.

Neither is the political allegory in *World War Hulk*, in which the Hulk is back from his exile in outer space with an alien army behind him, to seek revenge against the Illuminati. Smashing ensues.

A multisided war of galactic empires has been going on in the background during all of this. The Skrulls, barely clinging to shreds of their former might, have infiltrated Earth, which their religious leaders tell them they are destined to occupy; they promise to turn the planet into a peaceful, free-of-want utopia. Humans demand self-determination, of course, and *Secret Invasion* concerns their rout of the Skrulls.

That story's resolution leads into the political disaster that plays out over the course of 2009 in "Dark Reign," as the goes-horribly-wrong part of the superhuman-registration plan kicks in, and sociopathic Norman Osborn temporarily becomes the central character of Marvel's story. Following a conflict between the X-Men and Osborn, Cyclops declares that the tiny remaining mutant community is seceding from America, and moves it to an island off the California coast, which he names—you may have guessed this by now—Utopia.

The crises keep arriving, now often several at a time. There's another little wave of horror: the ongoing conflict in space brings about the opening of a portal to a Cancerverse, from which awful Lovecraftian creatures spew forth and are beaten back by Death's champion, Thanos. The mutants of Utopia deal with a vampire invasion of San Francisco, which the undead have decided could be their own paradise; then a schism between mutant factions emerges. *Fear Itself* is… actually, *Fear Itself* doesn't make a lot of sense, but it occupies 145 issues of 37 different series and has a lot of punching in it.

We see yet another adult version of Franklin Richards in *Fantastic Four*, and we learn that Galactus, the all-consuming, terrible, and sublime god from space, is *his* herald.

In the long-foreshadowed, mammoth crossover *Avengers vs. X-Men*, the Phoenix force returns to Earth, and the mutants possessed by it start fixing the world in a way that bears a strong similarity to what the Skrulls had promised in *Secret Invasion*: ameliorating food and power shortages, ending wars, and so forth. The Avengers, whose suspicion of utopias often puts them on the wrong side of conflicts, fight them. In the end, the Phoenix-possessed Scott Summers kills his father figure, Charles Xavier (Xavier's brain is saved, but that's a whole other thing), and the Phoenix goes away again.

Everyone takes a breath for a minute, and then the story's players reconfigure themselves into new teams. There's a big new Avengers group, put together by Tony Stark and Steve Rogers, who have rebuilt their alliance. The new lineup includes Carol Danvers, the former Ms. Marvel, who has finally bloomed into the vision she saw of her ideal self during *House of M*. She's now calling herself Captain Marvel, and building a reputation for leadership. As an indirect consequence of an interstellar war in which Danvers gets involved, a teenage Inhuman from Jersey City, Kamala Khan, becomes a new Ms. Marvel.

In the course of this period's final year, 2014–2015, every narrative thread accelerates into a flickering string of revelations and disasters. The Watcher, the alien who observes everything and is forbidden to act on his knowledge,* is found murdered on the moon; now there's nobody left who can see and understand the entirety of the Marvel story. One of his eyes is stolen; it explodes, revealing long-buried secrets. In particular, Thor learns a secret that makes him "unworthy," so he can no longer lift his hammer Mjolnir. His former girlfriend Jane Foster becomes the new Thor, which exacerbates the cancer that's killing her. The elderly Nick Fury takes over the role of the Watcher, while his son, who conveniently

---

*This makes him half a god: omniscient and impotent. The Beyonder is effectively his opposite number, clueless and omnipotent.

looks a lot like Samuel L. Jackson, assumes Fury's name and former role in Marvel's comics.

Steve Rogers, who's suddenly a very old man, gives up the identity of Captain America yet again, this time handing it over to his longtime associate Sam Wilson, the Falcon. Thanks to some shenanigans involving the Red Skull and Charles Xavier's brain, a group of heroes and villains are "inverted," changing moral polarity (as if there had been specific polarities to begin with). Iron Man, now more arrogant than ever, moves to the Bay Area and proclaims his own technocapitalist utopia. Wolverine dies, and there's a protracted squabble among his various doubles, clones, and children about whom will take over for him. Every version of Spider-Man ever teams up.

Amid the chaos, we see one beautiful, calm vision: a garden tended by the mature Franklin Richards, five thousand years or so in the future, as humanity has expanded beyond the Earth.

The earlier phase shifts within the Marvel story have all come about accidentally and are evident only in retrospect. The one that happens in 2015 is deliberate, obvious, and coordinated. Every narrative strand is tied off or severed, and every series concludes. The universe ends.

VI. 2015–

Then, after Doctor Doom saves everything, it resumes again, slightly after the point where it left off. This is the one shift between the Marvel story's narrative phases that is deliberate, for commercial reasons: the company's entire superhero line is relaunched with new first issues. The conceit of the beginning of this phase is that all the characters' circumstances have changed during an eight-month break: the deranged mercenary Deadpool has become a wealthy, beloved hero, for instance, and Daredevil's identity is secret again, and Spider-Woman is eight months pregnant.

The sixth movement of the big Marvel story is still ongoing. It will probably be hard to see its central themes clearly until we've got some distance from it, but so far, it's been leaning pretty hard on the idea of heirs and inheritances. There are new versions of lots of familiar characters, but they're less doubles or shadow selves than young people assuming their elders' roles.

There's also now an omnipresent terror that everyone is being presented with disinformation and deceptive spin all the time. The antagonists of this part of the story—the entities that seem worth struggling against in popular storytelling—seem to be people who are trying to control how the world is understood, especially retroactively. (One glib way of putting that is to say that villains, right now, spread "fake news.")

The first crisis of the current phase comes in early 2016. In *Standoff,* S.H.I.E.L.D. has used a reality-altering Cosmic Cube to create a prison for supervillains, rewriting their reality so that they believe they're among the cheerful residents of an idyllic American small town, Pleasant Hill, and don't remember their former lives; then they do. Pleasant Hill is unmade, and the Cosmic Cube restores Steve Rogers to his youth and health so he can be Captain America again (although Sam Wilson continues to be another Captain America, for a while). It also magically rewrites his past and his personal narrative, so that he has now always been a sleeper agent of the fascist organization Hydra.

Meanwhile, there's a new cold war between mutants and Inhumans, since the continued survival of either group will apparently doom the other. A long *Doctor Strange* sequence concerns the destruction of the world's magic by entities called, in a rather on-the-nose way, the Empirikul. And there's a second *Civil War*, in which an Inhuman called Ulysses can see visions of a probable future, and the superhero community divides again between Carol Danvers (who favors proactive interference) and Tony Stark (who thinks that's a terrible idea). Again, the wrong side is the one that's trying to seize control of the narrative and to insist that the infallibility of prophecy allows them to react to things that haven't yet happened.

In the wake of that conflict (and the deaths of Bruce Banner and War Machine, and Stark's absence after Danvers beats him comatose), there's a schism between the main Avengers team's younger and older members; the younger ones form their own group, the Champions, recycling the name of a short-lived team from the mid-1970s. Two new "Iron Men" arise as well: Victor Von Doom, who, having been a villain, an emperor, and a god, figures he might as well try being a hero, and Riri Williams, a Black teenage inventor who has an artificial-intelligence version of Stark in her armor.

The retroactively reconstructed Steve Rogers makes his move, isolating or neutralizing most of the forces that could oppose him, then takes over America as the leader of Hydra. In *Secret Empire*, the country swiftly settles into its new status as a fascist state, replacing the old history books with new ones in which the supposed fall of fascism was a huge lie that had been propagated until Hydra came back to save everyone. The young heroes, including those associated with the Champions, organize a resistance movement; Hydra razes Las Vegas as punishment for protecting them. Eventually, the original version of Rogers reappears, fights his double, and wins; the false history Hydra had impressed on everyone is refuted; and America is made whole again (except for the dead residents of Las Vegas, who still have to wait a bit).

The story goes on, ceaselessly, growing by almost twenty thousand pages a year, looping and expanding. Bruce Banner and War Machine return from the dead, and Tony Stark gets better too. Jane Foster dies and is resurrected, then becomes a new Valkyrie after the old ones are massacred when an army of dark elves invades Earth. Loki becomes Sorcerer Supreme, then hands the title back to Stephen Strange, who resurrects Las Vegas, which in turn starts some trouble with Mephisto.

Mutants establish a new nation on Krakoa and start to resurrect all of their own who have ever died. The current, post–*Secret Wars* version of reality turns out to be the eighth incarnation of the multiverse, and six of the previous seven multiverses, in personified form, are now a team themselves, "the Ultimate Ultimates."* And Linda Carter, the night nurse, who's just been doing what good she can since we first saw her, has had her clinic's building bought for her by the grateful billionaire superhero Iron Fist. A new crisis is approaching; it always is.

---

*The language of the sequence that introduces them repurposes resonant phrases from earlier phases of the Marvel story. The fourth multiverse, Al Ewing's captions note, "is missing. He is the pilgrim, the true believer who journeys into mystery." Stan Lee often addressed his readers as "Pilgrim" and "True Believer," and *Journey into Mystery* was the series that became *Thor*; the fourth universe's absence could also allude to Jack Kirby's "Fourth World" comics, which he created for DC when he left Marvel in the early 1970s. And the sixth multiverse is "the builder of the junction to everywhere," a phrase you may recall from chapter 4.

INDEX